ST THOMAS AQUINAS
SUMMA THEOLOGIÆ

ST THOMAS AQUINAS

SUMMA
THEOLOGIÆ

Latin text and English translation,
Introductions, Notes, Appendices
and Glossaries

NON NISI TE

BLACKFRIARS

IN CONJUNCTION WITH

EYRE & SPOTTISWOODE, LONDON, AND
McGRAW-HILL BOOK COMPANY, NEW YORK

PIÆ MEMORIÆ

JOANNIS

PP. XXIII

DICATUM

IN AN AUDIENCE, 13 December 1963, to a group representing the Dominican Editors and the combined Publishers of the New English *Summa*, His Holiness Pope Paul VI warmly welcomed and encouraged their undertaking. A letter from His Eminence Cardinal Cicognani, Cardinal Secretary of State, 6 February 1968, expresses the continued interest of the Holy Father in the progress of the work, 'which does honour to the Dominican Order, and the Publishers, and is to be considered without doubt as greatly contributing to the growth and spread of a genuinely Catholic culture', and communicates his particular Apostolic Blessing.

To

PAUL KEVIN MEAGHER O.P.

ST THOMAS AQUINAS

SUMMA THEOLOGIÆ
VOLUME 16

PURPOSE AND HAPPINESS
(1a2æ. 1-5)

Latin text, English translation, Introduction,
Notes, Appendices & Glossary

THOMAS GILBY O.P.
Blackfriars, Cambridge

NIHIL OBSTAT

HENRICUS ST JOHN O.P.
DROSTANUS MACLAREN O.P.

IMPRIMI POTEST

JOANNES HISLOP O.P.
Prior Provincialis Angliæ
die 26 Octobris 1968

NIHIL OBSTAT

NICHOLAS J. TRANTER S.T.L.
Censor

IMPRIMATUR

✠ PATRICK CASEY
Vic. Gen.
Westminster, 11 November 1968

PRINTED IN GREAT BRITAIN BY EYRE AND SPOTTISWOODE LIMITED

CONTENTS

EDITORIAL NOTES

THE TEXT AND TRANSLATION

The text is based on the Leonine, though occasionally other readings are adopted. Variations of any importance are indicated. The paragraphing in no printed edition is sacrosanct, and so, in order to make for clearer argument, it is more frequent here than elsewhere, and sometimes the better, so it has seemed to the editor, to mark the stages of the argument, the text runs on where others make a break. Punctuation is more sparingly used than by Continental printers. Since the translation can be readily checked against the original on the opposite page, it claims some freedom in such matters as number and tense and syncategorems; and, more for the sake of showing the analogies in St Thomas's thought than of elegant variation, attempts no rigid word for word equivalence on every appearance.

FOOTNOTES

Those signified by a superior number are the references given by St Thomas, with the exception of no. 1 to each article which usually refers to parallel texts in his writings. Those signified alphabetically are editorial references and explanatory remarks.

REFERENCES

Biblical references are to the Vulgate. Patristic references are to Migne (PG, Greek Fathers; PL, Latin Fathers). Abbreviations to St Thomas's works are as follows:

Summa Theologiæ, without title. Part, question, article, reply; e.g. 1a. 3, 2 ad 3. 1a2æ. 17, 6. 2a2æ. 180, 10. 3a. 35, 8.

Summa Contra Gentiles, CG. Book, chapter; e.g. *CG* 1, 28.

Scriptum in IV Libros Sententiarum, Sent. Book, distinction, question, article, solution or *quæstiuncula*, reply; e.g. III *Sent.* 25, 2, 3, ii ad 3.

Compendium Theologiæ, Compend. Theol.

Commentaries of Scripture (*lecturæ, expositiones*): Job, *In Job*; Psalms *In Psalm.*; Isaiah, *In Isa.*; Jeremiah, *In Jerem.*; Lamentations, *In Thren.*, St Matthew, *In Matt.*; St John, *In Joan.*; Epistles of St Paul, e.g. *In Rom.* Chapter, verse, *lectio* as required.

Philosophical commentaries: On the *Liber de Causis, In De causis*. Aristotle: *Peri Hermeneias, In Periherm.*; Posterior Analytics, *In Poster.*; Physics, *In Physic.*; *De Cælo et Mundo, In De Cæl.*; *De Generatione et Corruptione, In De gen.*; *Meteorologica, In Meteor.*; *De Anima, In De anima*; *De Sensu et Sensato, In De sensu*; *De Memoria et Reminiscentia, In De memor.*; Metaphysics, *In Meta.*; Nicomachean Ethics, *In Ethic.*; Politics, *In Pol.* Book, chapter, *lectio* as required, also for Expositions on Boëthius, *Liber de Hebdomadibus* and *Liber de Trinitate, In De hebd.* and *In De Trin.*, and on Dionysius *De Divinis Nominibus, In De div. nom. Quæstiones quodlibetales (de quolibet), Quodl.*

Main titles are given in full for other works, including the 10 series of *Quæstiones Disputatæ.*

References to Aristotle are given the Bekker notation; also, as with those to Proclus and Dionysius, the *lectio* number in St Thomas's exposition.

INTRODUCTION

THE SECOND, and by far the longest,[1] main part of the *Summa*, which opens with this volume, considers the returning home of human creatures to God by their own proper activities in the life of their grace-uplifted nature. It composes St Thomas's moral theology. But having said that, the need to qualify at once arises. For he certainly does not treat it as a special subject to be isolated, either in practice or still less in theory, from the whole body of *sacra doctrina*. His treatises range at large and are very unlike the tidy enclosures made by some later authors, particularly by those whose plan is built on an arrangement of precepts and sins. He gives both these topics special treatment,[2] but for the rest relegates them to corollaries appended to his examination of the living and positive content of acting for God and happiness through the virtues. It may be noted here how curiously absent is the note of legalism from the general discourse of the *Summa*, though its author was such a key figure in circles which included the papal canonists, perhaps the most ambitious group of lawyer-statesmen in European history, and was himself, as he showed on occasion, extremely proficient in their medium.

Instead its temper is rather to be described as biological; the *Prima Secundæ* in particular is like a living thing with an organic unity which can ingest a variety of elements often regarded as of no concern to moral theology. Thus the opening treatise, contained in the present volume, is about the human drive to happiness; it does not raise specifically moral questions at all, nor does the following treatise, on the structure of human acts. Not until Question 18[3] is morality considered as such, and then after four Questions the discourse shifts back to psychology with discussions on the human passions[4] and active dispositions.[5] Then not until Question 55[6] does it broach the matter of living according to virtue, and even so the treatises will include those on original sin[7] and grace[8] which are commonly reckoned to come under dogmatic, not moral theology.

St Thomas drives no deep division between the two disciplines. And in

---

[1]*Prima Secundæ*, 114 Questions; *Secunda Secundæ*, 189 Questions: a total of 303, compared with 119 for the *Prima Pars*, and 90 for the uncompleted *Tertia Pars*. In this series 32 vols out of 60.
[2]1a2æ. 71–80. Vol. 25 & 1a2æ. 90–7. Vol. 28
[3]Vol. 18
[4]Vols 19–21
[5]Vol. 22
[6]Vol. 23
[7]1a2æ. 81–85. Vol. 26
[8]1a2æ. 106–114. Vol. 30

fact the singleness in variety of his thought might be more readily appreciated if, despite the exigencies of a curriculum, no separation were made at all, and the *Summa* read through from beginning to end. He makes clear at the beginning that Christian theology is one science[9] because its medium is the light of divine revelation. It is all about God,[10] yet human topics are not thereby excluded. For if creatures are to be seen as they really are, then it must be as true and good in themselves yet at the same time as wholly from and to God.[11]

How is unity maintained in such diversity? Quite seriously it is all done by mirrors. Not in the manner of Maskelyne and Devant at the Egyptian Hall to produce illusions, but by showing the analogies that run through the whole of reality, from top to bottom and criss-cross. And sometimes it is very much to bottom, for St Thomas is not so high-minded as to disdain the lowlier levels of experience.

So then it is quite of a piece with his entire approach to look for the origins of right and wrong in the human desire for happiness, which comprehends the pleasurable, and even the sensuously pleasurable. First settle the 'can', he thinks, then afterwards the 'ought'. Accordingly the present treatise is less about our duties than our opportunities, for though moral questions are anticipated, notably when the rightness of will required in happiness is considered,[12] it is mainly about the pre-moral condition of being able to act for an end and the post-moral condition of being happy with it.

Moreover the treatise is written in his customary rather dead-pan manner; some may have the impression, from a hasty scanning of these pages, that it purveys somewhat sober stuff, doubtless improving, yet civic and Aristotelean and not very generous. Where the leap, the abandon, the fire in face of divinity? They will have missed the climax of each Question, which breaks out of the gates of the City of Reason, not in a desperate sortie, but at full strength and equipment, a theology with all of its philosophy intact.

The treatise was composed in 1269, when St Thomas was forty-four years old and at the height of his powers. He was beginning his second professorship at the University of Paris, and was soon to write the decisive tracts, *De unitate intellectus contra Averroistas* and *De æternitate mundi contra murmurantes*. He had been summoned to Paris, partly to defend the academic status of the Dominicans, partly, and more importantly, to

[9]Ia. 1, 3. Vol. 1
[10]Ia. 1, 7
[11]Ia. 45, 3. Vol. 8
[12]Ia2æ. 4, 4

counter a lay-minded Aristoteleanism which was attacking the entrench-ments of clerical theology. With much of the contemporary movement he was in agreement, especially as regards the recovery of profane values, the hard-headed rationalism, and the appeal to earthy evidences. That was his strength, and it enabled him to defend so effectively the authentic truths and values of the theological tradition by using the very resources of those who were questioning it.

He had gone over the field of the present treatise in earlier works,[13] but now he had mastered the new material provided by Robert Grosseteste, Albert of Cologne, and William of Moerbeke, and was completing his own careful analysis of the *Nicomachean Ethics*. His late office at the papal court gave him prestige, his collaboration with the Hellenists there gave him assurance.

The purpose of this treatise is to establish a basis for moral theory by an examination of the nature of human activity, or, as he will put it, of what belongs *ad genus naturæ*, not *ad genus moris*.[14] Thence moral theory can mainly proceed in accordance with the inner formation of man's being and acting by nature and grace, and not by his configuration to extrinsic and positive laws.

---

[13]I *Sent.* 1; IV, 49. *CG* III. 2-63
[14]cf 1a2æ. 18, 2 ad 1, 4; 20, 6

Prologus

QUIA, SICUT DAMASCENUS DICIT,[1] homo factus ad imaginem Dei dicitur, secundum quod per imaginem significatur intellectuale et arbitrio liberum et per se potestativum, postquam prædictum est de exemplari, scilicet de Deo, et de his quæ processerunt ex divina potestate secundum ejus voluntatem,[2] restat ut consideremus de ejus imagine, idest de homine secundum quod et ipse est suorum operum principium, quasi liberum arbitrium habens et suorum operum potestatem.

Ubi primo considerandum occurrit de ultimo fine humanæ vitæ, et deinde de his per quæ homo ad hunc finem pervenire potest vel ab eo deviare: ex fine enim oportet accipere rationes eorum quæ ordinantur ad finem. Et quia ultimus finis humanæ vitæ ponitur esse beatitudo, oportet primo considerare de ultimo fine in communi, deinde de beatitudine.

---

[1]*De fide orthodoxa* II, 12. PG 94, 920
[2]1a.2. Introduction
[a]God's image. The rich theological background here, largely filled by St Augustine, relates to man's likeness to God, not only as a footprint, *vestigium*, but also as an image, *imago*, able to reflect him by knowledge and love: cf 1a.93. Vol. 13 of this series, ed. E. Hill. Man's relationship to God is then not purely causal, of creature to creator, of effect to cause, but also objectual, of knower to known, and lover to beloved: cf 1a. 45, 7. Vol. 8, ed. T. Gilby. This theme, which will crop up frequently during the present treatise, shapes the doctrine that God's indwelling in his friends is a special mode of divine presence: cf 1a, 8, 3. Vol. 2, ed. T. McDermott. God is the final cause for moral action; how he is also the object will be developed when the theological virtues are considered: 1a2æ. 62 & 2a2æ. 1–46. A gap still remains to be filled in theological literature by a study of the meaning of *intentio* at full strength: cf 1a2æ. 18, 7 & 19, 7, 8. Vol. 18, ed. T. Gilby, Appendices 13 & 14.
[b]St John of Damascus, d. 749. The last of the Greek Fathers. A twelfth-century Latin translation of his *De fide orthodoxa* had come out of Italian trade with the Levant, and was a prized theological text in the high Middle Ages.
[c]Exemplar: the idea of a thing in the mind of its maker. For the divine Ideas, cf 1a. 15, 1–3. Vol. 4, ed. T. Gornall. Also 1a. 44, 3. Vol. 8.
[d]Production through will, not natural emanation: cf 1a. 19, 4. Vol. 5, ed. T. Gilby.
[e]Is such a course just theological anthropology? No matter. St Thomas would be perturbed no more than if the first half of the *Prima Pars* were to be set down as

Foreword

MAN IS MADE TO GOD'S IMAGE,[a] and since this implies, so Damascene tells us,[1b] that he is intelligent and free to judge and master of himself, so then, now that we have agreed that God is the exemplar cause[c] of things and that they issue from his power through his will,[2d] we go on to look at this image, that is to say, at man as the source of actions which are his own and fall under his responsibility and control.[e]

The first matter to come up is the destiny of human life, and next how it may be reached or missed:[f] remember, all our plans get their meaning from their final purpose. Happiness is set down as being this;[g] accordingly we shall start with human teleology in general (1), and then relate it to happiness (2-5).

---

anthropological theology: cf 1a. 1. Vol. 1, ed. T. Gilby. 1a. 13. Vol. 3, ed. H. McCabe. What he has done in the second half of the *Prima Pars* is to consider the human creature for what it is in itself, that is, wholly from God: cf 1a. 45, 3. Vol. 8. Now he considers the same thing, but as wholly to God, and so begins the second part, *Secunda Pars*, of the *Summa*. Yet his moral theology does not represent a switch to a field other than that of dogmatic theology: the separate treatment of the two disciplines calls for more safeguards than is customarily accorded. *Sacra doctrina* is centred on God, and loses nothing of its single-mindedness when it also extends to his friends and creatures: 1a. 1, 3 & 7.

Note, too, from the start, that man will be taken throughout as he really is within the economy of divine Providence, that is, compact of natural claims and of supernatural needs for grace and mercy, not in a hypothetical state of pure nature, though this may appear as a methodological abstract to furnish a point of reference. Hence the constant appeal will be to God's revelation transmitted by the Christian Church, though the discourse will quite easily gather in teachings from Plato and Aristotle, and St Augustine's meditations on Cicero, *De vita beata*.

[f]The treatises onward from 1a2æ. 6, on human acts, until the end of the *Secunda Secundæ*.

[g]Namely by Aristotle. Happiness, *beatitudo, eudaimonia*. The author here declares his hand, though it will not be until 1a2æ. 18, Vol. 18, ed. T. Gilby, that an explicit moral theory will enter into eudemonism.

Quæstio 1. de ultimo fine hominis

CIRCA PRIMUM quæruntur octo:

1. utrum hominis sit agere propter finem;
2. utrum hoc sit proprium rationalis naturæ;
3. utrum actus hominis recipiant speciem a fine;
4. utrum sit aliquis ultimus finis humanæ vitæ;
5. utrum unius hominis possint esse plures ultimi fines;
6. utrum homo ordinet omnia in ultimum finem;
7. utrum idem sit finis ultimus omnium hominum;
8. utrum in illo ultimo fine omnes aliæ creaturæ conveniant.

articulus 1. utrum homini conveniat agere propter finem

AD PRIMUM sic proceditur:[1] 1. Videtur quod homini non conveniat agere propter finem. Causa enim naturaliter prior est. Sed finis habet rationem ultimi, ut ipsum nomen sonat. Ergo finis non habet rationem causæ. Sed propter illud agit homo, quod est causa actionis: cum hæc præpositio *propter* designet habitudinem causæ. Ergo homini non convenit agere propter finem.

2. Præterea, illud quod est ultimus finis non est propter finem. Sed in quibusdam actiones sunt ultimus finis; ut patet per Philosophum in *Ethic.*[2] Ergo non omnia homo agit propter finem.

3. Præterea, tunc videtur homo agere propter finem quando deliberat. Sed multa homo agit absque deliberatione, de quibus etiam quandoque nihil cogitat; sicut cum aliquis movet pedem vel manum aliis intentus, vel fricat barbam. Non ergo homo omnia agit propter finem.

SED CONTRA, omnia quæ sunt in aliquo genere derivantur a principio illius generis. Sed finis est principium in operabilibus ab homine; ut patet per Philosophum in *Physic.*[3] Ergo homini convenit omnia agere propter finem.

---

[1]cf 1a2æ. 6, 1. *CG* III, 2   [2]*Ethics*, I, 1. 1094a4
[3]*Physics*. II. 9. 200a34
[a]End, an analogical term: take here as final cause or objective purpose. cf Glossary, also Appendix 1.

Readings for this Question. J. Rohmer, *La finalité chez les théologiens de saint Augustin à Duns Scotus*, Paris, 1939. O. Lottin, *Psychologie et morale aux XIIe. et XIIIe. siècles.* Vol. 1, *Problèmes de psychologie*, Louvain, 1942. V. de Broglie, *De fine ultimo humanæ vitæ*, Paris, 1948.

For scholastic commentaries on this part of the *Summa* two classical works are recommended. D. Bañez, *De fine ultimo et de actibus humanis*, unpublished until edited by V. Beltrán de Heredia, Salamanca, 1942. B. de Medina, *Expositio in 1am2æ Angelici Doctoris*, Salamanca, 1582.

2

Question 1. purpose in life

UNDER THIS HEADING there are eight points of inquiry:

1. whether we should speak of men acting for an end;[a]
2. whether this is peculiar to rational beings;
3. whether the end determines the kind of act they do;
4. whether human life has an ultimate goal;
5. whether an individual can have several final ends;
6. whether there is an over-riding purpose in all a man does;
7. whether this is the same for all;
8. and common to all creatures.[b]

article 1. does acting for an end apply to man?

THE FIRST POINT:[1] 1. It seems not. For of its nature a cause comes before an effect. Now an end, as the name indicates, means what comes last. Consequently its meaning is not that of being a cause. This with respect to a man's deeds is what he acts 'on account of': the preposition designates the causal relationship. His actions, therefore, are not on account of their endings.

2. Besides, an ultimate end is not for another end. Yet sometimes, as Aristotle shows,[2] actions themselves are ultimates.[c] And so not all a man does is for an end.

3. In addition, then apparently does a man plan for an end when he acts deliberately. However he does many things without deliberation, sometimes even without thinking about them, as when absently he makes a gesture or shifts his feet or rubs his chin. Not all he does, then, are of set purpose.

ON THE OTHER HAND, all specimens of a class have a common root.[d] Now, as Aristotle points out,[3] men's deeds originate from having an aim. And so this is why they are performed.

---

[b]The Question falls into two groups of articles; that there is a final aim of activity (to art. 4), and that it is single, namely God (5-8).
[c]That is, are values, *honesta*, or are pleasurable, *delectabilia*, and therefore not just means, *utilia*, to something else: cf 1a. 5, 6. The point will recur.
[d]A common *principium*: a broader term than element or cause, it stands for any kind of start, beginning, origin, or source, whether in reality or just in the logical order of thought: cf 1a. 33, 1.
Note that a *sed contra* is usually a statement of position, sometimes a gambit, sometimes an appeal to authority, sometimes put forward as a persuasion, by showing what is fitting, *conveniens*, or otherwise would be odd, *inconveniens*.

3

RESPONSIO: Dicendum quod actionum quæ ab homine aguntur, illæ solæ proprie dicuntur *humanæ* quæ sunt propriæ hominis inquantum est homo. Differt autem homo ab aliis irrationalibus creaturis in hoc, quod est suorum actuum dominus. Unde illæ solæ actiones vocantur proprie humanæ quarum homo est dominus.

Est autem homo dominus suorum actuum per rationem et voluntatem: unde et liberum arbitrium esse dicitur *facultas voluntatis et rationis*.[4] Illæ ergo actiones proprie humanæ dicuntur quæ ex voluntate deliberata procedunt. Si quæ autem aliæ actiones homini conveniant, possunt dici quidem *hominis* actiones; sed non proprie humanæ, cum non sint hominis inquantum est homo.

Manifestum est autem quod omnes actiones quæ procedunt ab aliqua potentia causantur ab ea secundum rationem sui objecti. Objectum autem voluntatis est finis et bonum. Unde oportet quod omnes actiones humanæ propter finem sint.

1. Ad primum ergo dicendum quod finis, etsi sit postremus in executione, est tamen primus in intentione agentis. Et hoc modo habet rationem causæ.

2. Ad secundum dicendum quod, si qua actio humana sit ultimus finis, oportet eam esse voluntariam: alias non esset humana, ut dictum est.[5] Actio autem aliqua dupliciter dicitur voluntaria: uno modo quia imperatur a voluntate, sicut ambulare vel loqui; alio modo quia elicitur a voluntate, sicut ipsum velle. Impossibile autem est quod ipse actus a voluntate elicitus sit ultimus finis. Nam objectum voluntatis est finis, sicut objectum visus

---

[4]Peter Lombard, II *Sent.*, 24, 3   [5]In the body of the art.

[e]Psychologically the difference lies in intelligence and the ensuing rational appetite of will, which is self-determining with respect to objects which are for an end: morally it lies in responsibility with respect to what ought to be done. Morality will be restricted later to the field of human actions properly so called.

[f]Peter Lombard (1100–60), the Master of the *Sentences*, the text for many commentaries in the Middle Ages. Reason: take narrowly here for the mind as coming to conclusions or decisions, rather than as having insight, *intellectus*. A parallel distinction applies to the will, which should be understood here as *boulēsis*, deliberate willing, which adapts itself by choice of goods which are to an end, rather than as *thelēsis* which intends good as an end: cf 3a. 18, 3. The practical discourse is shared by mind and will: 1a. 79, 8 & 83, 4. 1a2æ. 12 & 13. The free decision is called *liberum arbitrium*, not always adequately rendered as 'freewill', which may slur over the practical rôle of reason. *Ethics* VI, 11. 1113a11. 1a. 83, 3.

[g]Shaped by its formal interest, literally 'caused by the nature of its object'. The principle, which runs throughout the *Summa*, will be significantly applied in the course of the treatise: cf note *a* to Foreword. All powers, dispositions, and activities relate to an object, which as a real thing in a sufficiently complete though undifferentiated situation is called the 'material object', and as offering that special aspect which engaged the power, disposition and activity is called the 'formal object'.

REPLY: Of the actions a man performs those alone are properly called *human* which are characteristically his as a man. He differs from non-intelligent creatures in this, that he is the master of what he does. Consequently those actions alone which lie under his control are properly called human.[e]

Now he is master through his mind and will, which is why his free decision is referred to as an ability *of reason and will*.[4f] Therefore those acts alone are properly called human which are of his own deliberate willing. Others that may be attributed to him may be called 'acts of a man', but not 'human acts', since they are not his precisely as a human being.

Clearly all activities a power elicits come from it as shaped by its formal interest.[g] And this, for the will, is being an end and good.[h] Consequently all human acts must be for the sake of an end.[1]

Hence: 1. Though last in respect to execution, an end comes first in respect to the agent's intention: it is thus that it has the force of a cause.[j]

2. A human act that were an ultimate would still have to be willed, otherwise, as we have observed,[5] it would not be human.[k] An act can be willed in two ways, first as being commanded by the will, thus speaking or walking; second as being elicited from the will, thus willing itself.[l] Let us start with this elicited act. For it to be itself the ultimate end is out of the question, since the end is its objective, as colour is sight's objective.

---

[h]On the will as a power of which the object is good-as-the-end, cf 1a2æ. 8.

[1]Notice the words of the conclusion. The teleological formula for this part of the *Summa* is that actions rather than things are for an end. cf Appendix 1, and Glossary *s.v.* 'end'.

[j]The order of intention, constituted by cognitional and appetitional relations to objects, which scale down from judging and willing ends to the deliberate choosing of what is for them. The order of execution, the subsequent carrying out of the decision. The twelve stages in the dynamic structure of a complete human act are examined 1a2æ. 8–17. See also Vol. 18, Appendix 5, note 5.

The end is a cause in the order of intention, nevertheless it is wanted as a thing, not as a thought of a thing. Cajetan *in loc*: to be intended is a condition of its causality, to be effectively reached coincides with its causality, to be real is of the essence of its causality.

[k]The *voluntarium*, or the nature of voluntary activity is discussed later, 1a2æ. 6. It has two requirements, that the activity is natural and spontaneous or from within (and so is not forced or artificial) and that it works through knowledge (and so is not blind or ignorant). Since some perception of ends is present in animals, their natural actions are in a sense voluntary, but in its proper sense the term is restricted to rational beings: 1a2æ. 6, 2. Note that it is not strictly speaking synonymous with human or moral acts, which are voluntary acts working through deliberation and choice: the terminology can prove confusing. All acting through mind and will, e.g. our seeing God in the beatific vision and loving, is not 'voluntary' in the sense of being free. cf note *f* above.

[l]*Actus elicitus*, here an act from and in the will; *actus imperatus*, an act from the will but in another power. The distinction will occur again, and applied to the hierarchy of the virtues. Thus religion may command what it does not elicit, e.g. almsdeeds.

est color: unde sicut impossibile est quod primum visibile sit ipsum videre, quia omne videre est alicujus objecti visibilis, ita impossibile est quod primum appetibile, quod est finis, sit ipsum velle. Unde relinquitur quod, si qua actio humana sit ultimus finis, quod ipsa sit imperata a voluntate. Et ita ibi aliqua actio hominis, ad minus ipsum velle, est propter finem. Quidquid ergo homo faciat, verum est dicere quod homo agit propter finem, etiam agendo actionem quæ est ultimus finis.

3. Ad tertium dicendum quod hujusmodi actiones non sunt proprie humanæ, quia non procedunt ex deliberatione rationis, quæ est proprium principium humanorum actuum. Et ideo habent quidem finem imaginatum, non autem per rationem præstitutum.

articulus 2. utrum agere propter finem sit proprium rationalis naturæ

AD SECUNDUM sic proceditur:[1] 1. Videtur quod agere propter finem sit proprium rationalis naturæ. Homo enim, cujus est agere propter finem, nunquam agit propter finem ignotum. Sed multa sunt quæ non cognoscunt finem: vel quia omnino carent cognitione, sicut creaturæ insensibiles, vel quia non apprehendunt rationem finis, sicut bruta animalia. Videtur ergo proprium esse rationalis naturæ agere propter finem.

2. Præterea, agere propter finem est ordinare suam actionem ad finem. Sed hoc est rationis opus. Ergo non convenit his quæ ratione carent.

3. Præterea, bonum et finis est objectum voluntatis. Sed *voluntas in ratione est*,[2] ut dicitur in *De Anima*. Ergo agere propter finem non est nisi rationalis naturæ.

SED CONTRA est quod Philosophus probat in *Physic.*[3] quod *non solum intellectus, sed etiam natura agit propter finem.*

RESPONSIO: Dicendum quod omnia agentia necesse est agere propter finem. Causarum enim ad invicem ordinatarum, si prima subtrahatur, necesse est alias subtrahi. Prima autem inter omnes causas est causa finalis. Cujus ratio est, quia materia non consequitur formam nisi secundum quod movetur ab agente: nihil enim reducit se de potentia in actum. Agens autem non movet nisi ex intentione finis. Si enim agens non esset determinatum ad

---

[1] cf Ia2æ. 12, 5. *CG* II, 23; III, 1, 2, 16 & 24. *De potentia* I, 5; III, 15. *In Meta.* V, lect. 16

[2] *De Anima* III, 9. 432b5   [3] *Physics* II, 5. 196b21

m Yet people can be in love with love, particularly in friendship, which is a supple, complex, and reflex activity, not moving rigidly in one direction: cf 2a2æ. 25, 2.

n The question will be pursued later, and a distinction will be drawn in the following Question between the end as a thing or object, *finis cujus gratia, to heneka*, and the

What is first visible cannot be the act of seeing, for this always lights on some visible object, and no more can the very act of loving be the first beloved, or the end.^m And so we are left to speculate whether the ultimate might not be an act commanded by the will. Yet even there the human act, at least on the part of the willing, will be on account of the end.ⁿ Therefore it is true to say that whatever a man does is for an end, even in the doing of an act which holds the ultimate end.

3. Semi-automatic movements of this sort are not human actions in the strict sense, for they do not come from reasoned deliberation, which sets the stage on which men act as men. Such ends as are present stay on the level of sense, and are not presented by reason.^o

article 2. is acting for an end proper to rational beings?

THE SECOND POINT:¹ 1. So it seems.^a Acting with purpose is a function of a human being, and he never does so without knowing what he is about. Yet many beings are not aware of an end, for either they are quite without consciousness, thus insentient things, or they do not recognize the meaning of end and purpose, thus brute animals. Apparently, then, acting with purpose is exclusively for rational beings.

2. Moreover, to aim at an end is to direct activity towards it. This is the work of reason. And is not therefore found in things without reason.

3. Further, being an end and good is the object of willing. Now willing, as Aristotle notes,² *is in the reason*. And so acting for an end is for none but a being of a rational nature.

ON THE OTHER HAND Aristotle proves that *nature as well as intelligence acts for a purpose*.³

REPLY: All efficient causes must needs act for an end. In an ordered system of causes, strike out the first, and the others have to go too. And the first of all causes is the final cause or end. Our reasoning goes as follows: matter does not achieve form unless it be changed by an efficient cause, for nothing potential is self-actualizing.^b Now an efficient cause does not start this change except by intending an end. For were it not shaped towards pro-

---

end-condition of the subject obtaining it, *finis quo*. That the act of possession can be an act of will is later denied: 1a2æ. 3, 4.
^oSee note *k* above.
^aProper, i.e. peculiar or exclusive to: rational beings, i.e. creatures with intelligence. The argument will be for the need of a final cause before any other type of cause can come into play, not for an ultimate in a series of final causes, for which see below, art. 4. Yet though the end comes first in causing, it comes last in the thing caused: 1a. 5, 4.
^bA cardinal principle, first stated 1a. 2, 3. Here applied to material taking shape.

aliquem effectum, non magis ageret hoc quam illud: ad hoc ergo quod determinatum effectum producat, necesse est quod determinetur ad aliquid certum, quod habet rationem finis. Hæc autem determinatio, sicut in rationali natura fit per rationalem appetitum, qui dicitur voluntas, ita in aliis fit per inclinationem naturalem, quæ dicitur appetitus naturalis.

Tamen considerandum est quod aliquid sua actione vel motu tendit ad finem dupliciter: uno modo sicut seipsum ad finem movens, ut homo; alio modo sicut ab alio motum ad finem, sicut sagitta tendit ad determinatum finem ex hoc quod movetur a sagittante, qui suam actionem dirigit in finem. Illa ergo quæ rationem habent, seipsa movent ad finem: quia habent dominium suorum actuum per liberum arbitrium, quod est *facultas voluntatis et rationis*.[4] Illa vero quæ ratione carent tendunt in finem per naturalem inclinationem, quasi ab alio mota, non autem a seipsis: cum non cognoscant rationem finis, et ideo nihil in finem ordinare possunt, sed solum in finem ab alio ordinantur. Nam tota irrationalis natura comparatur ad Deum sicut instrumentum ad agens principale, ut supra habitum est.[5]

Et ideo proprium est naturæ rationalis ut tendat in finem quasi se agens vel ducens ad finem, naturæ vero irrationalis quasi ab alio acta vel ducta, sive in finem apprehensum, sicut bruta animalia, sive in finem non apprehensum, sicut ea quæ omnino cognitione carent.

1. Ad primum ergo dicendum quod homo, quando per seipsum agit propter finem, cognoscit finem: sed quando ab alio agitur vel ducitur, puta cum agit ad imperium alterius, vel cum movetur altero impellente, non est necessarium quod cognoscat finem. Et ita est in creaturis irrationalibus.

---

[4]Peter Lombard, II *Sent.*, 24, 3   [5]1a. 22, 2 ad 4

cA nature is its end, says Aristotle, thereby indicating how his natural philosophy is no mere classification of static types. Accordingly the definition of a thing should cast forward to its purpose, whether proposed by a governing mind or embodied in the immediate agent, rather than in its result, which may be arrested or open itself out for other indefinite ends. Thus a clockmaker proposes to make an instrument for telling the time, yet it may be used as an antique piece of furniture: laying a fertilized egg has the biological purpose of perpetuating the species, but other purposes, culinary or cosmetic, may supervene; yet the internal finality of the hen is not directed to making an omelette or beauty-cream. cf art. 1, note *j*. The 'intention' referred to in the text is not, of course, necessarily appreciated by the immediate agent at work.

dAppetite, *orexis:* a relationship, *habitudo*, to the good; in creatures a bent or tendency, *inclinatio*, to a good other than themselves, arising from their forms, which make them actual beings, not active beings. To reach their good they have to be not merely being but also acting. cf art. 3, note *c*.

Their natural form originates a natural appetite, a *pondus naturæ*, which as such is unconscious. A form they possess by understanding, *forma intelligibilis*, originates a voluntary or rational appetite. cf 1a. 19, 1. Vol. 5, ed. T. Gilby. 1a. 59, 1. Vol. 19, ed. K. Foster. 1a. 60, 1.

ducing a determinate effect, it would not produce this rather than that, and to produce a determinate effect it must be set on something defined, which is what an end, *finis*, implies.[c] In rational beings this determinateness is attained through the rational appetite, termed will, in other beings through an inborn bent, termed natural appetite.[d]

Observe all the same that a thing in its acting and moving may tend towards an end in two ways. First, by setting itself in motion towards it, thus a man; second, by being set in motion towards it, thus an arrow flighted by an archer to the target. Now things possessing intelligence set themselves in motion towards an end, for they are masters of their acts through their own free decision, of which they are capable by reason and will,[4] whereas things without intelligence tend towards their ends by their natural bent stimulated by another, not by themselves; they do not grasp what being an end means, and therefore cannot plan, but can only be planned for a purpose as such.[e] In fact, as we have established,[5] the whole of non-rational nature is compared to God as an instrumental to a principal cause.[f]

Our conclusion is that to be self-acting and bringing oneself to an end is proper to rational beings, whereas non-rational beings are acted on and brought there, whether with some purposive perception, as in brute animals, or without it, as in things quite devoid of sensation.[g]

Hence: 1. When a man is self-acting for an end he appreciates what it is, but not necessarily when he is led or driven by another—he may be carrying out orders blindly or submitting to force, like non-rational creatures.

The terms 'nature' and 'natural' have varying meanings in the *Summa*, which can be decided only from the context. Here natural appetite is contrasted with voluntary appetite, a natural agent, *agens per naturam*, with a will-agent, *agens per voluntatem*. Elsewhere the contrast may be, with the violent or forced, or with the artificial, or with the civilized, or with the juridical, or with the supernatural, or with the preternatural.

[e]What an end means, *ratio finis*. This does not require that the end-object is comprehended or even recognized in its true nature, but that it is at least inferred as an x to which other objects are subordinate (cf by analogy our rational knowledge of the existence of God. 1a. 2, 1 & 2. Vol. 2). That it be perceived or anticipated by sense as the last item of a process to be initiated, that is to say as a term of action, is not enough; it has to be an object of action. Though animals are not machines, but exhibit inner and sense purposes, they are without teleological thinking. 1a2æ. 6, 2. Art. 1, notes *j* & *k*. Note *c* above.

[f]Yet note that while there is no instrumentality in God's creative activity, 1a. 45, 5, nevertheless creatures are true principal causes in their own order, 1a. 105, 5.

[g]This activity, not merely of consciously willing, but also of making up one's own mind and carrying out a decision, is analysed in the following treatise, 1a2æ. 6–17. Vol. 17.

2. Ad secundum dicendum quod ordinare in finem est ejus quod seipsum agit in finem. Ejus vero quod ab alio in finem agitur est ordinari in finem. Quod potest esse irrationalis naturæ, sed ab aliquo rationem habente.

3. Ad tertium dicendum quod objectum voluntatis est finis et bonum in universali. Unde non potest esse voluntas in his quæ carent ratione et intellectu, cum non possint apprehendere universale: sed est in eis appetitus naturalis vel sensitivus, determinatus ad aliquod bonum particulare. Manifestum autem est quod particulares causæ moventur a causa universali; sicut rector civitatis, qui intendit bonum commune, movet suo imperio omnia particularia officia civitatis. Et ideo necesse est quod omnia quæ carent ratione moveantur in fines particulares ab aliqua voluntate rationali, quæ se extendit in bonum universale, scilicet a voluntate divina.

articulus 3. *utrum actus hominis recipiant speciem ex fine*

AD TERTIUM sic proceditur:[1] 1. Videtur quod actus humani non recipiant speciem a fine. Finis enim est causa extrinseca. Sed unumquodque habet speciem ab aliquo principio intrinseco. Ergo actus humani non recipiunt speciem a fine.

2. Præterea, illud quod dat speciem oportet esse prius. Sed finis est posterior in esse. Ergo actus humanus non habet speciem a fine.

3. Præterea, idem non potest esse nisi in una specie. Sed eundem numero actum contingit ordinari ad diversos fines. Ergo finis non dat speciem actibus humanis.

SED CONTRA est quod dicit Augustinus,[2] *Secundum quod finis est culpabilis vel laudabilis, secundum hoc sunt opera nostra culpabilia vel laudabilia.*

RESPONSIO: Dicendum quod unumquodque sortitur speciem secundum actum, et non secundum potentiam: unde ea quæ sunt composita ex materia et forma constituuntur in suis speciebus per proprias formas.

---

[1]cf 1a2æ. 18, 6; 72, 3. II *Sent.* 40, 1. *De virtutibus* I, 2 ad 3; II, 3
[2]*De moribus Eccl. et Manich.* II, 13. PL 32, 1356
[h]Universal value, cause. Common good. There is a wealth of suggestion here, but to keep to the thread of the argument the reader need take universal to mean here no more than not restricted to, though implied in, any one exemplification particularized in space and time. The analogy from the sovereign ruler rather weakens the argument if the common good suggests only the collective good, or the good of the majority. But see 1a2æ. 90, 2. Vol. 28, ed. T. Gilby, Appendix 4.
[1]cf 1a. 19, 4. Vol. 5.

2. To plan things for an end is the function of an agent which activates itself with respect to it, to be shaped to an end is that of one which is activated with respect to it. Purpose, therefore, can run through non-rational nature, though it derives from some agent with intelligence.

3. The object of the will is end-goodness as a universal value. Consequently will is absent from things without intelligence or reason, since they cannot apprehend a universal. Yet they have within them a natural appetite or a sense appetite set towards some particular good. Now it is clear that particular causes are moved by a universal cause—they are like departmental officials directed by a sovereign ruler who intends the common good.[h] The conclusion is inescapable that all things without intelligence are set in motion to their particular ends by an intelligent will which comprehends each and every good, and this is the divine will.[1]

article 3. are human acts what they are by reason of their end?

THE THIRD POINT:[1] 1. Apparently not.[a] For an end is an extrinsic cause, whereas essential character is determined by an intrinsic principle. Therefore a human act's essential character is not determined by its end.

2. Besides, what stamps is prior to what is stamped. Yet the end is posterior in reality to the human act, and in consequence does not stamp it.

3. Again, one and the same thing can belong only to one species. However, a single act can happen to have various aims. The species of a human act, therefore, is not settled by its aim.

ON THE OTHER HAND there is Augustine saying that *according as their aim is worthy of blame or praise so are our deeds worthy of blame or praise.*[2]

REPLY: A thing gets its specific character from being actual, not potential.[b] This is why things composed of matter and form are constituted in their species by their own proper forms.

---

[a]We are still on the threshold of moral theology, and the inquiry is whether the end determines the nature of a human act, not whether it determines its morality: this is discussed later, 1a2æ. 18, 6, 7 & 19, 7, 8. Vol. 18. Nevertheless, as often happens in the *Summa*, a coming question casts its shadow before.

The article is about the immediate and essential purpose of a human act, *finis operis*, not about a supervening and incidental personal motive brought into play, *finis operantis*.

[b]A thing's specific character is signified by its definition, and this, in zoology for instance, applies to an adult and not an embryonic specimen.

Et hoc etiam considerandum est in motibus propriis. Cum enim motus quodammodo distinguatur per actionem et passionem, utrumque horum ab actu speciem sortitur: actio quidem ab actu qui est principium agendi, passio vero ab actu qui est terminus motus. Unde calefactio actio nihil aliud est quam motio quædam a calore procedens, calefactio vero passio nihil aliud est quam motus ad calorem: definitio autem manifestat rationem speciei.

Et utroque modo actus humani, sive considerentur per modum actionum sive per modum passionum, a fine speciem sortiuntur. Utroque enim modo possunt considerari actus humani; eo quod homo movet seipsum et movetur a seipso.

Dictum est autem supra[3] quod actus dicuntur humani inquantum procedunt a voluntate deliberata. Objectum autem voluntatis est bonum et finis. Et ideo manifestum est quod principium humanorum actuum, inquantum sunt humani, est finis.

Et similiter est terminus eorundem: nam id ad quod terminatur actus humanus est id quod voluntas intendit tanquam finem; sicut in agentibus naturalibus forma generati est conformis formæ generantis.

Et quia, ut Ambrosius dicit *mores proprie dicuntur humani*,[4] actus morales proprie speciem sortiuntur ex fine: nam idem sunt actus morales et actus humani.

1. Ad primum ergo dicendum quod finis non est omnino aliquid extrinsecum ab actu, quia comparatur ad actum ut principium vel terminus; et hoc ipsum est de ratione actus, ut scilicet sit ab aliquo quantum ad actionem, et ut sit ad aliquid quantum ad passionem.

2. Ad secundum dicendum quod finis secundum quod est prior in intentione, ut dictum est,[5] secundum hoc pertinet ad voluntatem. Et hoc modo dat speciem actui humano sive morali.

3. Ad tertium dicendum quod idem actus numero, secundum quod semel egreditur ab agente, non ordinatur nisi ad unum finem proximum, a quo habet speciem: sed potest ordinari ad plures fines remotos, quorum unus est finis alterius. Possibile tamen est quod unus actus secundum speciem naturæ ordinetur ad diversos fines voluntatis: sicut hoc ipsum quod est occidere hominem, quod est idem secundum speciem naturæ, potest ordinari sicut in finem ad conservationem justitiæ et ad

---

[3] art. 1 above   [4]*Super Lucam*, Foreword. PL 15, 1612   [5]art. 1, ad 1
[c]The argument now moves from the 'first actuality' of things, namely their form in being, to the 'second actuality', namely their form in acting. cf below 1a2æ. 3, 2. Here this is described in terms of motion or change, yet the argument rests on common notions, and there is no need to explore Aristotelean kinetics. The 'passion' referred to is the category correlative to action, *actio-passio*, not the emotional feeling.

The same consideration also governs their proper motions.[c] There are as it were[d] two sides in a motion or change, the acting and the being acted on, and the character of each is decided by what is actual, the character of the action by that which actively starts the change, the character of the passion by the act which is its finish; for instance, heating in its active sense is a sort of certain change coming from heat, and in its passive sense one going to heat. Such definition makes a specific meaning clear.

Now to apply this to the present inquiry. A human act can be looked at as a manner of action and also of passion, since a man both sets himself in motion and is set in motion by himself.[e] Looked at either way it gets its specific character from the end.

We have already noted[3] that acts are called human inasmuch as they proceed from deliberate willing. Now the object of will is being an end and good, and so it is clear that this is the determining principle of human acts as such.[f]

Likewise it is their achievement as well, for it is the finish the will intends, as, to strike an analogy from physical causation, the form of a thing generated matches the form of the thing generating.[g]

Ambrose[h] writes that *morals are properly called human*.[4] Indeed moral acts and human acts are the same. So then we may add that the end also provides moral acts with their proper specific character.[i]

Hence: 1. The end is not altogether extrinsic to the act, but is related to it as its origin and destination, and so enters into its very nature, for as an action it is from something and as a passion it is towards something.

2. We have observed[5] that the end affects the will as prior by intention, and in this way does it give specific character to a human or moral act.

3. An act done but once is not directed except to one immediate end, and from this it gets its specific character, but it can be meant for several further ends, of which one is designed for another. All the same it is possible for an act of one physical kind to be willed for diverse ends; for instance the taking of human life considered as a physical event is generically always the same, yet considered as a moral act it can be of specifically different kinds

---

[d]A distinction of a sort, *quodammodo*, for in a real situation acting on and being acted on coincide. Vol. 2, Appendix 3.

[e]As when he decides to read a book. Or indeed when he performs any 'imperated' act. cf art. 1 ad 2 above.

[f]In other words, the end is the shaping principle of will because it is the object of will.

[g]The rightness of will is to be judged by what is intended, and only by what results, *eventus sequens*, in so far as this is somehow intended: cf 1a2æ. 20, 5. Vol. 18.

[h]St Ambrose of Milan (340–397). Invited St Augustine to read Isaiah, not Plotinus (*Confessions* IX, 5); his importance as a moral theorist is doubtful.

[i]cf 1a2æ. 18, 4, 6; 19, 7.

satisfaciendum iræ. Et ex hoc erunt diversi actus secundum speciem moris: quia uno modo erit actus virtutis, alio modo erit actus vitii. Non enim motus recipit speciem ab eo quod est terminus per accidens, sed solum ab eo quod est terminus per se. Fines autem morales accidunt rei naturali; et e converso ratio naturalis finis accidit morali. Et ideo nihil prohibet actus qui sunt iidem secundum speciem naturæ esse diversos secundum speciem moris, et e converso.

articulus 4. utrum sit aliquis ultimus finis humanae vitae

AD QUARTUM sic proceditur:[1] 1. Videtur quod non sit aliquis ultimus finis humanæ vitæ, sed procedatur in finibus in infinitum. Bonum enim, secundum suam rationem, est diffusivum sui, ut patet per Dionysium.[2] Si ergo quod procedit ex bono ipsum etiam est bonum oportet quod illud bonum diffundat aliud bonum: et sic processus boni est in infinitum. Sed bonum habet rationem finis. Ergo in finibus est processus in infinitum.

2. Præterea, ea quæ sunt rationis in infinitum multiplicari possunt: unde et mathematicæ quantitates in infinitum augentur. Species etiam numerorum propter hoc sunt infinitæ, quia, dato quolibet numero, ratio alium majorem excogitare potest. Sed desiderium finis sequitur apprehensionem rationis. Ergo videtur quod etiam in finibus procedatur in infinitum.

3. Præterea, bonum et finis est objectum voluntatis. Sed voluntas infinities potest reflecti supra seipsam: possum enim velle aliquid, et velle me velle illud, et sic in infinitum. Ergo in finibus humanæ voluntatis proceditur in infinitum, et non est aliquis ultimus finis humanæ voluntatis.

SED CONTRA est quod Philosophus dicit,[3] quod *qui infinitum faciunt auferunt naturam boni.* Sed bonum est quod habet rationem finis. Ergo contra rationem finis est quod procedatur in infinitum. Necesse est ergo ponere unum ultimum finem.

RESPONSIO: Dicendum quod, per se loquendo, impossibile est in finibus

---

[1]cf *In Meta.* II, *lect. 4. In Ethic.* I, *lect.* I
[2]*De divinis nominibus* 4. PG 3, 719 (cf 694 & 698) St Thomas, *lect.* I
[3]*Metaphysics* I, 2. 994b12
ʲThe later teaching of Ia2æ. 18, 4 is offered as justification for the free translation. cf Vol. 18, Appendices 10, *The Form of Moral Good,* and 11, *Moral Objectives.* Moral objects depend on natural objects, and moral judgments (ought) on psychological judgements (can), but are not to be resolved into them.
ᵃThis article, which pushes beyond the preceding ones to show that the final end is a thing, not just a real meaning, introduces the succeeding articles which culminate by establishing that this is God, art. 8. It supposes the conclusion arrived at in previous discussions on the infinite, Ia. 7 (Vol. 2) and on an infinite causal series,

when the purpose is upholding justice or when satisfying anger: one is an act of virtue, the other an act of vice. Now an action receives its specific character from a term that is essential to it, not incidental. Moral purposes lie outside merely natural processes, and conversely the purpose there does not constitute moral situations.[j] And so there is nothing to stop acts of the same physical category from belonging to diverse moral categories, and vice versa.

article 4. has human life an ultimate goal?

THE FOURTH POINT:[1] 1. No, for its aims stretch out indefinitely.[a] It is clear from Dionysius[b] that to spread itself is of the nature of good.[2] If that which springs from good is itself good, then this in its turn should pour itself out in another good, and so on with never a stop. But a good implies the meaning of aim. Therefore there can be a series of aims without limit.

2. Further, mental entities can be infinitely multiplied; thus mathematical quantities can be infinitely increased, and numbers too, for given one figure a greater can always be thought of. Now the will's desire for an end follows the thought of it in the reason. Consequently it seems there can be an infinite progression of purposes.

3. Then also, to be a good and an end is what engages the will. Now the willing can revolve on itself indefinitely, for I can will something, and will to will it, and so on and so on. Hence ends for human willing can stretch out ceaselessly without any one of them being ultimate.

ON THE OTHER HAND there is Aristotle teaching that *to maintain an indefinite is to deny it the nature of good,*[3c] which means being an end. The prospect of going on indefinitely is tantamount to this. Hence the need of positing an ultimate end.

REPLY: Whichever way you look at it, whether from the point of view of

---

1a. 2, 3 & 1a. 46, 2 ad 7 (Vols. 2 & 8): the distinction should be borne in mind between the indefinite, the non-defined by form, and the true infinite, the non-defined by matter or potentiality, 1a. 7, 1. Also that between a series of causes in essential and in incidental subordination. A succession of causal items may be interminable, at least on the grounds of their causality. Thus the catalogue of Don Juan's amours in Leporello's celebrated aria has to be curtailed, not because the causality in profligacy has to come to a stop with any intermediate object, but because of the limits of one man's life and one piece of music.
[b]The Pseudo-Dionysius. At one time was thought to be the Areopagite of *Acts* 15. Possibly a Syrian monk of the fifth century.
[c]Aristotle proves this statement from what St Thomas is setting out to prove. However, no vicious circle is involved.

procedere in infinitum, ex quacumque parte. In omnibus enim quæ per se habent ordinem ad invicem, oportet quod, remoto primo, removeantur ea quæ sunt ad primum. Unde Philosophus probat,[4] quod non est possibile in causis moventibus procedere in infinitum, quia jam non esset primum movens, quo subtracto alia movere non possunt, cum non moveant nisi per hoc quod moventur a primo movente.

In finibus autem invenitur duplex ordo, scilicet ordo intentionis et ordo executionis: et in utroque ordine oportet esse aliquid primum.

Id enim quod est primum in ordine intentionis est quasi principium movens appetitum: unde, subtracto principio, appetitus a nullo moveretur. Id autem quod est principium in executione est unde incipit operatio: unde, isto principio subtracto, nullus inciperet aliquid operari. Principium autem intentionis est ultimus finis: principium autem executionis est primum eorum quæ sunt ad finem.

Sic ergo ex neutra parte possibile est in infinitum procedere: quia si non esset ultimus finis nihil appeteretur, nec aliqua actio terminaretur, nec etiam quiesceret intentio agentis; si autem non esset primum in his quæ sunt ad finem nullus inciperet aliquid operari, nec terminaretur consilium, sed in infinitum procederet.

Ea vero quæ non habent ordinem per se, sed per accidens sibi invicem conjunguntur, nihil prohibet infinitatem habere: causæ enim per accidens indeterminatæ sunt. Et hoc etiam modo contingit esse infinitatem per accidens in finibus, et in his quæ sunt ad finem.

1. Ad primum ergo dicendum quod de ratione boni est quod aliquid ab ipso effluat, non tamen quod ipsum ab alio procedat. Et ideo, cum bonum habeat rationem finis, et primum bonum sit ultimus finis, ratio ista non probat quod non sit ultimus finis; sed quod a fine primo supposito procedatur in infinitum inferius versus ea quæ sunt ad finem. Et hoc quidem competeret si consideraretur sola virtus primi boni, quæ est infinita. Sed quia primum bonum habet diffusionem secundum intellectum, cujus est secundum aliquam certam formam* profluere in causata; aliquis certus modus adhibetur bonorum efflexui a primo bono, a quo omnia alia bona participant virtutem diffusivam. Et ideo diffusio bonorum non procedit in infinitum, sed, sicut dicitur Sap.,[5] Deus omnia disposuit *in numero, pondere et mensura.*

2. Ad secundum dicendum quod in his quæ sunt per se, ratio incipit a

---

*Piana: *causam certam*, determinate causality
[4]*Physics* VIII, 5. 256a17
[5]*Wisdom* 11, 21
[d]That is, as regards intention and execution. cf above art. 1, note *j*. The order of intention includes wishing, willing, deliberating, and choosing; the order of execution the effective command of the mind, *imperium*, the active application, *usus*

intention or from that of execution,[d] an infinite series of essentially related ends is out of the question. In the case of all objects forming a natural working system, if you rule out what is first then you also rule out all the others subordinate to it. Accordingly Aristotle shows[4] that you cannot indefinitely prolong such a series of efficient causes, for then there would be no first to set the others moving, and they would effect nothing, since they do not act save by being acted on by the first cause.

This holds true also of final causality, and for the double pattern of intention and of execution; for each we must set up something that comes first.

In the order of intention it is that which originally moves desire; take this away, and desire would be moved by nothing. In the order of execution it lies in that whence the activity starts; take this away, and no one would begin to do anything. The plan starts with the final aim; the performance with the first step towards it.

So then on neither side is the process infinite. Were there no ultimate end, nothing would be desired, no activity would be finished, no desire would come to rest. Were there no first step to the end, no one would start doing anything or make up his mind, but instead would deliberate interminably.[e]

Notice that we are not arguing against an infinity of things which just happen to be connected and compose no essential order of dependence, for accidental causes are indeterminate. In this sense there could be an infinity of ends and steps to ends in a series of items.

Hence: 1. That something flows from it is of the nature of good, not that it flows from something else. Well then, since being an end means being a good, and the ultimate end is the first good, the objection does not prove there is no ultimate end, but only that from this, already supposed, there could issue in descending scale an infinite series of subordinate values— quite an acceptable view if we took into account merely the infinite power of the first good. In point of fact, however, the fount of good pours forth according to a shaping intelligence so that a certain measure is established among the derivative goods which stream out and draw from it their generous virtue of giving of themselves.[f] Accordingly this propagation of good is not indefinite, for, as *Wisdom* says, God hath disposed all things *by measure and number and weight*.[5]

2. Reasoning advances from naturally evident premises to conclusions

---

activus, of will to the doing, the actual doing, *usus passivus*, and the consequent pleasure, *delectatio*, *quies*.

[e]i.e. would not move from intention to execution by effective decision, *imperium*: cf 1a2æ. 17, 3.

[f]God's goodness is the cause of the distinctiveness of things: 1a. 47, 1. Vol. 8.

principiis naturaliter notis, et ad aliquem terminum progreditur. Unde Philosophus probat,[6] quod in demonstrationibus non est processus in infinitum, quia in demonstrationibus attenditur ordo aliquorum per se ad invicem connexorum, et non per accidens. In his autem quæ per accidens connectuntur, nihil prohibet rationem in infinitum procedere. Accidit autem quantitati aut numero præexistenti, inquantum hujusmodi, quod ei addatur quantitas aut unitas. Unde in hujusmodi nihil prohibet rationem procedere in infinitum.

3. Ad tertium dicendum quod illa multiplicatio actuum voluntatis reflexæ supra seipsam per accidens se habet ad ordinem finium. Quod patet ex hoc, quod circa unum et eundem finem* indifferenter semel vel pluries supra seipsam voluntas reflectitur.

articulus 5. utrum unius hominis possint esse plures ultimi fines

AD QUINTUM sic proceditur:[1] 1. Videtur quod possibile sit voluntatem unius hominis in plura ferri simul, sicut in ultimos fines. Dicit enim Augustinus[2] quod quidam ultimum hominis finem posuerunt in quatuor, scilicet *in voluptate, in quiete, in primis naturæ, et in virtute.* Hæc autem manifeste sunt plura. Ergo unus homo potest constituere ultimum finem suæ voluntatis in multis.

2. Præterea, ea quæ non opponuntur ad invicem se invicem non excludunt. Sed multa inveniuntur in rebus quæ sibi invicem non opponuntur. Ergo si unum ponatur ultimus finis voluntatis, non propter hoc alia excluduntur.

3. Præterea, voluntas per hoc quod constituit ultimum finem in aliquo suam liberam potentiam non amittit. Sed antequam constitueret ultimum finem suum in illo, puta in voluptate, poterat constituere finem suum ultimum in alio, puta in divitiis. Ergo etiam postquam constituit aliquis ultimum finem suæ voluntatis in voluptate, potest simul constituere ultimum finem in divitiis. Ergo possibile est voluntatem unius hominis simul ferri in diversa, sicut in ultimos fines.

SED CONTRA, illud in quo quiescit aliquis sicut in ultimo fine, hominis affectui dominatur: quia ex eo totius vitæ suæ regulas accipit. Unde de gulosis dicitur *Philipp.*,[3] *Quorum deus venter est:* quia scilicet constituunt ultimum finem in deliciis ventris. Sed sicut dicitur *Matt.*,[4] *nemo potest*

---

*Piana: *actum,* one and the same act
[6]*Posterior Analytics* I, 3. 72b7 (cf 84a11)
[1]cf Ia. 2, 3
[2]*De civit. Dei* XIX, 1 & 4. PL 41, 622 & 627

when the terms are essentially related. On these grounds Aristotle proves[6] that no infinite regress can be pursued in demonstration, for there the mind attends to necessary implications, not incidental connections. As for terms which come together only contingently, there is nothing to stop reasoning from going on for ever. For it so happens that given any fixed number or quantity you can always add to it; such cases can be reasoned about without your ever coming to a halt.

3. The multiplication in question, namely of acts of will reflecting on itself, is quite incidental to an order of purposes, as is evident when you consider that it is a matter of indifference how often the will reflects upon itself in willing the same end.[g]

article 5. can one individual have several ultimate ends?

THE FIFTH POINT.[1] It seems possible for a man to set his heart simultaneously on various things as ultimate ends.[a] Augustine records four to which people commit themselves, namely *pleasure, tranquillity, the riches of nature, and virtue.*[2] Obviously these represent various aims. Therefore one man can place his ultimate end in many things.

2. Again, non-opposites are not mutually exclusive. And many things, we find, are not opposites. If one be taken as our final goal, why should others be thereby excluded?

3. In addition, by setting your heart on one thing as a final aim your will does not lose its ability to choose. Before doing so, committing yourself, let us say, to pleasure, you could have gone elsewhere, let us say, to riches. But even after doing so you can still at the same time make riches your aim. Consequently for one man's will to be simultaneously intent upon diverse final ends is possible.

ON THE OTHER HAND, an object on which his desire finally rests dominates a man's affections, and sways his whole life. St Paul writes of gluttons whose *god is their belly,*[3] for they make its pleasures their main pre-occupation. Now, according to the Gospel, *No man can serve two masters,*[4]

---

[3]*Philippians* 3, 19
[4]*Matthew* 6, 24
[g]Thus the repetition of caresses in Catullus, *Carmen* v. *Ad Lesbiam.* And of saying prayers, 2a2æ. 83, 14.
[a]The beginning of the second set of articles in the Question, which show that the ultimate end is single (art. 5), sovereign (art. 6), universal for all men (art. 7), and all creatures (art. 8).

duobus dominis servire, ad invicem scilicet non ordinatis. Ergo impossibile est esse plures ultimos fines unius hominis ad invicem non ordinatos.

RESPONSIO: Dicendum quod impossibile est quod voluntas unius hominis simul se habeat ad diversa, sicut ad ultimos fines. Cujus ratio potest triplex assignari.

Prima est quia, cum unumquodque appetat suam perfectionem, illud appetit aliquis ut ultimum finem, quod appetit, ut bonum perfectum et completivum sui ipsius. Unde Augustinus dicit,[5] *Finem boni nunc dicimus, non quod consumatur ut non sit, sed quod perficiatur ut plenum sit.* Oportet igitur quod ultimus finis ita impleat totum hominis appetitum, quod nihil extra ipsum appetendum relinquatur. Quod esse non potest, si aliquid extraneum ad ipsius perfectionem requiratur. Unde non potest esse quod in duo sic tendat appetitus, ac si utrumque sit bonum perfectivum* ipsius.

Secunda ratio est quia, sicut in processu rationis principium est id quod naturaliter cognoscitur, ita in processu rationalis appetitus, qui est voluntas, oportet esse principium id quod naturaliter desideratur. Hoc autem oportet esse unum: quia natura non tendit nisi ad unum. Principium autem in processu rationalis appetitus est ultimus finis. Unde oportet id in quod tendit voluntas sub ratione ultimi finis esse unum.

Tertia ratio est quia, cum actiones voluntariæ ex fine speciem sortiantur, sicut supra habitum est,[6] oportet quod a fine ultimo, qui est communis, sortiantur rationem generis: sicut et naturalia ponuntur in genere secundum formalem rationem communem. Cum igitur omnia appetibilia voluntatis, inquantum hujusmodi, sint unius generis, oportet ultimum finem esse unum. Et præcipue quia in quolibet genere est unum primum principium: ultimus autem finis habet rationem primi principii, ut dictum est. Sicut autem se habet ultimus finis hominis simpliciter ad totum humanum

---

*Leonine: *perfectum*, complete

[5]*De civit. Dei* XIX, 1. PL 41, 621   [6]art. 3 above

[b]Cajetan, *in loc.*, raises the doubt: grave sin is the turning away from God for some mortal good, and this is its last end. But a man may intend two grave sins, and the two may be disparate and unco-ordinated. He replies that both converge on the sinner's undue love of himself, amounting to the contempt of God; a unity in disorder which constitutes the City of Babylon, not the order in love of Jerusalem.

[c]Billuart, a useful eighteenth-century commentator, remarks that the first argument is sufficient, while the others are rather recondite. Cajetan shows their convergence. Ramirez regards them as plain sailing, *facillimæ*, but his lengthy attempts at explanation, like those of John of St Thomas, in effect rather gainsay his opinion.

[d]Naturally known, that is, known as self-evident without a process of reasoning.

[e]Desired naturally: but not by natural desire as meaning unconscious appetite. cf art. 2, note *d*.

[f]On the Aristotelean principle of defining a nature *phusis*, by its end, *telos*; hence a single nature has a single end.

that is to say, when they are not partners. Impossible, then, for a man to have several unco-ordinated ultimate aims.[b]

REPLY: That is to say, at one and the same time. We set out the following three reasons.[c]

First, because in all things whatsoever there is an appetite for completion, the final end to which each move marks its own perfect and fulfilling good. Augustine says, *In speaking of the culminating good, we mean, not that it passes away so as to be no more, but that it is so brought to completion as to be fulfilled.*[5] The ultimate end ought so to fulfil a man's whole desire that nothing is left beside for him to desire. Now this would not be the case were something else outside it still wanted. Hence it cannot be that desire should go out to two things as though each were its fulfilment.

The second reason draws a parallel. As the process of reasoned thought starts from that which is natively known,[d] so the process of reasoned love in the will starts from that which is natively desired.[e] This principle has to be single, for a nature has a unifying tendency.[f] In rational desire it is the ultimate end. Consequently that to which the will tends as to its ultimate end has to be one.

The third reason develops a point already raised.[6] Voluntary actions are classified according to species by their ends, and consequently according to genus by their ultimate end, the causality of which runs throughout all their purposes:[g] thus also natural species are grouped together in a genus by an essential meaning they share in common. Now since all the objects the will can desire are, as such, of one generic class, it follows that the ultimate end ought to be one; and all the more because in each genus there is a single dominant, and we have just observed how the ultimate end has that force.[h] Now as the ultimate end of man as such is to the whole human

---

[g]Literally, their genus should be assigned from an ultimate end which is common to them all.

[h]This third argument has to be read cautiously. For genus and species, properly so called, are univocal classifications: a genus remains a fixed constant under the addition of specific differences; it is, as it were, expanded from outside. Whereas the notions of the universal good and particular good are analogical, what is here called the 'generic' end receives nothing from outside by the various particular goods which are the more proximate objects of desire. The interested reader is referred to the commentators for the elucidation of the argument, which in fact uses 'generic' to signify a comprehensive cause, *universale in causando*, rather than a common classification, *universale in prædicando*. In other words, the discourse is better left as a sort of parable, convincing enough, rather than pursued as an allegory. It may be noted here that moral science will treat of the specific kinds of good shaped by the immediate objects of activity, and will relate them to the more generic good arising from the end intended. cf 1a2æ. 18, 7 & 19, 7. Vol. 18.

SUMMA THEOLOGIÆ, Ia2æ. 1, 6

genus, ita se habet ultimus finis hujus hominis ad hunc hominem. Unde oportet quod, sicut omnium hominum est naturaliter unus finis ultimus, ita hujus hominis voluntas in uno ultimo fine statuatur.

1. Ad primum ergo dicendum quod omnia illa plura accipiebantur in ratione unius boni perfecti ex his constituti, ab his qui in eis ultimum finem ponebant.

2. Ad secundum dicendum quod, etsi plura accipi possint quæ ad invicem oppositionem non habeant, tamen bono perfecto opponitur quod sit aliquid de perfectione rei extra ipsum.

3. Ad tertium dicendum quod potestas voluntatis non habet ut faciat opposita esse simul. Quod contingeret, si tenderet in plura disparata sicut in ultimos fines, ut ex dictis patet.

articulus 6. *utrum homo omnia quæ vult velit propter ultimum finem*

AD SEXTUM sic proceditur:[1] 1. Videtur quod non omnia quæcumque homo vult propter ultimum finem velit. Ea enim quæ ad finem ultimum ordinantur, seriosa dicuntur, quasi utilia. Sed jocosa a seriis distinguuntur. Ergo ea quæ homo jocose agit non ordinat in ultimum finem.

2. Præterea, Philosophus dicit, in principio *Meta.*,[2] quod scientiæ speculativæ propter seipsas quæruntur. Nec tamen potest dici quod quælibet earum sit ultimus finis. Ergo non omnia quæ homo appetit, appetit propter ultimum finem.

3. Præterea, quicumque ordinat aliquid in finem aliquem, cogitat de illo fine. Sed non semper homo cogitat de ultimo fine in omni eo quod appetit aut facit. Non ergo omnia homo appetit aut facit propter ultimum finem.

SED CONTRA est quod dicit Augustinus,[3] *Illud est finis boni nostri, propter quod amantur cetera, illud autem propter seipsum.*

RESPONSIO: Dicendum quod necesse est quod omnia quæ homo appetit appetat propter ultimum finem. Et hoc apparet duplici ratione.

Primo quidem, quia quidquid homo appetit appetit sub ratione boni. Quod quidem si non appetitur ut bonum perfectum, quod est ultimus finis, necesse est ut appetatur ut tendens in bonum perfectum: quia semper inchoatio alicujus ordinatur ad consummationem ipsius; sicut patet tam in his quæ fiunt a natura quam in his quæ fiunt ab arte. Et ideo omnis inchoatio perfectionis ordinatur in perfectionem consummatam, quæ est per* ultimum finem.

---

*Piana: *propter*, on account of
[1]IV *Sent.* 49, 1, 3, iv. *CG* I, 101   [2]*Metaphysics* I, 2. 982a14 & 28
[3]*De civit. Dei* XIX, 1. PL 41, 621

22

race so is the ultimate end of a man to this particular individual. Accordingly as there is one ultimate end for all men by their nature, so also should one individual's will be set on one ultimate end.

Hence: 1. The allusion is to those who include various objects in their final end and take them as collectively comprising the ideal of one perfect good.

2. Although several particular things can be embraced together so long as there is no opposition between them, nevertheless that anything required for a thing's perfection should lie outside its perfect good is out of the question.

3. It is not within the will's power to make opposites co-exist simultaneously, which would be the case were it to commit itself to several disparate objects as final ends: this has appeared from our discussion.[1]

article 6. is everything a man wills for an ultimate end?

THE SIXTH POINT:[1] 1. Apparently not. For what is done for an ultimate end is a serious matter and serves a purpose. We draw a distinction between it and a matter of play. Accordingly what is done in play serves no ultimate aim.

2. Moreover, early in the *Metaphysics* it is said that the theoretical sciences are sought for their own sake.[2] But you cannot contend that any of them is our final goal. Therefore not all human interests are pursued with that in view.

3. Further, whoever plans for an end takes thought about it. But does a man think about ultimates in all he plans and contrives? No. Then neither does he always act for an ultimate end.

ON THE OTHER HAND Augustine says, *That is our ending-good for the sake of which all else is loved, but itself for its own sake.*[3]

REPLY: It needs must be that all a man's desires are on account of his love for the ultimate end. Two reasons make this clear.

First, whatever a man desires is because of its evidence of good. If not desired as the perfect good, that is, the ultimate end, then it is desired as tending to that,[a] for a start is made in order to come to a finish, as appears in the products of nature and art alike. And so every initial perfection anticipates the consummate perfection which comes with the final end.

---

[1]Nevertheless, as will appear in the following Questions, it is man's tragic lot to be able to separate the thought of happiness, its *ratio formalis*, from the reality, *res*, in which it is truly found.

[a]As tending to complete good; not that the object of desire is thereby a pure means, *bonum utile*, for it may be a good in itself, though incomplete, and therefore an end, though intermediate. Creatures as real things can be *bona honesta et delectabilia*.

Secundo, quia ultimus finis hoc modo se habet in movendo appetitum sicut se habet in aliis motionibus primum movens. Manifestum est autem quod causæ secundæ moventes non movent nisi secundum quod moventur a primo movente. Unde secunda appetibilia non movent appetitum nisi in ordine ad primum appetitibile, quod est ultimus finis.

1. Ad primum ergo dicendum quod actiones ludicræ non ordinantur ad aliquem finem extrinsecum; sed tamen ordinantur ad bonum ipsius ludentis, prout sunt delectantes vel requiem præstantes. Bonum autem consummatum hominis est ultimus finis ejus.

2. Et similiter dicendum ad secundum de scientia speculativa; quæ appetitur ut bonum quoddam speculantis, quod comprehenditur sub bono completo et perfecto, quod est ultimus finis.

3. Ad tertium dicendum quod non oportet ut semper aliquis cogitet de ultimo fine quandocumque aliquid appetit vel operatur: sed virtus primæ intentionis, quæ est respectu ultimi finis, manet in quolibet appetitu cujuscumque rei, etiam si de ultimo fine actu non cogitetur. Sicut non oportet quod qui vadit per viam, in quolibet passu cogitet de fine.

articulus 7. utrum sit unus ultimus finis omnium hominum

AD SEPTIMUM sic proceditur:[1] 1. Videtur quod non omnium hominum sit unus finis ultimus. Maxime enim videtur hominis ultimus finis esse incommutabile bonum. Sed quidam avertuntur ab incommutabili bono, peccando. Non ergo omnium hominum est unus ultimus finis.

2. Præterea, secundum ultimum finem tota vita hominis regulatur. Si igitur esset unus ultimus finis omnium hominum, sequeretur quod in hominibus non essent diversa studia vivendi. Quod patet esse falsum.

3. Præterea, finis est actionis terminus. Actiones autem sunt singularium. Homines autem, etsi conveniant in natura speciei, tamen differunt secundum ea quæ ad individua pertinent. Non ergo omnium hominum est unus ultimus finis.

---

[1]cf *In Ethic.* I, *lect.* 9
[b]cf above art. 4, note *a*.
[c]*Secunda appetibilia* in the flow of final causality derive their attractiveness from the *primum appetibile*, and in themselves are objects of desire, though from and to the *summum bonum*.
[d]The topic of play and game is here somewhat cursorily dismissed in answering the objection. So also when the virtue of playfulness, *eutrapelia*, is discussed; 2a2æ. 168, 2. In truth there is more to play than the taking of recreation, or of unbending from the strain of life, as will appear when it is discussed in terms of enjoyment, *frui*, Ia2æ. 11, and delight, *delectatio*, Ia2æ. 31–4, and even the fruits of the Spirit, Ia2æ. 70, the joy and peace which are the effects of *agape*, 2a2æ. 28 & 29. There St Thomas shows that it is an ultimate, and expects no further purpose, though

Secondly, the final end with respect to rousing desire is like the first mover with respect to other motions.[b] There, manifestly, secondary causes do not set in motion except as set in motion by the first cause. Likewise secondary objects of desire[c] do not attract except as subordinate to the supreme good, which is the final end.

Hence: 1. Games are not meant to serve any purpose outside themselves; all the same they are salutary to the player, by delighting him and affording relaxation.[d] And his complete good is his ultimate end.

2. The second objection calls for a similar answer. Even the disinterested knowledge of theoretic science is loved as good for the one who pursues it; moreover it is caught up in the complete and perfect good which is his ultimate end.[e]

3. We are not expected always to be thinking of our last end whenever we desire or do something in particular. The force of our first intention with respect to it persists in each desire of any other thing, even though it is not adverted to.[f] For example, in walking somewhere one does not have to be reminding oneself of one's destination at every step.

article 7. is there one ultimate end for all human beings?

THE SEVENTH POINT:[1] 1. Apparently not. Above all else man's ultimate end seems to be eternal good.[a] And yet some turn away from it by sinning. How, then, is there one ultimate end for all?

2. Again, an ultimate end rules the whole of life. Were it the same for all, men would not choose diverse walks of life, whereas in point of fact they do.

3. In addition, an aim marks the term of an action. Now actions are individual affairs. Though men agree in their common specific nature, they are quite diverse in their personal proclivities. Consequently their chief aims are not identical.

---

as he will point out in this section, 1a2æ. 2, 6 & 4, 1, it does not constitute the real object of desire.

[e]cf 1a2æ. 3, 7 below.

[f]The following division of intention (cf Glossary *s.v.* 'Intention') is useful—there are other divisions more complicated, especially in sacramental theology. An intention is said to be actual when it is consciously attended to and sets off the performance of a deed, and to be virtual when it is not so present in consciousness. A virtual intention is explicit when the doer is working from a previous actual intention which has not been retracted, as in the example, or implicit when what he is doing is of itself calculated to have that purpose, as when in an emergency you rescue a stranger from drowning, giving no thought but to keep him from struggling and to get him to the bank. The teaching of the reply applies to distractions in prayer.

[a]*Bonum incommutabile*, contrast with *bonum commutabile*, subject to change.

SED CONTRA est quod Augustinus dicit,[2] quod omnes homines conveniunt in appetendo ultimum finem, qui est beatitudo.

RESPONSIO: Dicendum quod de ultimo fine possumus loqui dupliciter: uno modo secundum rationem ultimi finis; alio modo secundum id in quo finis ultimi ratio invenitur.

Quantum igitur ad rationem ultimi finis, omnes conveniunt in appetitu finis ultimi: quia omnes appetunt suam perfectionem adimpleri, quæ est ratio ultimi finis, ut dictum est.[3]

Sed quantum ad id in quo ista ratio invenitur, non omnes homines conveniunt in ultimo fine: nam quidam appetunt divitias tanquam consummatum bonum, quidam autem voluptatem, quidam vero quodcumque aliud. Sicut et omni gustui delectabile est dulce, sed quibusdam maxime delectabilis est dulcedo vini, quibusdam dulcedo mellis, aut alicujus talium. Illud tamen dulce oportet esse simpliciter melius delectabile in quo maxime delectatur qui habet optimum gustum. Et similiter illud bonum oportet esse completissimum quod tanquam ultimum finem appetit habens affectum bene dispositum.

1. Ad primum ergo dicendum quod illi qui peccant avertuntur ab eo in quo vere invenitur ratio ultimi finis: non autem ab ipsa ultimi finis intentione, quam quærunt falso in aliis rebus.

2. Ad secundum dicendum quod diversa studia vivendi contingunt in hominibus propter diversas res in quibus quæritur ratio summi boni.

3. Ad tertium dicendum quod, etsi actiones sint singularium, tamen primum principium agendi in eis est natura, quæ tendit ad unum, ut dictum est.[4]

articulus 8. utrum in illo ultimo fine aliæ creaturæ conveniant

AD OCTAVUM sic proceditur:[1] 1. Videtur quod in ultimo fine hominis etiam omnia alia conveniant. Finis enim respondet principio. Sed illud quod est principium hominum, scilicet Deus, est etiam principium omnium aliorum. Ergo in ultimo fine hominis omnia alia communicant.

2. Præterea, Dionysius dicit[2] quod *Deus convertit omnia ad seipsum tanquam ad ultimum finem.* Sed ipse est etiam ultimus finis hominis: quia solo ipso fruendum est, ut Augustinus dicit.[3] Ergo in fine ultimo hominis etiam alia conveniunt.

---

[2]*De Trinitate* XIII, 3. PL 42, 1018
[3]art. 5 above
[4]ibid
[1]cf 1a. 103, 2. *CG* III, 17 & 25. *De veritate* v, 6 ad 4. II *Sent.* 38, 1, 2
[2]*De div. nom.* 4. PG 3, 700. St Thomas, *lect.* 3
[3]*De doctr. Christ.* I, 5 & 22. PL 34, 21 & 25

ON THE OTHER HAND Augustine observes that all agree in desiring that ultimate which is happiness.[2]

REPLY: We can speak of the ultimate end in two senses, namely to signify first what it means, and second that in which it is realized.[b]

As for the first, all are at one here, because all desire their complete fulfilment, which, as we have noted,[3] is what final end means.

As for the second, however, all are not unanimous, for some want riches, others a life of pleasure, others something else. We draw a comparison here with the palatable,[c] which is pleasurable to every taste. Some find this in wine most of all, others in sweetstuffs or something of the sort. All the same, by and large, we esteem that most palatable which most appeals to cultivated tastes. And likewise we ought to account that good the most complete which is finally sought by those with well-tempered affections.

Hence: 1. When men sin they turn away from that in which the idea of the ultimate end is truly realized, not from the intention of reaching it, which mistakenly they seek elsewhere.[d]

2. Different views of how life should be lived arise from the various objects in which the idea of complete good is sought.

3. Although actions are engaged with individual situations they are rooted in a nature, which, as we have said,[4] tends to a unified end.[e]

article 8. do men and other creatures share the same ultimate end?

THE EIGHTH POINT:[1] 1. So it seems.[a] For ends match beginnings. Men begin from God, and so do all other things. Hence all in common reach out to the same ultimate end.

2. Moreover, Dionysius says that *God turns all things to himself as to their final end.*[2] Now he is man's final end, who, as Augustine tells us,[3] alone is to be enjoyed. Men, therefore, and other things join in the same final end.

---

[b]The idea of happiness and the happy-making thing; approximately happiness in the abstract and in the concrete.

[c]*Dulce*, the sweet. An important consideration in the Middle Ages when most people relied for their sugar-intake on honey, fruit, and wine. To take a lowly example in a high discussion is characteristic of St Thomas.

[d]Where the last end is found in fact is the topic of the following Question.

[e]The moral theory to be developed later will consider human acts not only as personal by their intentions and individual by their circumstances but also as being of certain kinds according to their objects: 1a2æ. 18. Vol. 18.

[a]The article is to be read in conjunction with art. 2 above, of which it is the complement.

3. Præterea, finis ultimus hominis est objectum voluntatis. Sed objectum voluntatis est bonum universale, quod est finis omnium. Ergo necesse est quod in ultimo fine hominis omnia conveniant.

SED CONTRA est quod ultimus finis hominum est beatitudo, quam omnes appetunt, ut Augustinus dicit.[4] Sed *non cadit in animalia rationis expertia ut beata sint*, sicut Augustinus dicit in libro *Octogintatrium Quæst.*[5] Non ergo in ultimo fine hominis alia conveniunt.

RESPONSIO: Dicendum quod, sicut Philosophus dicit,[6] finis dupliciter dicitur, scilicet *cujus*, et *quo*, idest ipsa res in qua ratio boni invenitur, et usus sive adeptio illius rei. Sicut si dicamus quod motus corporis gravis finis est vel locus inferior ut res, vel hoc quod est esse in loco inferiori, ut usus: et finis avari est vel pecunia ut res, vel possessio pecuniæ ut usus.

Si ergo loquamur de ultimo fine hominis quantum ad ipsam rem quæ est finis, sic in ultimo fine hominis omnia alia conveniunt: quia Deus est ultimus finis hominis et omnium aliarum rerum. Si autem loquamur de ultimo fine hominis quantum ad consecutionem finis, sic in hoc fine hominis non communicant creaturæ irrationales. Nam homo et aliæ rationales creaturæ consequuntur ultimum finem cognoscendo et amando Deum: quod non competit aliis creaturis, quæ adipiscuntur ultimum finem inquantum participant aliquam similitudinem Dei, secundum quod sunt, vel vivunt, vel etiam cognoscunt.

Et per hoc patet responsio ad objecta: nam beatitudo nominat adeptionem ultimi finis.

---

[4]*De Trin.* XIII, 3. PL 42, 1018
[5]*Lib. 83 Quæst.* 5 PL 40, 12
[6]*Physics* II, 2. 194a35. *De Anima* II, 4. 415b2 & 20
[b]*Beatitudo*, the first appearance of the term in the text of the discussions: the topic of the four following Questions.
[c]The *finis cujus gratia* and the *finis quo*, the why and the how. Henceforth to be related to objective and subjective happiness respectively.
[d]The text—which can be left as an illustration, without entering into the cosmology —refers to the place as a thing, *res*, and to reaching of it as *usus*. For the technical meaning of this term in human activity, cf 1a2æ. 16.

3. Further, the will's object is the ultimate end, and also it is universal good, and this is the end for all. And so all must share in man's ultimate end.

ON THE OTHER HAND, man's ultimate end is happiness,[b] which, according to Augustine, all things desire.[4] Yet he also remarks that *it is not the lot of animals lacking intelligence to be happy.*[5] Hence other things do not meet in man's final end.

REPLY: An end, says Aristotle,[6] has a double reference, the 'because of which' and the 'by which', that is, respectively, the thing itself in which the nature of good is found and the actual condition of reaching and holding it.[c] For instance, we might say that for local movement the ending is a bottom place in the first sense and the gravitating there in the second sense;[d] or again that the end for a miser is money as the thing and the hoarding of it as its execution.

Well then, if we speak of the ultimate end with respect to the thing itself, then human and all other beings share it together, for God is the ultimate end for all things without exception.[e] But if with respect to the act of gaining it, then the final end for man is not that of non-rational creatures.[f] For men and other rational creatures lay hold of it in knowing and loving God, which non-rational creatures are not capable of doing, for they come to their final end through sharing in some likeness of God,[g] inasmuch as they actually exist, or live, and even know after their fashion.[h]

Here lies the answer to the objections, for the inquiry is about the happiness which means actively possessing the ultimate end.

---

[e]Alpha and Omega. *Revelations* 1, 8; 21, 6; 22, 13.

[f]God acts 'for' his essential goodness: 1a. 19, 5. His goodness is the end for the universe: 1a. 65, 2. His glory is our happiness: 1a2æ. 2, 3 ad 1.

[g]God as object to our knowing and loving, not merely as cause to us as effects. The thought will reappear in the treatise, and underlies the theology of his presence to us by grace and glory. cf Foreword, note *a*.

[h]An echo of Dionysius: see below 1a2æ. 2, 5 ad 2.

DEINDE CONSIDERANDUM est de beatitudine:
primo quidem, in quibus sit;
secundo, quid sit;
tertio, qualiter eam consequi possimus.

Quæstio 2. de his in quibus hominis beatitudo consistit

CIRCA PRIMUM quæruntur octo:

1. utrum beatitudo consistat in divitiis;
2. utrum in honoribus;
3. utrum in fama, sive in gloria;
4. utrum in potestate;
5. utrum in aliquo corporis bono;
6. utrum in voluptate;
7. utrum in aliquo bono animæ;
8. utrum in aliquo bono creato.

articulus 1. utrum beatitudo hominis consistat in divitiis

AD PRIMUM sic proceditur:[1] 1. Videtur quod beatitudo hominis in divitiis consistat. Cum enim beatitudo sit ultimus finis hominis, in eo consistit quod maxime in hominis affectu dominatur. Hujusmodi autem sunt divitiæ: dicitur enim *Eccles.*,[2] *Pecuniæ obediunt omnia.* Ergo in divitiis beatitudo hominis consistit.

2. Præterea, secundum Boëtium,[3] beatitudo est *status omnium bonorum aggregatione perfectus.* Sed in pecuniis omnia possideri videntur: quia, ut Philosophus dicit in *Ethic.*,[4] ad hoc nummus est inventus, ut sit quasi fidejussor habendi pro eo quodcumque homo voluerit. Ergo in divitiis beatitudo consistit.

3. Præterea, desiderium summi boni, cum nunquam deficiat, videtur esse infinitum. Sed hoc maxime in divitiis invenitur: quia *avarus*

---

[1]cf *CG* III, 30. *In Ethic.* I, *lect.* 5   [2]*Ecclesiastes* 10, 19
[3]*De consolatione philosophiæ* III, 2. PL 63, 724   [4]*Ethics* v, 5. 1133b12
[a]Happiness; etymology, by hap, or good luck, which is similar to the Greek, *eudaimonia, eu/daimon.* TheLatin indicates a more stable condition or state: *beatitudo, beatitas,* blessedness, bliss, from *beare,* possibly from *benum,* an archaic form of *bonum.* Also *felicitas,* perhaps cognate to *fecunditas.* Appendix 2.
Question 2: where it is, as it were the material cause. Question 3: what it is

HAPPINESS comes next under discussion, and
first, where it is (2);
second, what it is (3-4);
third, how it can be gained (5).[a]

Question 2. objective beatitude

UNDER THIS FIRST HEADING there are eight points of inquiry:

1. whether happiness lies in riches;
2. or in honours;
3. or in fame and glory;
4. or in having power;
5. in any bodily endowment;
6. or in pleasure;
7. or in any endowment of soul;
8. or in any created value.[b]

article 1. *does happiness lie in riches?*

THE FIRST POINT:[1] 1. It seems so. For since happiness is man's final end it
must be looked for where his affections are held above all. And such is
wealth, as *Ecclesiastes* remarks, *All things obey money.*[2] And so happiness is
found in wealth.

2. Moreover, according to Boethius, happiness is *a state made complete
by the accumulation of all good things.*[3] Wealth can ensure the possession of
goods of every kind: Aristotle notices how money was invented to guarantee
a man's obtaining whatever he might want.[4] Therefore wealth provides his
happiness.

3. Further, desire for the highest good appears to be boundless because
it is never exhausted. Desire for riches is a conspicuous example; the

---

essentially, the formal cause. Question 4: what it required for its integrity. Question
5: how is it gained, the efficient cause.
For these Questions see: A. Mansion, *L'eudémonisme aristotélicien et la morale
thomiste.* Rome, 1925. K. E. Kirk, *The Vision of God,* the Christian Doctrine of the
Summum Bonum. London, 2nd ed. 1932. J. Ramirez, *De hominis beatitudine,* 3 vols.
Madrid, 1942, 1943, 1947.
[b]Arts 1-4, about external goods, need only to be read through; arts 5-7 about
internal endowments; art. 8 is the culmination of the Question. Not until art. 6
does it get well under way: the earlier discussions echo the *Nicomachean Ethics.*

non implebitur pecunia, ut dicitur *Eccles.*[5] Ergo in divitiis beatitudo consistit.

SED CONTRA, bonum hominis in retinendo beatitudinem magis consistit quam in emittendo ipsam. Sed sicut Boëtius dicit,[6] *Divitiæ effundendo, magis quam coacervando, melius nitent: siquidem avaritia semper odiosos, claros largitas facit.* Ergo in divitiis beatitudo non consistit.

RESPONSIO: Dicendum quod impossible est beatitudinem hominis in divitiis consistere. Sunt enim duplices divitiæ, ut Philosophus dicit,[7] scilicet naturales et artificiales. Naturales quidem divitiæ sunt, quibus homini subvenitur ad defectus naturales tollendos: sicut cibus, potus, vestimenta, vehicula et habitacula, et alia hujusmodi. Divitiæ autem artificiales sunt, quibus secundum se natura non juvatur, ut denarii; sed ars humana eos adinvenit propter facilitatem commutationis, ut sint quasi mensura quædam rerum venalium.

Manifestum est autem quod in divitiis naturalibus beatitudo hominis esse non potest. Quæruntur enim hujusmodi divitiæ propter aliud, scilicet ad sustentandam naturam hominis: et ideo non possunt esse ultimus finis hominis, sed magis ordinantur ad hominem sicut ad finem. Unde in ordine naturæ omnia hujusmodi sunt infra hominem, et propter hominem facta; secundum illud *Psalm.,*[8] *Omnia subjecisti sub pedibus eius.*

Divitiæ autem artificiales non quæruntur nisi propter naturales: non enim quærerentur nisi quia per eas emuntur res ad usum vitæ necessariæ. Unde multo minus habent rationem ultimi finis. Impossibile est igitur beatitudinem, quæ est ultimus finis hominis, in divitiis esse.

1. Ad primum ergo dicendum quod omnia corporalia obediunt pecuniæ quantum ad multitudinem stultorum, qui sola corporalia bona cognoscunt quæ pecunia acquiri possunt. Judicium autem de bonis humanis non debet sumi a stultis, sed a sapientibus: sicut et judicium de saporibus ab his qui habent gustum bene dispositum.

2. Ad secundum dicendum quod pecunia possunt haberi omnia venalia: non autem spiritualia, quæ vendi non possunt. Unde dicitur *Prov.,*[9] *Quid prodest stulto divitias habere, cum sapientiam emere non possit?*

3. Ad tertium dicendum quod appetitus naturalium divitiarum non est infinitus, quia secundum certam mensuram naturæ sufficiunt. Sed appetitus

---

[5]*Ecclesiastes* 5, 9
[6]*De consol.* II, 5. PL 63, 690
[7]*Politics* I, 3. 1257a4
[8]*Psalms* 8, 8
[9]*Proverbs* 17, 16
cAnicius Manlius Severinus Boethius, born about 476. A Roman statesman under

Preacher declares, *The covetous man is never satisfied with what he has.*[5] And so happiness is found in riches.

ON THE OTHER HAND the good for man means holding on to happiness, not getting rid of it. Yet, as Boethius notes, *Wealth shines in spending, not amassing: to be close-fisted is hateful, to be open-handed splendid.*[6c] Consequently happiness does not rest on wealth.

REPLY: Aristotle puts riches into two classes, natural and artificial.[7] Natural wealth comprises the things which relieve our natural wants, for example, food, drink, clothing, means of transport, shelter, and the like. Artificial wealth comprises the things which of themselves directly satisfy no natural need, for example, money, which is a human contrivance to serve as a means of exchange, as a sort of measure of the value of things for sale.

Man's happiness clearly cannot consist in natural riches. For they are sought for the sake of something else, namely the support of human life, and so are subordinate to its ultimate end, not the end itself. They are made for man, not man for them. In the natural order of things they rank beneath him; according to the Psalmist, *Thou hast set all things under his feet.*[8]

Still less ultimate are artificial riches, for they are sought only for the sake of natural wealth; there would be no demand for them except to procure the requirements for good living.[d]

The happiness, then, of man's ultimate end cannot consist in wealth.

Hence: 1. That money can do everything is the mass-opinion of silly people who recognize only the material goods which can be bought. To estimate human values, however, we should consult the wise, not the foolish, just as for matters gastronomical we go to those with well-educated tastes.

2. Anything for sale can be had for money, but not spiritual values, which cannot be bought.[e] Hence in *Proverbs* it is written, *What doth it avail a fool to have riches, since he cannot buy wisdom?*[9]

3. The appetite for natural wealth is not unlimited, for a fixed measure is enough for nature. The appetite for artificial wealth, however, may know

---

Theodoric the Ostrogoth, but executed by him about 525. During his long imprisonment he wrote the *De consolatione philosophiæ*, a favourite book of the Middle Ages, which was translated by Chaucer.

For the development of his 'integral' definition, as it is called, see *CG* III, 26–48.

[d]A collector of pictures and precious stones might demur, when his intention is not that of making a capital investment. Nevertheless his appreciation, though disinterested, normally fits into the needs of gracious living.

[e]Simony, 2a2æ. 100.

divitiarum artificialium est infinitus, quia deservit concupiscentiæ inordinatæ, quæ non modificatur, ut patet per Philosophum in I *Polit*.[10]
Aliter tamen est infinitum desiderium divitiarum, et desiderium summi boni. Nam summum bonum quanto perfectius possidetur tanto ipsummet magis amatur, et alia contemnuntur; quia quanto magis habetur, magis cognoscitur. Et ideo dicitur *Eccli.*,[11] *Qui edunt me, adhuc esurient*. Sed in appetitu divitiarum, et quorumcumque temporalium bonorum, est e converso: nam quando jam habentur ipsa contemnuntur et alia appetuntur; secundum quod significatur *Joann.*,[12] cum Dominus dicit, *Qui bibit ex hac aqua*, per quam temporalia significantur, *sitiet iterum*. Et hoc ideo, quia eorum insufficientia magis cognoscitur cum habentur. Et ideo hoc ipsum ostendit eorum imperfectionem, et quod in eis summum bonum non consistit.

articulus 2. utrum beatitudo hominis consistat in honoribus

AD SECUNDUM sic proceditur:[1] 1. Videtur quod beatitudo hominis in honoribus consistat. Beatitudo enim, sive felicitas, est *præmium virtutis*, ut Philosophus dicit.[2] Sed honor maxime videtur esse id quod est virtutis præmium, ut Philosophus dicit.[3] Ergo in honore maxime consistit beatitudo.

2. Præterea, illud quod convenit Deo et excellentissimis maxime videtur esse beatitudo, quæ est bonum perfectum. Sed hujusmodi est honor, ut Philosophus dicit in *Ethic*.[4] Et etiam I *Tim*. dicit Apostolus,[5] *Soli Deo honor et gloria*. Ergo in honore consistit beatitudo.

3. Præterea, illud quod est maxime desideratum ab hominibus est beatitudo. Sed nihil videtur esse magis desiderabile ab hominibus quam honor; quia homines patiuntur jacturam in omnibus aliis rebus ne patiantur aliquod detrimentum sui honoris. Ergo in honore beatitudo consistit.

SED CONTRA, beatitudo est in beato. Honor autem non est in eo qui honoratur, sed *magis in honorante*, qui reverentiam exhibet honorato, ut Philosophus dicit.[6] Ergo in honore beatitudo non consistit.

RESPONSIO: Dicendum quod impossibile est beatitudinem consistere in honore. Honor enim exhibetur alicui propter aliquam ejus excellentiam; et ita est signum et testimonium quoddam illius excellentiæ quæ est in honorato. Excellentia autem hominis maxime attenditur secundum beatitudinem, quæ est hominis bonum perfectum; et secundum partes ejus, idest secundum illa bona quibus aliquid beatitudinis participatur. Et ideo honor potest quidem consequi beatitudinem, sed principaliter in eo beatitudo consistere non potest.

---

[10]*Politics* I, 3. 1258a1   [11]*Ecclesiasticus*, 24, 29   [12]*John* 4, 13

1530114

no bounds, but pander to an unregulated concupiscence which, as Aristotle brings out, is without measure.[10]

Yet note that is not the boundlessness of desire for the supreme good. The more fully that is possessed the more is it loved and substitutes disdained, for the more it is possessed the more it is known.[f] And so in *Ecclesiasticus* it is written,[11] *They that eat me shall yet hunger.* Whereas with riches and other temporal goods it is the reverse, for when they are possessed they are despised and other things craved instead. Hence the words of our Lord, *Whosoever drinks of this water*, which signifies temporal benefits, *will thirst again.*[12] When we have obtained them we recognize how incomplete they are and how far short of our highest good.

article 2. does happiness lie in honours?

THE SECOND POINT:[1] 1. Yes, apparently. For to Aristotle happiness or felicity is the crown of virtue.[2] Also honour above all is the crown of virtue.[3] Accordingly happiness lies greatly in being honoured.[a]

2. Besides, that which befits God and the most sublime beings is happiness and the highest good. Such is being honoured, as Aristotle recognizes,[4] and so does St Paul; *To the only God be honour and glory.*[5] Happiness, therefore, consists in honour.

3. Then again, happiness is what men prize above all things. And this is their honour, for they would lose everything else rather than have that impugned. Accordingly honour is happiness.

ON THE OTHER HAND, happiness is inside the person who is happy. Now Aristotle notes[6] that honour is not in the one who receives it but in the one who gives it. Hence being honoured does not constitute being happy.

REPLY: A person is honoured because of some excellence he has, for honour is a sign or recognition of his worth. Now it is this excellence which composes his happiness, namely his perfect well-being and the blessings which go to make it up,[b] namely those particular goods which draw him into some semblance of happiness. And so honour may indeed be a result, but is not the main head of happiness.

---

[1]cf *CG* III, 28. *In Ethic.* I, lect. 5   [2]*Ethics* I, 9. 1099b16   [3]*Ethics* IV, 3. 1123b35
[4]ibid 1123b20   [5]I *Timothy* I, 17   [7]*Ethics*, I, 5. 1095b24
[f]The author shows his hand: he will argue later that the decisive moment in happiness is holding the good by mind, not living it by will, 1a2æ. 3, 4.
[a]For *honestas* and the condition of being honourable in relation to the virtue of temperance see 2a2æ. 145. Vol. 43, ed. T. Gilby.
[b]Man's perfect good: in the concrete is not isolated in an *apex animæ*, but comprehends his whole well-being, or *consistentia naturalis.* cf 1a2æ. 10, 1. Also below 1a2æ. 4.

1. Ad primum ergo dicendum quod, sicut Philosophus ibidem dicit, honor non est præmium virtutis propter quod virtuosi operantur: sed accipiunt honorem ab hominibus loco præmii, *quasi a non habentibus aliquid majus ad dandum.* Verum autem præmium virtutis est ipsa beatitudo, propter quam virtuosi operantur. Si autem propter honorem operarentur, jam non esset virtus, sed magis ambitio.

2. Ad secundum dicendum quod honor debetur Deo et excellentissimis in signum vel testimonium excellentiæ præexistentis: non quod ipse honor faciat eos excellentes.

3. Ad tertium dicendum quod ex naturali desiderio beatitudinis, quam consequitur honor, ut dictum est, contingit quod homines maxime honorem desiderant. Unde quærunt homines maxime honorari a sapientibus, quorum judicio credunt se esse excellentes vel felices.

articulus 3. utrum beatitudo hominis consistat in fama, sive gloria

AD TERTIUM sic proceditur:[1] 1. Videtur quod beatitudo hominis consistat in gloria. In eo enim videtur beatitudo consistere, quod redditur sanctis pro tribulationibus quas in mundo patiuntur. Hujusmodi autem est gloria: dicit enim Apostolus,[2] *Non sunt condignæ passiones hujus temporis ad futuram gloriam, quæ revelabitur in nobis.* Ergo beatitudo consistit in gloria.

2. Præterea, bonum est diffusivum sui, ut patet per Dionysium.[3] Sed per gloriam bonum hominis maxime diffunditur in notitiam aliorum: quia gloria, ut Ambrosius dicit,[4] nihil aliud est quam *clara cum laude notitia.* Ergo beatitudo hominis consistit in gloria.

3. Præterea, beatitudo est stabilissimum bonorum. Hoc autem videtur esse fama vel gloria, quia per hanc quodammodo homines æternitatem sortiuntur. Unde Boëtius dicit,[5] *Vos immortalitatem vobis propagare videmini, cum futuri famam temporis cogitatis.* Ergo beatitudo hominis consistit in fama seu gloria.

SED CONTRA, beatitudo est verum hominis bonum. Sed famam seu gloriam contingit esse falsam: ut enim dicit Boëtius,[6] *plures magnum sæpe nomen falsis vulgi opinionibus abstulerunt. Quo quid turpius excogitari potest? Nam qui falso prædicantur, suis ipsi necesse est laudibus erubescant.* Non ergo beatitudo hominis consistit in fama seu gloria.

---

[1]cf *CG* III, 29
[2]*Romans* 8, 18
[3]*De div. nom.* 4. PG 3, 719; cf 694 & 698
[4]cf Augustine, *Contra Maxim.* II, 13. PL 42, 770
[5]*De consol.* II, 7. PL 63, 711
[6]*De consol.* III, 6. PL 63, 745

Hence: 1. Aristotle there notices that honour is not the reward of virtue as though it were the motive from which men of virtue act; it is what they receive rather than what they deserve from men *who have nothing better to give*. Virtue's true reward is happiness itself, and good men aim at this. To act for honour would be ambition, not virtue.[c]

2. Honour is due to God and sublime beings in sign and testimony of the excellence which is theirs already; it does not make them excellent.

3. Because of their native desire for happiness, of which, as we have remarked, honour is a consequence, men desire to be honoured. And especially by the wise and experienced, in whom they find assurance of their worth and good estate.[d]

article 3. does happiness consist in fame or glory?

THE THIRD POINT:[1] 1. It would seem so.[a] For does not happiness lie in the recompense rendered the saints for the trials they have undergone in this world? And is not this glory? St Paul tells us that *the sufferings of this time are not to be compared to the glory that is to be revealed in us.*[2] Beatitude, therefore, is glory.

2. Moreover, Dionysius says the good is self-diffusive.[3] Now by glory a man's goodness is spread abroad and acknowledged. Glory, Ambrose says, *is clear recognition with praise.*[4b] To receive this, then, is to be happy.

3. Furthermore, of all blessings happiness is the steadiest. This seems to be the note of fame or glory which perpetuates a person so that he achieves a sort of immortality.[c] Boethius writes, *When you think of your renown in future ages you seem to beget eternity unto yourselves.*[5d] Accordingly happiness lies in fame or glory.

ON THE OTHER HAND, happiness is man's true good. Whereas fame or glory may happen to be illusory, Boethius writes, *Many owe their renown to lying reports broadcast to the multitude. Can anything more shameful be thought of? Those who are falsely celebrated must needs blush at the praise.*[6] Therefore man's happiness does not consist in fame or glory.

---

[c]Ambition, a vice against courage and magnanimity, 2a2æ. 131. Vol. 42, ed. A. Ross & P. G. Walsh.

[d]Yet flattery is sweet even when known to be insincere. *Adulatio* a sin against friendliness, *affabilitas*: 2a2æ. 115.

[a]Glory adds to honour the note of public acknowledgment. The glory of which grace, the manifestation of God's favour, is the seed is touched on in the article. For the *lumen gloriæ* see 1a. 12, 5. Vol. 3, ed. H. McCabe.

[b]In fact St Augustine, not St Ambrose.

[c]Thus *les immortelles* of the French Academy.

[d]Boethius' own disgrace under Theodoric lends special force to these reflections.

RESPONSIO: Dicendum quod impossibile est beatitudinem hominis in fama seu gloria humana consistere. Nam gloria nihil aliud est quam *clara notitia cum laude*,[7] ut Ambrosius dicit. Res autem cognita aliter comparatur ad cognitionem humanam, et aliter ad cognitionem divinam: humana enim cognitio a rebus cognitis causatur, sed divina cognitio est causa rerum cognitarum. Unde perfectio humani boni, quæ beatitudo dicitur, non potest causari a notitia humana: sed magis notitia humana de beatitudine alicujus procedit et quodammodo causatur ab ipsa humana beatitudine, vel inchoata vel perfecta. Et ideo in fama vel in gloria non potest consistere hominis beatitudo.

Sed bonum hominis dependet, sicut ex causa, ex cognitione Dei. Et ideo ex gloria quæ est apud Deum dependet beatitudo hominis sicut ex causa sua: secundum illud *Psalm.*,[8] *Eripiam eum, et glorificabo eum, longitudine dierum replebo eum, et ostendam illi salutare meum.*

Est etiam aliud considerandum, quod humana notitia sæpe fallitur, et præcipue in singularibus contingentibus, cujusmodi sunt actus humani. Et ideo frequenter humana gloria fallax est. Sed quia Deus falli non potest, ejus gloria semper vera est. Propter quod dicitur, II *ad Cor.*,[9] *Ille probatus est, quem Deus commendat.*

1. Ad primum ergo dicendum quod Apostolus non loquitur ibi de gloria quæ est ab hominibus, sed de gloria quæ est a Deo coram Angelis ejus. Unde dicitur *Marc.*,[10] *Filius hominis confitebitur eum in gloria Patris sui, coram angelis ejus.*

2. Ad secundum dicendum quod bonum alicujus hominis quod per famam vel gloriam est in cognitione multorum si cognitio quidem vera sit, oportet quod derivetur a bono existente in ipso homine: et sic præsupponit beatitudinem perfectam vel inchoatam. Si autem cognitio falsa sit, non concordat rei; et sic bonum non invenitur in eo cujus fama celebris habetur. Unde patet quod fama nullo modo potest facere hominem beatum.

3. Ad tertium dicendum quod fama non habet stabilitatem: immo falso rumore de facili perditur. Et si stabilis aliquando perseveret, hoc est per accidens. Sed beatitudo habet per se stabilitatem, et semper.

articulus 4. utrum beatitudo hominis consistat in potestate

AD QUARTUM sic proceditur:[1] 1. Videtur quod beatitudo consistat in potestate. Omnia enim appetunt assimilari Deo, tanquam ultimo fini et primo principio. Sed homines qui in potestatibus sunt, propter similitudinem potestatis, maxime videntur esse Deo conformes: unde et in Scriptura *dii*

---

[7]loc cit, note 4
[8]*Psalms* 90, 15–16

REPLY: We speak of human fame or glory, which, according to the quotation,[7] is being well recognized and praised. That this should make happiness is impossible. Things known are related otherwise to the human mind and to God's, for they cause our knowledge but are caused by his.[e] Therefore the complete human good of blessedness cannot depend on other people recognizing it; instead their recognition rises from and is caused by its being there, whether as dawning or full happiness. And so men's happiness does not lie in their being famous or glorious.

Their blessedness depends on God's knowledge as on its cause,[f] and on the favour and glory they have with him; thus the verse in the *Psalms*, *I will deliver him and I will glorify him; I will fill him with length of days, and I will show him my salvation.*[8]

Bear in mind also that human knowledge is often mistaken, particularly about such individual and contingent events as human deeds, and so human glory is frequently illusory. But God cannot be deceived, and his glory is always true; accordingly St Paul writes, *He is approved whom God commendeth.*[9]

Hence: 1. The Apostle is referring to the glory which is from God before his angels, not from man. Accordingly we read, *The Son of Man shall acknowledge him in the glory of his Father before his angels.*[10][g]

2. When a man achieves popular fame or glory, either the praise is well-founded and based on his real worth, and presupposes his being blessed, either initially or completely, or it is not, and his celebrity is hollow. It is evident that a man's happiness in neither case comes from his fame.

3. Fame does not endure, but is soon dissipated by lying reports. And when it is lasting, that is just by chance, whereas happiness essentially remains and for ever.[h]

article 4. does man's happiness lie in power?

THE FOURTH POINT:[1] 1. It would appear to. There is a drive within all things towards some likeness to God, who is their first beginning and final end. Now men in the seats of power seem to be most like God because of

---

[9]II *Corinthians* 10, 18
[10]*Mark* 8, 38. *Luke* 12, 8
[1]cf *CG* III, 31. *In Matt.* 5. *Se regimine principum* I, 8. *Compend. Theol.* II, 9
[e]cf 1a. 14, 8. Vol. 4, ed. T. Gornall.
[f]Depends on, not is constituted by, comments Cajetan. Our happiness consists in knowing God, not in being known by him. See 1a2æ. 3, 1 below. Also 1a. 12, 4.
[g]St Thomas runs *Luke* 12, 8 and *Mark* 8, 38 together, possibly because he is quoting from memory.
[h]Below 1a2æ. 5, 4.

vocantur, ut patet *Exod.*,[2] *Diis non detrahes.* Ergo in potestate beatitudo consistit.

2. Præterea, beatitudo est bonum perfectum. Sed perfectissimum est quod homo etiam alios regere possit, quod convenit his qui in potestatibus sunt constituti. Ergo beatitudo consistit in potestate.

3. Præterea, beatitudo, cum sit maxime appetibilis, opponitur ei quod maxime est fugiendum. Sed homines maxime fugiunt servitutem, cui contraponitur potestas. Ergo in potestate beatitudo consistit.

SED CONTRA, beatitudo est perfectum bonum. Sed potestas est maxime imperfecta. Ut enim dicit Boëtius,[3] *Potestas humana sollicitudinum morsus expellere, formidinum aculeos vitare nequit.* Et postea: *Potentem censes cui satellites latus ambiunt, qui quos terret, ipse plus metuit?* Non igitur beatitudo consistit in potestate.

RESPONSIO: Dicendum quod impossible est beatitudinem in potestate consistere, propter duo. Primo quidem, quia potestas habet rationem principii, ut patet in *Meta.*[4] Beatitudo autem habet rationem ultimi finis. Secundo, quia potestas se habet ad bonum et ad malum. Beatitudo autem est proprium et perfectum hominis bonum. Unde magis posset consistere beatitudo aliqua in bono usu potestatis, qui est per virtutem, quam in ipsa potestate.

Possunt autem quatuor generales rationes induci ad ostendendum quod in nullo præmissorum exteriorum bonorum beatitudo consistat.

Quarum prima est quia, cum beatitudo sit summum hominis bonum, non compatitur secum aliquod malum. Omnia autem prædicta possunt inveniri et in bonis et in malis.

Secunda ratio est quia, cum de ratione beatitudinis sit quod sit *per se sufficiens,* ut patet in *Ethic.*,[5] necesse est quod, beatitudine adepta, nullum bonum homini necessarium desit. Adeptis autem singulis præmissorum, possunt adhuc multa bona homini necessaria deesse, puta sapientia, sanitas corporis, et hujusmodi.

Tertia, quia, cum beatitudo sit bonum perfectum, ex beatitudine non potest aliquod malum alicui provenire. Quod non convenit præmissis: dicitur enim *Eccles.*,[6] quod divitiæ interdum conservantur *in malum domini sui;* et simile patet in aliis tribus.

Quarta ratio est quia ad beatitudinem homo ordinatur per principia interiora, cum ad ipsam naturaliter ordinetur. Præmissa autem quatuor bona

---

[2]*Exodus* 22, 28   [3]*De consol.* III, 5. PL 63, 741
[4]*Metaphysics* V, 4. 1019a15   [5]*Ethics* I, 7. 1097b8
[6]*Ecclesiastes* 5, 12

their lordship; even Scripture speaks of them as gods, *Thou shalt speak no ill of the gods.*[2a] Therefore happiness resides in power.

2. Further, happiness is the perfect good. Man's highest perfection is to rule others well, and this is the office of those in power. And so happiness lies in wielding power.

3. Again, as happiness is the most to be desired, so its opposite is the most to be shunned. For man this is slavery, the opposite of having power, and in consequence of holding happiness.

ON THE OTHER HAND, whereas happiness is perfect good, power is highly imperfect. Boethius writes, *Human power cannot drive away the gnawings of worry, nor escape the thorns of dread.* He goes on to ask, *Think you a man powerful when he is surrounded by courtiers, whom he inspires with fear indeed, though he is more fearful of them?*[3]

REPLY: Being powerful is not being happy, and for two reasons. First, because the essential notions are distinct, for power means an origin of activity[b] as stated in the *Metaphysics*,[4] whereas happiness means its achievement. Second, because power is held both for good and ill, whereas happiness is a man's proper and complete good. Hence the happiness to be found in power lies rather in its good use, which is through virtue, than in power itself.

We may set forth four general reasons to show that happiness lies in none of the four external goods so far discussed, namely wealth, honours, fame or glory, and power.[c]

First: each of them can be present both in a good and a bad man, whereas happiness is complete well-being and incompatible with any evil.

Second: it is clear from the *Ethics*[5] that to be self-sufficient is of the very nature of happiness;[d] in consequence once he has gained it a man can lack for nothing. Whereas after obtaining each or all of the four we have enumerated he may still be found wanting in many indispensable gifts, such as wisdom, health of body, and so forth.

Third: no misfortune can crop up from happiness, since it is complete fulfilment. So much cannot be said of the four blessings we have considered; for instance *Ecclesiastes* warns us that sometimes riches are held *to the hurt of their owner.*[6] And the same holds true of the other three.

Fourth: man's instinct for happiness is from within by the dynamism of his nature. All the four foregoing, however, are due to extrinsic causes,

---

[a]Vulgate: *diis non detrahes.* RSV, *nor curse a ruler of your people.*
[b]*Principium*, a beginning, start, source.
[c]arts 1–4.
[d]self-sufficient, *autarkēs*, needing no aid, supplying itself, wants no imports.

magis sunt a causis exterioribus, et ut plurimum a fortuna: unde et bona fortunæ dicuntur.

Unde patet quod in præmissis nullo modo beatitudo consistit.

1. Ad primum ergo dicendum quod divina potestas est sua bonitas: unde uti sua potestate non potest nisi bene. Sed hoc in hominibus non invenitur. Unde non sufficit ad beatitudinem hominis quod assimiletur Deo quantum ad potestatem, nisi etiam assimiletur ei quantum ad bonitatem.

2. Ad secundum dicendum quod, sicut optimum est quod aliquis utatur bene potestate in regimine multorum, ita pessimum est si male utatur. Et ita potestas se habet et ad bonum et ad malum.

3. Ad tertium dicendum quod servitus est impedimentum boni usus potestatis: ed ideo naturaliter homines eam fugiunt, et non quasi in potestate hominis sit summum bonum.

articulus 5. utrum beatitudo hominis consistat in aliquo corporis bono

AD QUINTUM sic proceditur:[1] 1. Videtur quod beatitudo hominis consistat in bonis corporis. Dicitur enim *Eccl.*,[2] *Non est census supra censum salutis corporis*. Sed in eo quod est optimum consistit beatitudo. Ergo consistit in corporis salute.

2. Præterea, Dionysius dicit[3] quod esse est melius quam vivere, et vivere melius quam alia quæ consequuntur. Sed ad esse et vivere hominis requiritur salus corporis. Cum ergo beatitudo sit summum bonum hominis, videtur quod salus corporis maxime pertineat ad beatitudinem.

3. Præterea, quanto aliquid est communius tanto ab altiori principio dependet, quia quanto causa est superior tanto ejus virtus ad plura se extendit. Sed sicut causalitas causæ efficientis consideratur secundum influentiam, ita causalitas finis attenditur secundum appetitum. Ergo sicut prima causa efficiens est quæ in omnia influit, ita ultimus finis est quod ab omnibus desideratur. Sed ipsum esse est quod maxime desideratur ab omnibus. Ergo in his quæ pertinent ad esse hominis, sicut est salus corporis, maxime consistit ejus beatitudo.

SED CONTRA, secundum beatitudinem homo excellit omnia alia animalia. Sed secundum bona corporis a multis animalibus superatur: sicut ab elephante in diuturnitate vitæ, a leone in fortitudine, a cervo in cursu. Ergo beatitudo hominis non consistit in bonis corporis.

---

[1]cf *CG* III, 32. *In Ethic.* I, *lect.* 10. IV *Sent.* 49, 1, 1, i. *Compend. Theol.* II, 9
[2]*Ecclesiasticus* 30, 16
[3]*De div. nom.* 5. PG 3, 817. St Thomas, *lect.* 1
[e]Note the naturalness or within-ness of happiness. For good fortune see the *Liber*

and most often to good luck, for which reason they are called the goods of fortune.[e]

And so it is evident that happiness in no way reposes in any of them.

Hence: 1. God's power is his goodness,[f] accordingly he cannot apply his power otherwise than well. Such is not the case with men. Therefore to show some reflection of God by their power does not approach to happiness, unless they also become like him in goodness.

2. As the good use of power in ruling many is the best, so its abuse is the worst that can befall.[g] Mere might as such is neutral between good and evil.

3. Slavery is a bar to the right exercise of power; that is why man's nature is to flee it, not because the possession of power is his supreme good.

article 5. does our happiness lie in well-being of body?

THE FIFTH POINT:[1] 1. So it would seem.[a] For in *Ecclesiasticus* we read, *There is no wealth above health of body*.[2] Since happiness is the optimum, health is where it is found.

2. Again, Dionysius says[3] that to be is better than to live, and to live is better than all the succeeding stages. Health is demanded for man's being and living, and therefore seems to be the main part of happiness, which is his highest good.

3. Again, the higher the cause the wider its reach, and correspondingly the more universal a reality the more ultimate the principle on which it depends. Now as efficient causality is looked at as a flowing in of activity, so final causality is looked at as a drawing out by desire. Accordingly the first efficient cause is that which runs into all, and the final end is that which all desire. What is this unless existence itself? Therefore man's happiness consists above all in the components of his existence, and such is his health of body.[b]

ON THE OTHER HAND, it is by happiness that man surpasses the other animals. Yet many surpass him in physical qualities, for instance the elephant in longevity, the lion in strength, the buck in speed. Therefore his happiness does not lie in his bodily qualities.

---

de bona fortuna, an excerpt from the *Eudemian Ethics*, a favourite mediæval text.
[f]Divine power, 1a. 25. Vol. 5, ed. T. Gilby.
[g]Ruling under law, 1a2æ. 95–97. Vol. 28. Practical wisdom in government, 2a2æ. 50. Vol. 36.
[a]Physical health and beauty; physical pleasure is discussed in the following article.
[b]Components of well-being, *consistentia naturalis*, 1a2æ. 10, 1.

RESPONSIO: Dicendum quod impossibile est beatitudinem hominis in bonis corporis consistere, propter duo.

Primo quidem, quia impossibile est quod illius rei quæ ordinatur ad aliud sicut ad finem ultimus finis sit ejusdem conservatio in esse. Unde gubernator non intendit, sicut ultimum finem, conservationem navis sibi commissæ; eo quod navis ad aliud ordinatur sicut ad finem, scilicet ad navigandum. Sicut autem navis committitur gubernatori ad dirigendum, ita homo est suæ voluntati et rationi commissus; secundum illud quod dicitur *Eccl.*,[4] *Deus ab initio constituit hominem, et reliquit eum in manu consilii sui.* Manifestum est autem quod homo ordinatur ad aliquid sicut ad finem: non enim homo est summum bonum. Unde impossibile est quod ultimus finis rationis et voluntatis humanæ sit conservatio humani esse.

Secundo quia, dato quod finis rationis et voluntatis humanæ esset conservatio humani esse, non tamen posset dici quod finis hominis esset aliquod corporis bonum. Esse enim hominis consistit in anima et corpore: et quamvis esse corporis dependeat ab anima, esse tamen humanæ animæ non dependet a corpore, ut supra ostensum est;[5] ipsumque corpus est propter animam, sicut materia propter formam, et instrumenta propter motorem ut per ea suas actiones exerceat. Unde omnia bona corporis ordinantur ad bona animæ, sicut ad finem. Unde impossibile est quod in bonis corporis beatitudo consistat, quæ est ultimus hominis finis.

1. Ad primum ergo dicendum quod, sicut corpus ordinatur ad animam sicut ad finem, ita bona exteriora ad ipsum corpus. Et ideo rationabiliter bonum corporis præfertur bonis exterioribus, quæ per *censum* significantur, sicut et bonum animæ præfertur omnibus bonis corporis.

2. Ad secundum dicendum quod esse simpliciter acceptum, secundum quod includit in se omnem perfectionem essendi, præeminet vitæ et omnibus subsequentibus; sic enim ipsum esse præhabet in se omnia subsequentia. Et hoc modo Dionysius loquitur. Sed si consideretur ipsum esse prout participatur in hac re vel in illa, quæ non capiunt totam perfectionem essendi, sed habent esse imperfectum, sicut est esse cujuslibet creaturæ, sic manifestum est quod ipsum esse cum perfectione superaddita est eminentius. Unde et Dionysius ibidem dicit quod viventia sunt meliora existentibus, et intelligentia viventibus.

3. Ad tertium dicendum quod, quia finis respondet principio, ex illa ratione probatur quod ultimus finis est primum principium essendi, in quo est omnis essendi perfectio: cujus similitudinem appetunt, secundum suam

---

[4]*Ecclesiasticus* 15, 14
[5]Ia. 75, 2; 76. 1 ad 5 & 6; 90, 2 ad 2
[c]Nevertheless, as appears from the contexts to which the author refers, man is one single thing, from which only by abstraction do we form the notions of one part

REPLY: That man's happiness cannot be centred on his body may be supported by two arguments.

First, when a thing is made for something other than itself, then its ultimate end cannot be constituted by its own continuance in existence. A commanding officer's final purpose is not to save his ship, since she is part of a wider plan indicated in his sailing orders. Yet he is responsible for her course and speed. So likewise man is entrusted with his own reason and will; according to *Ecclesiasticus*,[4] *God made man in the beginning, and left him in the hand of his own counsel.* Manifestly man is destined to an end beyond himself, for he himself is not the supreme good. And therefore the final goal for his reason and will cannot just be his own continuance.

Second, even granted this were the case, it could not be argued that it lay in some bodily endowment. For man's being consists of body and soul, and though the existence of the body depends on that of the soul, the existence of the soul does not depend on that of the body: we have already explained the implications.[5c] The body is for the soul, as matter for form, and instruments for a principal cause to work through. Likewise blessings of body are meant for blessings of soul. And so they cannot contain man's happiness, which is his final end.

Hence: 1. The body is for the soul rather as external possessions are for the body. With good reason, then, the welfare of the body is rated more important than the ownership of property—signified by *riches*, and the welfare of the soul than that of the body.

2. If we think of existence wholly and simply, that is including every perfection of being real, then it surpasses life and all that biologically involves; signified thus, as elsewhere by Dionysius, it anticipates all that is developed from it. But if we think of existence precisely as participated and as realized in this or that, then it is limited, as is the existence of each and every creature: signified thus, as in the present passage cited from Dionysius, in the objection, it is clear that mere existence is heightened by an additional value. And in this sense we should read his statement that living beings are better than existing beings, and intelligent beings better than living beings.[d]

3. It is true that the end is in the beginning, and the argument can prove that the final cause is the first cause[e] from which existence holds every perfection of reality.[f] All in their own proportion pursue its likeness,

---

acting like a principal and another like an instrumental cause. For the civil and despotic rule of lower by higher powers, cf 1a. 81, 3.

[d]*Esse*. Its minimal meaning signifies that a thing just exists. It is taken more fully to stand for the actuality of any perfection, 1a. 2, 1; 3, 4; 4, 2.

[e]1a. 44, 1 & 4. Vol. 8.

[f]God anticipates, *præhabet*, every perfection, 1a. 6, 4. Vol. 2. 1a. 26, 4. Vol. 5.

proportionem, quædam quidem secundum esse tantum, quædam secundum esse vivens, quædam secundum esse vivens et intelligens et beatum. Et hoc paucorum est.

articulus 6. utrum beatitudo hominis consistat in voluptate

AD SEXTUM sic proceditur:[1] 1. Videtur quod beatitudo hominis in voluptate consistat. Beatitudo enim, cum sit ultimus finis, non appetitur propter aliud, sed alia propter ipsam. Sed hoc maxime convenit delectationi: *ridiculum est enim ab aliquo quærere propter quid velit delectari*, ut dicitur in *Ethic*.[2] Ergo beatitudo maxime in voluptate et delectatione consistit.

2. Præterea, *causa prima vehementius imprimit quam secunda*, ut dicitur in *Libro de causis*.[3] Influentia autem finis attenditur secundum ejus appetitum. Illud ergo videtur habere rationem finis ultimi quod maxime movet appetitum. Hoc autem est voluptas: cujus signum est quod delectatio intantum absorbet hominis voluntatem et rationem quod alia bona contemnere facit. Ergo videtur quod ultimus finis hominis, qui est beatitudo, maxime in voluptate consistat.

3. Præterea, cum appetitus sit boni, illud quod omnia appetunt videtur esse optimum. Sed delectationem omnia appetunt, et sapientes et insipientes, et etiam ratione carentia. Ergo delectatio est optimum. Consistit ergo in voluptate beatitudo, quæ est summum bonum.

SED CONTRA est quod Boëtius dicit,[4] *Tristes exitus esse voluptatum, quisquis reminisci libidinum suarum volet, intelliget. Quæ si beatos efficere possent, nihil causæ est quin pecudes quoque beatæ esse dicantur.*

RESPONSIO: Dicendum quod, *quia delectationes corporales pluribus notæ sunt, assumpserunt sibi nomen voluptatum*, ut dicitur *Ethic.*,[5] cum tamen sint aliæ delectationes potiores. In quibus tamen beatitudo principaliter non consistit.

Quia in unaquaque re aliud est quod pertinet ad essentiam ejus, aliud est proprium accidens ipsius: sicut in homine aliud est quod est animal rationale mortale, aliud quod est risibile. Est igitur considerandum quod omnis delectatio est quoddam proprium accidens quod consequitur beati-

---

[1]cf *CG* III, 27 & 33. *Compend. Theol.* 108. IV *Sent.* 44, 1, 3, iv ad 3 & 4. *In Ethic.* I, lect. 5
[2]*Ethics* X, 2. 1172b22   [3]1. Bardenhewer 163
[4]*De consol.* III, 7. PL 63, 749   [5]*Ethics* VII, 13. 1153b33
[a]*Voluptas* is here taken in no pejorative sense: the discussion will broaden out to pleasure as such, and will be resumed later, 1a2æ. 4, 2. Appendix 3.
[b]The *Book of Causes, Liber de causis, Liber bonitatis puræ, Aphorismi de essentia*

some as just being, others as also being alive, others as also being intelligent, and others—a minority these—as also being blessed.

article 6. does happiness consist in pleasures of sense?

THE SIXTH POINT:[1] 1. It would seem so.[a] For since happiness is the ultimate end, it is not desired for the sake of something else; rather others are desired for its sake. Now this is the dominant note in pleasure especially; Aristotle remarks *how absurd it is to ask somebody why he wishes to enjoy himself.*[2] Therefore happiness lies chiefly in pleasure and delight.

2. Moreover, the *Liber de causis*[3b] teaches that the impression of a first cause is stronger than that of a second. The causality of an end comes from its being desired, and consequently that end will be final which most strongly moves desire. Such is pleasure. That it can so absorb mind and heart that in comparison other goods count for little is one sign of its power. And so it seems that in man's ultimate end, which is his happiness, pleasure is the dominant.

3. Again, since desire is for good, that which all desire would seem to be the best. All desire pleasure, whether they be wise and foolish, or even beings without intelligence. And therefore pleasure is best, and holds happiness, the supreme good.

ON THE OTHER HAND Boethius writes,[4] *Anyone who chooses to reflect on past excesses will appreciate how pleasures have sad endings. And if they can render a person happy, there is no reason why we should not say that the very beasts are happy too.*

REPLY: Aristotle observes[5] how bodily pleasures have engrossed the name of pleasure, because they are commonly experienced, whereas in point of fact there are other delights more potent. Even these, however, are not what make happiness.

These are our grounds. A distinction is to be drawn between what is part of a thing's essence and what is a consequent property: take man, for instance; his being a rational mortal animal is not exactly the same as his having a sense of humour.[c] Now note that pleasure is a sort of property

---

summæ bonitatis, a compilation of extracts from the *Elements of Theology* by Proclus (411–85) by an unknown hand. Translated into Latin, either from the Greek or the Arabic, perhaps by Gerard of Cremona (d. 1187). An influential medieval text, commented on by St Thomas; both he and St Albert recognized that it was not the work of Aristotle. The book opens with the statement quoted. For Proclus see introduction to translation of *Elements* by E. R. Dodds, 1933.
[c]The comparison now to be made should not be pressed beyond the bounds of analogy.

tudinem, vel aliquam beatitudinis partem: ex hoc enim aliquis delectatur quod habet bonum aliquod sibi conveniens, vel in re vel in spe vel saltem in memoria. Bonum autem conveniens, si quidem sit perfectum, est ipsa hominis beatitudo, si autem sit imperfectum, est quædam beatitudinis participatio, vel propinqua vel remota vel saltem apparens. Unde manifestum est quod nec ipsa delectatio quæ consequitur bonum perfectum, est ipsa essentia beatitudinis; sed quoddam consequens ad ipsam sicut per se accidens.

Voluptas autem corporalis non potest etiam modo prædicto sequi bonum perfectum. Nam sequitur bonum quod apprehendit sensus, qui est virtus animæ corpore utens. Bonum autem quod pertinet ad corpus, quod apprehenditur secundum sensum, non potest esse perfectum hominis bonum. Cum enim anima rationalis excedat proportionem materiæ corporalis, pars animæ quæ est ab organo corporeo absoluta quandam habet infinitatem respectu ipsius corporis et partium animæ corpori concretarum: sicut immaterialia sunt quodammodo infinita respectu materialium, eo quod forma per materiam quodammodo contrahitur et finitur, unde forma a materia absoluta est quodammodo infinita. Et ideo sensus, qui est vis corporalis, cognoscit singulare, quod est determinatum per materiam: intellectus vero, qui est vis a materia absoluta, cognoscit universale, quod est abstractum a materia, et continet sub se infinita singularia. Unde patet quod bonum conveniens corpori, quod per apprehensionem sensus delectationem corporalem causat, non est perfectum bonum hominis, sed est minimum quiddam in comparatione ad bonum animæ. Unde *Sap.*[6] dicitur quod *omne aurum, in comparatione sapientiæ, arena est exigua*. Sic igitur neque voluptas corporalis est ipsa beatitudo, nec est per se accidens beatitudinis.

1. Ad primum ergo dicendum quod ejusdem rationis est quod appetatur bonum et quod appetatur delectatio, quæ nihil est aliud quam quietatio appetitus in bono: sicut ex eadem virtute naturæ est quod grave feratur deorsum et quod ibi quiescat. Unde sicut bonum propter seipsum appetitur, ita et delectatio propter se, et non propter aliud appetitur, si ly *propter* dicat causam finalem. Si vero dicat causam formalem, vel potius motivam, sic delectatio est appetibilis propter aliud, idest propter bonum, quod est delectationis objectum, et per consequens est principium ejus, et dat ei

---

[6]*Wisdom* 7, 9
[d]*Consequens sicut per se accidens.* The passage argues the classical case against hedonism, such as was recapitulated by Bishop Butler in the eighteenth century. Briefly it is that happiness makes pleasure, not pleasure happiness. The criticism of hedonism, at least in its refined form of Epicureanism, is, in fact, psychological, not moral. Later the *Summa* will take spiritual pleasure as a good test for virtue: 1a2æ. 34, 2–4. The implication here and in the following paragraph against Aristippus of

resulting from being happy, in whole or in part; a person delights by responding to a good he holds, whether in reality or in hope or at least in memory. And it is in this good which meets his desire that his happiness lies—pure happiness if this be complete good, some share in happiness, close or distant or at least by shadow, if it be incomplete. And so it is manifest that not even the delight resulting from the perfect good is the decisive point of happiness, but a sort of essential property or result of it.[d]

Sensuous pleasure lacks even this essential connection, for it arises from a good experienced by sense, a power of soul working through body, which good cannot be man's complete good. Since the rational soul outstretches the reach of bodily matter, that part of it which is not bound to a corporeal organ has a sort of limitlessness with respect to the body and those parts of the soul having solidarity with the body. Thus spiritual things are as it were unbounded compared with material things. This is because material forms in a manner are constricted by and confined in matter, whereas forms independent of matter are, so to speak, at large. Sense, which is a bodily power, perceives an individual pinned down to space and time through matter, whereas the intelligence, which is a power unenclosed by matter, perceives a universal which is lifted above matter and embraces any number of individuals.[e] So then it is clear that a good matching the body and affording bodily pleasure when sensuously experienced is not man's full good, but is trifling compared with a good for the soul. Accordingly we read of wisdom, *All gold compared with her is like a little sand.*[6] Consequently bodily pleasure is neither the heart nor an essential property of happiness.

Hence: 1. It is for the same impulse that a value is desired and that pleasure is desired, as it is by the same force of nature that a body gravitates and stays in its place. Correspondingly as good is desired on its own account, so too is pleasure desired and not on account of anything else, if the term 'on account of'[f] spells final causality. If, however, it spells formal causality or, better, efficient causality, then pleasure is desired on account of something other than itself, namely the good which is the object providing delight; and consequently this thing is its source of delight and gives it

---

Cyrene, and the Cyrenaics generally, also Protagoras of Abdera, is that a distinction is to be drawn between the human appreciation of the good which gives delight and the actual enjoyment of it. The *ratio finis delectabilis* is a *bonum honestum*. See note g below. Also Appendix 3. For the sin of *delectatio morosa*, see 1a2æ. 74, 6; for an analysis of dwelling on pleasure, ibid. 8. Vol. 25, ed. J. Fearon.

[e]The epistemology can be left as here briefly indicated; it is enough to show that the ultimate is not to be found in an object individualized by matter.

[f]*Ly propter; ly* a transliteration of the Arabic article *el*. The equivalent of the Greek *to*. The two sense of *propter* are important for psychological and moral theory.

formam: ex hoc enim delectatio habet quod appetatur, quia est quies in bono desiderato.

2. Ad secundum dicendum quod vehemens appetitus delectationis sensibilis contingit ex hoc quod operationes sensuum, quia sunt principia nostræ cognitionis, sunt magis perceptibiles. Unde etiam a pluribus delectationes sensibiles appetuntur.

3. Ad tertium dicendum quod eo modo omnes appetunt delectationem, sicut et appetunt bonum: et tamen delectationem appetunt ratione boni, et non e converso, ut dictum est.[7] Unde non sequitur quod delectatio sit maximum et per se bonum: sed quod unaquæque delectatio consequatur aliquod bonum, et quod aliqua delectatio consequatur id quod est per se et maximum bonum.

articulus 7. *utrum beatitudo hominis consistat in aliquo bono animæ*

AD SEPTIMUM sic proceditur:[1] 1. Videtur quod beatitudo consistat in aliquo bono animæ. Beatitudo enim est quoddam hominis bonum. Hoc autem per tria dividitur, quæ sunt bona exteriora, bona corporis, et bona animæ. Sed beatitudo non consistit in bonis exterioribus, neque in bonis corporis, sicut supra ostensum est.[2] Ergo consistit in bonis animæ.

2. Præterea, illud cui appetimus aliquod bonum magis amamus quam bonum quod ei appetimus: sicut magis amamus amicum cui appetimus pecuniam, quam pecuniam. Sed unusquisque quodcumque bonum sibi appetit.* Ergo seipsum amat magis quam omnia alia bona. Sed beatitudo est quod maxime amatur: quod patet ex hoc quod propter ipsam omnia alia amantur et desiderantur. Ergo beatitudo consistit in aliquo bono ipsius hominis. Sed non in bonis corporis. Ergo in bonis animæ.

3. Præterea, perfectio est aliquid ejus quod perficitur. Sed beatitudo est quædam perfectio hominis. Ergo beatitudo est aliquid hominis. Sed non est aliquid corporis, ut ostensum est.[3] Ergo beatitudo est aliquid animæ. Et ita consistit in bonis animæ.

SED CONTRA, sicut Augustinus dicit,[4] *id in quo constituitur beata vita, propter se diligendum est*. Sed homo non est propter seipsum diligendus, sed quidquid est in homine, est diligendum propter Deum. Ergo in nullo bono animæ beatitudo consistit.

---

*Piana: adds *amat*, he loves for himself
[7]ad 1   [1]cf 1a2æ. 55, 1, 2; 60, 1; 57, 1.   [2]art. 4 & 5 above
[3]art. 5   [4]*De doctrina Christ.* 1, 24. PL 34, 25
[g]*Quies*, not the stillness of inertia, but the rest of being fully actual. cf the motionless first setter in motion of 1a. 2, 3. Vol. 2. Appendix 6.
[h]Again the distinction, which will be used later, 1a2æ. 4, 2, between the good in itself and the good as providing pleasure. And so pleasure itself is not the form of the desire or of the desirable, or even of the pleasurable as authentically a good. An

shape. Pleasure is the resting[g] with an object of desire, and it is because of this that pleasure itself is desired.[h]

2. Our sensations are the beginnings of our knowledge, and the fact that they are emphatically experienced contributes to the urgency of desire for the pleasures they harbour. This goes to explain why these are what a majority want.

3. The motions of appetite for the pleasurable and the good-in-itself[1] follow the same channel; all the same, the pleasurable is desired by reason of the good in itself, and not, as we have pointed out,[7] the other way round. Consequently it does not follow from the objection that pleasure is the sovereign and essential good, but that each pleasure results from some good, and a pleasure from the highest and essential good.

article 7. does a good quality of soul make a man's happiness?

THE SEVENTH POINT:[1] 1. So it seems.[a] For happiness is a good for man. This falls into three classes, external good, good of body, and good of soul. We have seen that the first two do not constitute happiness.[2] Therefore the third remains.

2. Moreover, we desire a thing more than the blessing we want it to have. Do we not love a friend rather than the wealth we wish him to enjoy? And whatever a man desires is a good for him; in this sense he loves himself more than other goods. Happiness is what is loved above all, while all other goods are loved and desired for its sake. Therefore it is a good within himself. But not of his body. Therefore of his soul.

3. Again, perfection is a condition of the thing made perfect. And happiness is a man's perfection of man, and therefore part of his condition. But, as we have agreed,[3] it is not a condition of his body, but of his soul. In other words, it consists in endowments of soul.

ON THE OTHER HAND Augustine says,[4] *That which constitutes blessed living is lovable for its own sake.* But man is not lovable for his own sake, though whatever is in him is to be loved for God's sake.[b] Therefore no good of soul constitutes happiness.

---

object we mistake for a good, *bonum apparens tantum*, of course offers its appropriate pleasure, but it is not wrong because of this, although the promise of it has been the incentive.

Keep in mind the caution of the opening of the reply, to be repeated in the reply to the third objection, against separating the drives to the good and the pleasurable.
[1]i.e. for the *delectabile* and the *honestum*.
[a]A good of soul, namely virtue. The article is critical of a position held by the Stoics, as the preceding article was critical of the Epicureans. Self-perfectioning is not the object in happiness.
[b]For his own sake, that is as a complete ultimate.

RESPONSIO: Dicendum quod, sicut supra dictum est,[5] finis dupliciter dicitur: scilicet ipsa res quam adipisci desideramus; et usus, seu adeptio aut possessio illius rei.

Si ergo loquamur de ultimo fine hominis quantum ad ipsam rem quam appetimus sicut ultimum finem, impossibile est quod ultimus finis hominis sit ipsa anima, vel aliquid ejus. Ipsa enim anima, in se considerata, est ut in potentia existens: fit enim de potentia sciente actu sciens, et de potentia virtuosa actu virtuosa. Cum autem potentia sit propter actum, sicut propter complementum, impossibile est quod id quod est secundum se in potentia existens, habeat rationem ultimi finis. Unde impossibile est quod ipsa anima sit ultimus finis sui ipsius.

Similiter etiam neque aliquid ejus, sive sit potentia sive habitus sive actus. Bonum enim quod est ultimus finis, est bonum perfectum complens appetitum. Appetitus autem humanus, qui est voluntas, est boni universalis. Quodlibet bonum autem inhærens ipsi animæ, est bonum participatum, et per consequens particulatum. Unde impossibile est quod aliquod eorum sit ultimus finis hominis.

Sed si loquamur de ultimo fine hominis quantum ad ipsam adeptionem vel possessionem, seu quemcumque usum ipsius rei quæ appetitur ut finis, sic ad altimum finem pertinet aliquid hominis ex parte animæ: quia homo per animam beatitudinem consequitur.

Res ergo ipsa quæ appetitur ut finis, est id in quo beatitudo consistit, et quod beatum facit: sed hujus rei adeptio vocatur beatitudo. Unde dicendum est quod beatitudo est aliquid animæ; sed id in quo consistit beatitudo, est aliquid extra animam.

1. Ad primum ergo dicendum quod, secundum quod sub illa divisione comprehenduntur omnia bona quæ homini sunt appetibilia, sic bonum animæ dicitur non solum potentia aut habitus aut actus, sed etiam objectum, quod est extrinsecum. Et hoc modo nihil prohibet dicere id in quo beatitudo consistit esse quoddam bonum animæ.

2. Ad secundum dicendum, quantum ad propositum pertinet, quod beatitudo maxime amatur tanquam bonum concupitum: amicus autem amatur tanquam id cui concupiscitur bonum; et sic etiam homo amat seipsum. Unde non est eadem ratio amoris utrobique. Utrum autem amore amicitiæ aliquid homo supra se amet, erit locus considerandi cum de caritate agetur.[6]

---

[5]Ia2æ. 1, 8
[6]2a2æ. 26, 3
[e]This object-subject contrast will now run throughout the treatise.
[d]ability, *facultas*; disposition, *habitus*.
[e]What makes us happy is an object other than the self, and not some real quality of which we are the subject, that is an 'accident' in our substance, whether by way of

REPLY: As we have noticed,[5] there are two sides to an end, namely the very thing itself we want to possess and the actual reaching or holding of it.[c]

As for the first, namely the object desired as an ultimate end, then this cannot be our soul either as the thing itself or by anything which qualifies it. In itself it is a potential being, which becomes actually cognitive or virtuous from having been inactive beforehand. Since potentiality is for actuality, which is its fulfilment, it is not possible that a thing which of itself is potential should have the force of being an ultimate end. And consequently that the soul should be its own ultimate end.

Nor can this be any quality of soul, whether you take this as an aptitude, a disposition, or an activity.[d] For the good which is the ultimate end is complete and fulfils desire. Human desire or will is for unrestricted good, whereas a psychological entity is a derivative and therefore a particular good. None of them, consequently, can be man's ultimate end.[e]

If, however, by this we refer to the gaining or possessing, or to our being conjoined in any way with the thing on which we set our heart, then our ultimate end implies something within man and on the part of our soul, for it is then that we come to happiness.

To sum up: the thing itself desired as the final end is that which gives substance to happiness and makes a man happy, though happiness itself is defined by the holding of it.[f] The conclusion to be drawn is that happiness is a real condition of soul, yet is founded on a thing outside the soul.

Hence: 1. If the division is to cover all a man can desire, then the goods of soul should include not only aptitude, disposition, and activity, but also object from outside.[g] Understood in this sense there is no gainsaying the statement that happiness is a certain good of soul.

2. To keep to the point of our inquiry, we may say that happiness is loved above all as the good desired, and a friend as that for which it is desired; thus, too, does a man love himself. We allow for this variation on the meaning of love.[h] Whether a man loves another more than himself by friendship is a point that will be raised when we come to discuss charity.[6]

---

ability (faculty), disposition (habit), or activity (operation). St Thomas will insist on these creaturely categories in happiness, 1a2æ. 3, 1, as he does in grace, 1a2æ. 110, 1, and charity, 2a2æ. 23, 2; they are, however, but the subjective gear, as it were, required for attaining God as an object. But see reply to the first objection.

The discussions are still about objective beatitude; the following Questions will take up subjective or, as it is called, formal beatitude, i.e. our condition in having the object of bliss.

[f]i.e. formal happiness.

[g]Again the reference to object, though not here developed, which offers the key to the theological understanding of our identification with God in an objectual and not causal relationship. cf Foreword note *a*, and below art. 8, note *e*.

[h]Love is an analogical term.

3. Ad tertium dicendum quod beatitudo ipsa, cum sit perfectio animæ, est quoddam animæ bonum inhærens: sed id in quo beatitudo consistit, quod scilicet beatum facit, est aliquid extra animam, ut dictum est.

articulus 8. utrum beatitudo hominis consistat in aliquo bono creato

AD OCTAVUM sic proceditur:[1] 1. Videtur quod beatitudo hominis consistat in aliquo bono creato. Dicit enim Dionysius,[2] quod divina sapientia *conjungit fines primorum principiis secundorum:* ex quo potest accipi quod summum inferioris naturæ sit attingere infimum naturæ superioris. Sed summum hominis bonum est beatitudo. Cum ergo angelus naturæ ordine sit supra hominem, ut in *Primo*[3] habitum est; videtur quod beatitudo hominis consistat in hoc quod aliquo modo attingit ad angelum.

2. Præterea, ultimus finis cujuslibet rei est in suo opere perfecto: unde pars est propter totum, sicut propter finem. Sed tota universitas creaturarum, quæ dicitur *major mundus*, comparatur ad hominem, qui in VIII *Physic.*,[4] dicitur *minor mundus*, sicut perfectum ad imperfectum. Ergo beatitudo hominis consistit in tota universitate creaturarum.

3. Præterea, per hoc homo efficitur beatus, quod ejus naturale desiderium quietat. Sed naturale desiderium hominis non extenditur ad majus bonum quam quod ipse capere potest. Cum ergo homo non sit capax boni quod excedit limites totius creaturæ, videtur quod per aliquod bonum creatum homo beatus fieri possit. Et ita beatitudo hominis in aliquo bono creato consistit.

SED CONTRA est quod Augustinus dicit,[5] *Ut vita carnis anima est, ita beata vita hominis Deus est; de quo dicitur, Beatus populus cujus Dominus Deus ejus.*[6]

RESPONSIO: Dicendum quod impossibile est beatitudinem hominis esse in aliquo bono creato. Beatitudo enim est bonum perfectum, quod totaliter quietat appetitum: alioquin non esset ultimus finis si adhuc restaret aliquid appetendum.

Objectum autem voluntatis, quæ est appetitus humanus, est universale bonum; sicut objectum intellectus est universale verum. Ex quo patet quod nihil potest quietare voluntatem hominis nisi bonum universale. Quod non invenitur in aliquo creato, sed solum in Deo: quia omnis creatura habet bonitatem participatam. Unde solus Deus voluntatem hominis implere

---

[1]cf 1a. 12, 1. *CG* IV. 54. *De regimine principum* I, 8. *In Psalm.* 32. *Compendium Theol.* 108 & II, 9.
[2]*De div. nom.* 7. PG 3, 872   [3]1a. 96, 1 ad 1; 108, 2 ad 3 & 8 ad 2; III, 1
[4]*Physics* VIII, 2. 252b24   [5]*De civit. Dei* XIX, 26. PL 41, 656
[6]*Psalms* 143, 15

3. Happiness itself, as being a perfection of soul, is a particular good or quality inside the soul, but, as we have just explained, that on which it is centred, which causes a man to be happy, is outside the soul.

article 8. *is man's happiness realized in any created good?*

THE EIGHTH POINT:[1] 1. So it would seem.[a] Dionysius says that divine wisdom conjoins the ends and beginnings of prime and secondary creatures,[2] from which we gather that a lower nature at its peak touches a higher at its base. Man reaches his true height in happiness. And since angels are above men in the hierarchy of natures, as we have agreed,[3] it would seem that human happiness consists in somehow reaching to the angels.[b]

2. Further, each thing's final end is realized in its own full development; thus a part is for the sake of the whole, which is its purpose. The whole universe of creatures, called the macrocosm, is compared to man, called the microcosm, as the complete to the incomplete.[4] It is, therefore, as a part integrated within this whole that man realizes his happiness.

3. Again, man is made happy by an object which brings to rest his natural desire. This, however, does not reach out to more good than it can hold. Since he has not the capacity for a good beyond the bounds of all creation, it would seem that he can become happy through some created good, and here he finds his happiness.

ON THE OTHER HAND Augustine says, *As soul is life for the flesh, so God is the blessed life for man.*[5] And the Psalmist, *Happy the people whose god is the Lord.*[6]

REPLY: For man to rest content with any created good is not possible, for he can be happy only with complete good which satisfies his desire altogether: he would not have reached his ultimate end were there something still remaining to be desired.

The object of the will, that is the human appetite, is the Good without reserve, just as the object of the mind is the True without reserve. Clearly, then, nothing can satisfy man's will except such goodness, which is found, not in anything created, but in God alone. Everything created is a

---

[a]The culminating article of the Question, as the final article will be of the following Question: the two should be read together.

Note that St Thomas writes here explicitly as a Christian theologian, not just as a religious philosopher.

Note, too, the transition from the abstract to the concrete, from 'goodness without reserve' to the Good. On the use of abstract and concrete terms in divinity, cf Ia. 13, 1.

[b]An echo of the emanationist theories of Alexandrian and Neo-Platonist authors.

potest; secundum quod dicitur in *Psalm.*,[7] *Qui replet in bonis desiderium tuum.* In solo igitur Deo beatitudo hominis consistit.

1. Ad primum ergo dicendum quod superius hominis attingit quidem infimum angelicæ naturæ per quandam similitudinem; non tamen ibi sistit sicut in ultimo fine, sed procedit usque ad ipsum universalem fontem boni, qui est universale objectum* beatitudinis omnium beatorum, tanquam infinitum et perfectum bonum existens.

2. Ad secundum dicendum quod, si totum aliquod non sit ultimus finis, sed ordinetur ad finem ulteriorem, ultimus finis partis non est ipsum totum, sed aliquid aliud. Universitas autem creaturarum, ad quam comparatur homo ut pars ad totum, non est ultimus finis, sed ordinatur in Deum sicut in ultimum finem. Unde bonum universi non est ultimus finis hominis, sed ipse Deus.

3. Ad tertium dicendum quod bonum creatum non est minus quam bonum cujus homo est capax ut rei intrinsecæ et inhærentis: est tamen minus quam bonum cujus est capax ut objecti, quod est infinitum. Bonum autem quod participatur ab angelo, et a toto universo, est bonum finitum et contractum.

---

*Piana: *subjectum*, the subject in which the blessed find their bliss
[7]*Psalms* 102, 5
cA compression of Plato's dialectic of love. cf *Banquet* 211C.
dThe *bonum commune* of the universe is sometimes taken as the good of the whole, but more theologically, as here, as the all-good transcending yet sustaining it. cf Vol. 28, Appendix 4.

derivative good. He alone, *who fills with all good things thy desire*,[7] can satisfy our will, and therefore in him alone our happiness lies.[c]

Hence: 1. To say that the heights of human nature rise to the lower flanks of angelic nature is a metaphorical turn of speech. In truth men do not stay there as their utmost limit, but press upward to the universal fount of good, the unrestricted object of bliss for all the blessed, the infinite and complete subsisting good.

2. If the whole itself is not an ultimate but subordinate to a further end, then a person's ultimate end does not lie there but somewhere beyond. The universe of creatures, to which man is compared as part to whole, is not the ultimate end, but is ordered to God who is the ultimate end. And so man's final destiny is reached with God himself, not within the universe.[d]

3. The phrase, the good of which man is capable, can refer to the good as an intrinsic modification or quality of his being; in this sense a creaturely good does not exceed his capacity. And thus as a property of derivative being, the goodness of an angel, indeed of the entire universe, is finite and limited. But if it refers to an object, then in this sense creaturely good is less than a man's capacity, for he can reach out to the infinite.[e]

---

[e]The distinction is between a creature considered as an ontological and therefore limited entity and as open to an infinite object. It has already appeared in the subject-object contrast; e.g. art. 7, notes *d* & *e*. It is developed in the doctrine of the beatific vision. cf 1a2æ. 3, 8 below.

DEINDE CONSIDERANDUM est
quid sit beatitudo; et quæ requirantur ad ipsam.

Quæstio 3. quid sit beatitudo

CIRCA PRIMUM quæruntur octo:

1. utrum beatitudo sit aliquid increatum;
2. si est aliquid creatum, utrum sit operatio;
3. utrum sit operatio sensitivæ partis, an intellectivæ tantum;
4. si est operatio intellectivæ partis, utrum sit operatio intellectus, an voluntatis;
5. si est operatio intellectus, utrum sit operatio intellectus speculativi, aut practici;
6. si est operatio intellectus speculativi, utrum consistat in speculatione scientiarum speculativarum;
7. utrum consistat in speculatione substantiarum separatarum, scilicet angelorum;
8. utrum in sola speculatione Dei qua per essentiam videtur.

articulus 1. utrum beatitudo sit aliquid increatum

AD PRIMUM sic proceditur:[1] 1. Videtur quod beatitudo sit aliquid increatum. Dicit enim Boëtius,[2] *Deum esse ipsam beatitudinem necesse est confiteri.*

2. Præterea, beatitudo est summum bonum. Sed esse summum bonum convenit Deo. Cum ergo non sint plura summa bona, videtur quod beatitudo sit idem quod Deus.

3. Præterea, beatitudo est ultimus finis in quem naturaliter humana voluntas tendit. Sed in nullum aliud voluntas tanquam in finem tendere debet nisi in Deum; quo solo fruendum est, ut Augustinus dicit.[3] Ergo beatitudo est idem quod Deus.

---

[1]cf 1a. 26, 3. IV *Sent.* 49, 1, 2, i   [2]*De consol.* III, 10. PL 63, 766
[3]*De doctr. Christ.* I, 5 & 22. PL 34, 21 & 25
[a]The definition of happiness and its elements.
[b]A medieval tradition of Christian sufism forms part of the background for this and the following articles. Some of the earlier mystical theologians lacked the instruments for analysis that St Thomas uses, later writers sometimes did not care to use them, and others arrived at different conclusions with scholastic expertise. Some headings may be roughly indicated. For Hugh of St Victor (d. 1141) happiness was the uncreated knowledge of the Eternal Word; for Peter Lombard (d. 1173) the love of charity was the Holy Ghost. Others spoke of an *illapsus,* a flowing into, pene-

WE GO ON TO DISCUSS

what happiness is (3),
and what it requires (4).[a]

Question 3. what happiness is

HERE eight points of inquiry are raised:

1. whether happiness is something uncreated;
2. and if created, whether it is an activity;
3. whether on the sensory or only on the intelligent level;
4. and if the latter whether it is of mind or of will;
5. and if of mind whether it is contemplative or active;
6. and if contemplative whether it is theoretical;
7. whether it is in gazing at bodiless substances, namely angels;
8. or in the face to face vision of God himself.

article 1. is happiness non-creaturely?

THE FIRST POINT:[1] 1. Apparently yes.[b] For, according to Boethius, *we must confess that happiness itself is God.*[2]

2. Again, happiness is the sovereign good, a term we reserve to God alone. There are not several sovereign goods, and so it would seem that happiness is identified with God.

3. Besides, happiness is the final end to which the human will tends by nature. And it should tend to no other but God, who alone, says Augustine,[3] is to be enjoyed. Therefore happiness is identical with God.

---

tration, or descent of divinity into the essence of the soul. The Dionysian teaching of Hierotheus undergoing divine things, not learning about them, *patiens non discens divina* (cf 1a. 1, 6. Vol. 1) was pushed to excess by Miguel Molinos (d. 1696) and the Quietist teaching of the need for pure passivity.

Among the great scholastics St Bonaventure (d. 1274) and John Peckham (d. 1292), held that beatitude was a habit deifying the substance of the soul and thereby endowing it with the powers of appropriate activity, Henry of Ghent (d. 1293) and John Baconthorpe (d. 1348) that it was a relationship of presence. The *devotio moderna*, affected by Nominalism, considered such inquiries irrelevant to the mystical experience. The high Franciscan teaching on the primacy of love will be referred to under art. 4 below. Master Eckhart is a special case: he was credited with a pantheist doctrine of absorption into the divine, but he was well trained in the school of St Thomas, and should not be counted as standing outside it. St Thomas himself stresses the creaturely in union with God. cf the parallel articles, on grace, 1a2æ. 110, 1; on charity, 2a2æ. 23, 2.

SED CONTRA, nullum factum est increatum. Sed beatitudo hominis est aliquid factum: quia secundum Augustinum,[4] *illus rebus fruendum est quæ nos beatos faciunt.* Ergo beatitudo non est aliquid increatum.

RESPONSIO: Dicendum quod, sicut supra dictum est,[5] finis dicitur dupliciter. Uno modo, ipsa res quam cupimus adipisci: sicut avaro est finis pecunia. Alio modo, ipsa adeptio vel possessio, seu usus aut fruitio ejus rei quæ desideratur: sicut si dicatur quod possessio pecuniæ est finis avari, et frui re voluptuosa est finis intemperati.

Primo ergo modo, ultimus hominis finis est bonum increatum, scilicet Deus, qui solus sua infinita bonitate potest voluntatem hominis perfecte implere. Secundo autem modo, ultimus finis hominis est aliquid creatum in ipso existens, quod nihil est aliud quam adeptio vel fruitio finis ultimi. Ultimus autem finis vocatur beatitudo. Si ergo beatitudo hominis consideretur quantum ad causam vel objectum, sic est aliquid increatum: si autem consideretur quantum ad ipsam essentiam beatitudinis, sic est aliquid creatum.

1. Ad primum ergo dicendum quod Deus est beatitudo per essentiam suam: non enim per adeptionem aut participationem alicujus alterius beatus est, sed per essentiam suam. Homines autem sunt beati, sicut ibidem dicit Boëtius, per participationem; sicut et *dii* per participationem dicuntur. Ipsa autem participatio beatitudinis secundum quam homo dicitur beatus, aliquid creatum est.

2. Ad secundum dicendum quod beatitudo dicitur esse summum hominis bonum, quia est adeptio vel fruito summi boni.

3. Ad tertium dicendum quod beatitudo dicitur ultimus finis per modum quo adeptio finis dicitur finis.

articulus 2. utrum beatitudo sit operatio

AD SECUNDUM sic proceditur:[1] 1. Videtur quod beatitudo non sit operatio. Dicit enim Apostolus,[2] *Habetis fructum vestrum in sanctificationem, finem vero vitam æternam.* Sed vita non est operatio, sed ipsum esse viventium. Ergo ultimus finis, qui est beatitudo, non est operatio.

2. Præterea, Boëtius dicit,[3] quod beatitudo est *status omnium bonorum aggregatione perfectus.* Sed status non nominat operationem. Ergo beatitudo non est operatio.

---

[4]op cit 3. PL 34, 20   [5]1a2æ. 1, 8; 2, 7
[1]cf *CG* I, 100. *In Ethic.* I, lect. 10. *In Meta.* IX, lect. 8. IV *Sent.* 49, 1, 2, ii
[2]*Romans* 6, 22   [3]*De consol.* III, 2. PL 63, 724
[c]And therefore also to happiness. 1a. 26, 3.
[d]Again the distinction, the object and the category of being into which the subject

ON THE OTHER HAND, nothing that is made is uncreated. And human happiness is made; Augustine tells us to enjoy the things that make us happy.[4] Happiness, then, is something created.

REPLY: As we have noticed,[5] there are two sides to an end.[c] One, the thing itself we long for, thus money for the miser. Two, the getting, holding, or effective attainment and enjoyment of it, as hoarding for the miser, or self-indulging for a voluptuary.

As for the first, man's ultimate end is uncreated good, namely God, who alone can fill the will of man to the brim because of his infinite goodness. Yet as for the second, man's ultimate end is a creaturely reality in him, for what is it but *his* coming to God and *his* joy with God. This end defines his happiness. And so then, with respect to its object or cause happiness is uncreated reality, while with respect to its essence it is a creaturely reality.[d]

Hence: 1. What Boethius means is that God is happiness itself: he is happy by his essence, and not by coming to happiness or partaking of it from another.[e] He says in the same place that men are blessed by participation, rather as they are called divine gods by participation.[f] And this derivative bliss is a creature being.

2. Happiness is said to be man's highest good because it is the attainment and enjoyment of the sovereign good.[g]

3. Happiness is called the ultimate end in the way that reaching an end is called the end.

article 2. is happiness an activity?

THE SECOND POINT:[1] 1. It would seem not.[a] St Paul tells us, *You have fruit unto sanctification, and the end is life everlasting.*[2] Now life is not the acting but the very being of living things. Accordingly our final end, which is happiness, is not an activity.

2. Moreover, Boethius describes happiness as a state made complete by all good things being gathered together.[3] But a state does not denote an operation. And so happiness is not an operation.

---

falls, roughly between the 'epistemological' content and the psychological reality. cf 1a2æ. 2, 8, note *e* above. The Question will go on to show that happiness in us is an activity (*operatio*, a species of quality), furthermore an activity of the mind contemplating.
[e]1a. 26. On God's happiness and our sharing in it.
[f]cf 1a2æ. 2, 4 obj. 1 above.
[g]Man's formal happiness, *beatitudo formalis*, sometimes called subjective happiness, is his possession of the object of happiness, *beatitudo objectiva*.
[a]cf art. 1, notes *b* and *d*.

3. Præterea, beatitudo significat aliquid in beato* existens, cum sit ultima perfectio hominis. Sed operatio non significat ut aliquid existens in operante, sed magis ut ab ipso procedens. Ergo beatitudo non est operatio.

4. Præterea, beatitudo permanet in beato. Operatio autem non permanet, sed transit. Ergo beatitudo non est operatio.

5. Præterea, unius hominis est una beatitudo. Operationes autem sunt multæ. Ergo beatitudo non est operatio.

6. Præterea, beatitudo inest beato absque interruptione. Sed operatio humana frequenter interrumpitur puta somno, vel aliqua alia occupatione, vel quiete. Ergo beatitudo non est operatio.

SED CONTRA est quod Philosophus dicit,[4] quod *felicitas est operatio secundum virtutem perfectam.*

RESPONSIO: Dicendum quod, secundum quod beatitudo hominis est aliquid creatum in ipso existens necesse est dicere quod beatitudo hominis sit operatio. Est enim beatitudo ultima hominis perfectio.

Unumquodque autem intantum perfectum est inquantum est actu; nam potentia sine actu imperfecta est. Oportet ergo beatitudinem in ultimo actu hominis consistere. Manifestum est autem quod operatio est ultimus actus operantis; unde et *actus secundus* a Philosopho nominatur in II *De Anima.*[5] Nam habens formam potest esse in potentia operans, sicut sciens est in potentia considerans. Et inde est quod in aliis quoque rebus res unaquæque dicitur esse *propter suam operationem,* ut dicitur in II *De Cælo.*[6] Necesse est ergo beatitudinem hominis operationem esse.

1. Ad primum ergo dicendum quod vita dicitur dupliciter. Uno modo, ipsum esse viventis. Et sic beatitudo non est vita: ostensum est enim[7] quod esse unius hominis, qualecumque sit, non est hominis beatitudo; solius enim Dei beatitudo est suum esse. Alio modo dicitur vita ipsa operatio viventis, secundum quam principium vitæ in actum reducitur: et sic nominamus vitam activam, vel contemplativam, vel voluptuosam. Et hoc modo vita æterna dicitur ultimus finis. Quod patet per hoc quod dicitur *Joan.,*[8] *Hæc est vita æterna, ut cognoscant te, Deum verum unum.*

---

*Piana: *in bono,* in a person who is good

[4]*Ethics* I, 13. 1102a5. cf 1098a16   [5]*De Anima* II, I. 412a23
[6]*De cælo* II, 3. 286a8   [7]1a2æ. 2, 5   [8]*John* 17, 3
[b]The Aristotelean categories underlie this argument. A thing is a substance, a being, *ens,* and each of its various modifications is an 'of being', *entis,* and is called an 'accident'. Nine types are enumerated, among which is the category called quality. The activity with which the argument is concerned is a kind of quality: it is a perfection of the agent, and as such is immanent and not productive of an out-

3. Further, happiness means a real condition intrinsic to the one who is happy, since it is his ultimate fulfilment. Now his activity denotes a going out from him, not a condition within him. Consequently happiness is not activity.

4. Or put it like this: happiness remains in the person, whereas activity does not, but passes into another. Happiness, then, is not an activity.

5. Besides, for one man there is but one single happiness. Yet he has many activities. And so happiness and activity are not the same.

6. Then also, happiness is in the happy man without interruption. Not so his activity, for it is broken by sleep, by another occupation, or by just being at rest. Happiness, then, is not activity.

ON THE OTHER HAND there is Aristotle speaking of felicity as activity in accordance with consummate virtue.[4]

REPLY: In so far as man's happiness is a creaturely reality in him the inference must be that it is an activity. For that is the full expansion of his being.

Each thing is perfect inasmuch as it is actual, for what is potential is still imperfect. Happiness, therefore, must go with man's culminating actuality. Clearly this means his being active; indeed Aristotle speaks of activity as *second actuality*.[5] For what already is actually a being by having a form may yet be only potentially active, thus a man of science when not engaged with his field of study. That is why, in other things too, Aristotle says that each is for its activity.[6b] Therefore man's happiness has to be an activity.

Hence: 1. Life—the term may refer either to being or to acting.[c] Take it as the being of a living thing, then happiness is not life, since, as we have noticed,[7] a man's being, whatever it is, is not his happiness, for of God alone is it true that his very being is his being happy.[d] Take the term, however, to refer to the activity of a living thing, namely the full development of what has begun to live, then we speak of a life of contemplation, a life of practical affairs, a life of pleasure.[e] It is in this sense that eternal life is said to be our final end. Thus in the Gospel, *This is eternal life, that they may know thee, the only true God.*[8]

---

side effect. A transitive action belongs to the special heading called *actio*, and its being undergone by the subject to that called *passio*.
[c]cf 1a. 18, 2.
[d]cf 1a. 14, 4.
[e]cf 2a2æ. 179, on the diverse ways of life.

2. Ad secundum dicendum quod Boëtius, definiendo beatitudinem, consideravit ipsam communem beatitudinis rationem. Est enim communis ratio beatitudinis quod sit bonum commune perfectum; et hoc significavit cum dixit quod est *status omnium bonorum aggregatione perfectus*, per quod nihil aliud significatur nisi quod beatus est in statu boni perfecti. Sed Aristoteles expressit ipsam essentiam beatitudinis, ostendens per quid homo sit in hujusmodi statu, quia per operationem quandam.[9] Et ideo in *Ethic.*,[10] ipse etiam ostendit quod beatitudo est *bonum perfectum*.

3. Ad tertium dicendum quod, sicut dicitur in *Meta.*,[11] duplex est actio. Una quæ procedit ab operante in exteriorem materiam, sicut urere et secare. Et talis operatio non potest esse beatitudo: nam talis operatio non est actio et perfectio agentis, sed magis patientis, ut ibidem dicitur. Alia est actio manens in ipso agente, ut sentire, intelligere et velle: et hujusmodi actio est perfectio et actus agentis. Et talis operatio potest esse beatitudo.

4. Ad quartum dicendum quod, cum beatitudo dicat quandam ultimam perfectionem, secundum quod diversæ res beatitudinis capaces ad diversos gradus perfectionis pertingere possunt, secundum hoc necesse est quod diversimode beatitudo dicatur. Nam in Deo est beatitudo per essentiam: quia ipsum esse ejus est operatio ejus, qua non fruitur alio, sed seipso. In angelis autem beatis est ultima perfectio secundum aliquam operationem, qua conjunguntur bono increato: et hæc operatio in eis est unica et sempiterna. In hominibus autem, secundum statum præsentis vitæ, est ultima perfectio secundum operationem qua homo conjungitur Deo: sed hæc operatio nec continua potest esse, et per consequens nec unica est, quia operatio intercisione multiplicatur. Et propter hoc in statu præsentis vitæ, perfecta beatitudo ab homine haberi non potest. Unde Philosophus,[12] ponens beatitudinem hominis in hac vita, dicit eam imperfectam, post multa concludens, *Beatos autem dicimus ut homines.* Sed promittitur nobis a Deo beatitudo perfecta, quando erimus *sicut angeli in cælo*, sicut dicitur *Matt.*[13]

Quantum ergo ad illam beatitudinem perfectam, cessat objectio: quia una et continua et sempiterna operatione in illo beatitudinis statu mens hominis Deo conjungetur. Sed in præsenti vita, quantum deficimus ab unitate et continuitate talis operationis, tantum deficimus a beatitudinis perfectione. Est tamen aliqua participatio beatitudinis: et tanto major quanto operatio potest esse magis continua et una. Et ideo in activa vita, quæ circa multa occupatur, est minus de ratione beatitudinis quam in vita contemplativa, quæ versatur circa unum, idest circa veritatis contem-

[9]*Ethics* I, 13. 1102a5. cf 1098a16   [10]op cit I, 7. 1097a29
[11]*Metaphysics*, VIII, 8. 1050a30   [12]*Ethics* I, 10. 1101a20
[13]*Matthew* 22, 30

2. In designating happiness, Boethius covers all that goes with it in general, namely the completion in common of every good, and this he signified by a state made perfect by the bringing together of all goods, thus implying that a person in bliss is in a settled condition of full goodness.[f] Aristotle's definition,[9] however, is more pointed, and expresses the essence of happiness by marking what puts him in this state, namely an activity of some sort; and he follows this line in the *Ethics* to show that happiness is the crowning good.[10]

3. According to the *Metaphysics*[11] there are two sorts of activity, transitive and immanent. The first issues from the agent into external material; it is an action such as burning or cutting. Happiness cannot lie here, for, as Aristotle points out, such an action is less an actualizing of what acts than of what is acted on. The second activity stays within the agent itself, such as sensing, understanding, and willing, and is its completion and actualization.[g] And happiness can be in such inward operation.

4. Happiness denotes a certain ultimate completeness, and since different kinds of things mount to various degrees of perfection, the term admits variations of meaning.[h] God's is essential happiness; his very existing is his acting, and thereby he enjoys no other than himself. Final perfection for the blessed angels is the activity conjoining them to uncreated good, which activity in them is single and everlasting.[1] Final perfection for men in their present life is their cleaving to God by activity which, however, cannot be continuous or consequently single, for activity becomes multiple when interrupted. That is why we cannot possess perfect happiness now, as Aristotle admits; after a long discussion of the sort of happiness men can reach, he concludes, *We call them happy, but only as men.*[12] God, however, promises us complete happiness, *when we shall be as the angels in heaven.*[13]

With regard to that state, the objection has no force, for then by a single, uninterrupted and continuous act our minds will be united with God. In the meantime, in so far as we fall short of that lasting unity, so far do we fall short of perfect bliss. All the same we can already have some share in it, and so much the greater as our activity grows more single-minded and less distracted. Hence the active life, which is occupied with many things, has less of the nature of happiness than the contemplative life, which revolves round one thing, the gazing at truth. And if at times a man is not actually

---

[f]A state, not just a condition, but one that is stable and permanent. A Roman notion, 2a2æ. 183, 1.
[g]The distinction is between activity (immanent) and action (transitive). cf note *b* above.
[h]Happiness is an analogical term: see 1a2æ. 5, 2 below.
[1]cf 1a. 54, 1–3; 58, 1–4. Vol. 9, ed. K. Foster.

plationem. Et si aliquando homo actu non operetur hujusmodi opera-tionem, tamen quia in promptu habet eam semper operari; et quia etiam ipsam cessationem, puta somni vel occupationis alicujus naturalis, ad operationem prædictam ordinat; quasi videtur operatio continua esse.

5 & 6. Et per hoc patet solutio ad quintum, et ad sextum.

articulus 3. *Utrum beatitudo sit operatio sensitivæ partis, aut intellectivæ tantum*

AD TERTIUM sic proceditur:[1] 1. Videtur quod beatitudo consistat etiam in operatione sensus. Nulla enim operatio invenitur in homine nobilior opera-tione sensitiva nisi intellectiva. Sed operatio intellectiva dependet in nobis ab operatione sensitiva, quia *non possumus intelligere sine phantasmate*, ut dicitur in III *De Anima*.[2] Ergo beatitudo consistit etiam in operatione sensitiva.

2. Præterea, Boëtius dicit[3] quod beatitudo est *status omnium bonorum aggregatione perfectus*. Sed quædam bona sunt sensibilia quæ attingimus per sensus operationem. Ergo videtur quod operatio sensus requiratur ad beatitudinem.

3. Præterea, beatitudo est *bonum perfectum*, ut probatur in *Ethic.*,[4] quod non esset nisi homo perficeretur per ipsam secundum omnes partes suas. Sed per operationes sensitivas quædam partes animæ perficiuntur. Ergo operatio sensitiva requiritur ad beatitudinem.

SED CONTRA, in operatione sensitiva communicant nobiscum bruta animalia. Non autem in beatitudine. Ergo beatitudo non consistit in operatione sensitiva.

RESPONSIO: Dicendum quod ad beatitudinem potest aliquid pertinere trip-liciter: uno modo, essentialiter; alio modo, antecedenter; tertio modo, consequenter.

Essentialiter quidem non potest pertinere operatio sensus ad beatitu-dinem. Nam beatitudo hominis consistit essentialiter in conjunctione ipsius ad bonum increatum, quod est ultimus finis, ut supra ostensum est,[5] cui homo conjungi non potest per sensus operationem. Similiter etiam quia, sicut ostensum est,[6] in corporalibus bonis beatitudo hominis non consistit, quæ tamen sola per operationem sensus attingimus.

Possunt autem operationes sensus pertinere ad beatitudinem ante-cedenter et consequenter. Antecedenter quidem, secundum beatitudinem imperfectam, qualis in præsenti vita haberi potest: nam operatio intellectus præexigit operationem sensus. Consequenter autem, in illa perfecta beati-

---

[1]cf *CG* III, 33. *In Ethic.* I, *lect.* 10. *In Meta.* IX, *lect.* 8. *Compend. Theol.* II, 9

so engaged, nevertheless because he is ever open and ready, and since he turns even his very ceasing, because of sleep or natural business, to its service, his contemplation seems, as it were, to be continuous.[j]

5 & 6. This makes evident the answers to the other objections.

article 3. is happiness an activity of our sensitive or only of our intellective part?

THE THIRD POINT:[1] 1. It seems that sensitive activity enters also into happiness.[a] Intellective activity is in man the most noble of all, yet this is dependent on sensitive activity, for, according to the *De Anima*, we cannot think without imagining.[2b] Therefore sensitive activity enters into happiness.

2. Moreover, Boethius describes happiness as a state brought to completion by all goods being gathered together.[3] But some of them are disclosed in sensation, which, accordingly, seems to be part of happiness.

3. Further, happiness would not be the consummate good of the *Ethics*[4] unless it fulfilled every side of man. Some are fulfilled by sensing and feeling, which, therefore, are required for happiness.

ON THE OTHER HAND the beasts are not one with us in happiness, though they are in sensation. And so happiness is not composed of sensation.[c]

REPLY: A part can enter happiness in three ways, as a constituent, an antecedent, and a consequent.

Sensitive activity cannot be a constituent of happiness, which essentially consists, as we have shown,[5] in man being united to the uncreated good, his ultimate end, a union which cannot be achieved by activity on the level of sense and feeling. Nor likewise, as we have also shown,[6] is happiness a matter of possessing maternal good, and sensitive activity can reach no further.

Yet it comes into happiness as an antecedent and a consequent. In respect of partial happiness we can enjoy in our present life, it is a preliminary, for sensation is presupposed to understanding. In respect of the perfect happiness hoped for in heaven it is a result, for after the resurrection there

---

[2]*De Anima* III, 7. 431a16   [3]*De consol.* III, 2. PL 63, 724   [4]*Ethics* I, 7. 1097a29
[5]art. 1 above.   [6]Ia2æ. 2, 5
[j]*Though I sleep my heart waketh, Song of Songs;* 5, 2. The reply taps the theological teaching of the steady and habitual cleaving to God by charity. cf Ia. 87, 1–4; 2a2æ. 180, 6 & 8.
[a]Sensitive activity, i.e. of the external and internal senses and of the resulting emotions, Ia. 78 & 81.
[b]St Thomas accepts the position that we cannot understand our world without forming pictures about it, Ia. 84, 7.
[c]Not a decisive *sed contra*, for the objections have urged only that sensation enters into happiness, not that happiness is to be resolved into sensation.

tudine quæ expectatur in cælo: quia post resurrectionem, *ex ipsa beatitudine animæ*, ut Augustinus dicit,[7] *fiet quædam refluentia in corpus et in sensus corporeos, ut in suis operationibus perficiantur*; ut infra magis patebit, cum de resurrectione agetur.[8] Non autem tunc operatio qua mens humana Deo conjungetur, a sensu dependebit.

1. Ad primum ergo dicendum quod objectio illa probat quod operatio sensus requiritur antecedenter ad beatitudinem imperfectam, qualis in hac vita haberi potest.

2. Ad secundum dicendum quod beatitudo perfecta, qualem angeli habent, habet congregationem omnium bonorum per conjunctionem ad universalem fontem totius boni; non quod indigeat singulis particularibus bonis. Sed in hac beatitudine imperfecta requiritur congregatio bonorum sufficientium ad perfectissimam operationem hujus vitæ.

3. Ad tertium dicendum quod in perfecta beatitudine perficitur totus homo, sed in inferiori parte per redundantiam a superiori. In beatitudine autem imperfecta præsentis vitæ, e converso a perfectione inferioris partis proceditur ad perfectionem superioris.

articulus 4. utrum, si beatitudo est intellectivæ partis, sit operatio intellectus, an voluntatis

AD QUARTUM sic proceditur:[1] 1. Videtur quod beatitudo consistat in actu voluntatis. Dicit enim Augustinus,[2] quod beatitudo hominis in pace consistit: unde in *Psalmo*,[3] *Qui posuit fines tuos pacem*. Sed pax ad voluntatem pertinet. Ergo beatitudo hominis in voluntate consistit.

2. Præterea, beatitudo est summum bonum. Sed bonum est objectum voluntatis. Ergo beatitudo in operatione voluntatis consistit.

3. Præterea, primo moventi respondet ultimus finis: sicut ultimus finis totius exercitus est victoria, quæ est finis ducis, qui omnes movet. Sed primum movens ad operandum est voluntas: quia movet alias vires, ut infra dicetur.[4] Ergo beatitudo ad voluntatem pertinet.

4. Præterea, si beatitudo est aliqua operatio, oportet quod sit nobilissima operatio hominis. Sed nobilior operatio est dilectio Dei, quæ est actus voluntatis, quam cognitio, quæ est operatio intellectus: ut patet per Apostolum.[5] Ergo videtur quod beatitudo consistat in actu voluntatis.

5. Præterea, Augustinus dicit,[6] quod *beatus est qui habet omnia quæ vult, et nihil vult male*. Et post pauca subdit, *Propinquat beato qui bene vult*

---

[7]*Epist.* CXVIII *ad Dioscurum.* 3. PL 33, 439   [8]*Suppl.* 82
[1]cf Ia. 26, 2 ad 2. *CG* III, 26,*Quodl.* VIII, 9, 1. *Compend. Theol.* 107. IV *Sent.* 49, 1, I,ii
[2]*De civit. Dei* XIX, 10. PL 41, 636   [3]*Psalms* 147,3
[4]Ia2æ. 9, 1 & 3   [5]I *Corinthians* 13
[6]*De Trinitate* XIII, 6. PL 42, 1020

will be what Augustine describes, a flowing out from the beatitude of soul into the body and the senses such as to enhance their activities.[7d] We shall make this clearer later on when we come to discuss the resurrection.[8] All the same the act conjoining the human mind with God will not depend on sense.

Hence: 1. The objection proves that sensitive activity is a pre-condition of the incomplete happiness we can enjoy in the present life.

2. Perfect beatitude, such as the angels have, gathers all goods together because it is union with the universal fount of all good, not that it requires each and every individual good. Our present partial happiness requires good things enough to ensure the most developed activity this life allows.

3. In perfect bliss the whole man is fulfilled, his lower levels by the higher brimming over. In our present imperfect happiness the reverse is the case; the lower rises to fill the higher.

article 4. is happiness an activity of the understanding or of the will?

THE FOURTH POINT:[1] 1. An activity of will it would seem.[a] Augustine puts man's happiness in being at peace,[2] according to the *Psalm, He has set thy borders in peace.*[3] Now peace is a condition of the will. Therefore happiness as well.

2. Moreover, happiness is the highest good, and good is the object of will, and so also is happiness.

3. Further, a final aim corresponds to the intention of the chief executive power engaged, thus victory, which is what a whole army in the field is for, is the purpose above all of its commander who effectively brings all his forces to bear. Now the first executive power which sets us acting is the will, which, as will be shown,[4] commands all our human forces. Consequently happiness lies in the will.

4. Again, if happiness is an activity it ought to be the noblest. Such is the love of God, an activity of will, and not the knowledge of God, an activity of mind: St Paul is emphatic on the point in 1 *Corinthians.*[5] So then it is in loving that happiness consists.

5. Besides, Augustine remarks, *Blessed is the man who has all he wills, and wills nothing amiss.*[6] He goes on after a while, *Almost blessed is he who wills*

---

[d] cf 1a2æ. 4, 5 & 6. Also 1a. 12, 1–3.
[a] The article states a thesis steadily maintained in the Dominican school. Vasquez also subscribes to it. A Franciscan stress is on love-activity, a Carmelite on uncreated understanding, and a Jesuit, notably in Suarez, Molina, and Valentia, on knowledge and love together. Yet though St Thomas holds that knowing is the decisive moment in happiness, art. 6 and 8 below will make clear that this is no detached appreciation. And arts 1–4 of the following Question, which stress the love-condition in happiness, will also help to redress the balance of too one-sided an intellectualism. Appendix 4.

quodcumque vult: bona enim beatum faciunt quorum bonorum jam habet aliquid, ipsam scilicet bonam voluntatem. Ergo beatitudo in actu voluntatis consistit.

SED CONTRA est quod Dominus dicit,[7] *Hæc est vita æterna ut cognoscant te, Deum verum unum.* Vita autem æterna est ultimus finis, ut dictum est.[8] Ergo beatitudo hominis in cognitione Dei consistit, quæ est actus intellectus.

RESPONSIO: Dicendum quod ad beatitudinem, sicut supra dictum est,[9] duo requiruntur, unum quod est essentia* beatitudinis, aliud quod est quasi per se accidens ejus, scilicet delectatio ei adjuncta. Dico ergo quod, quantum ad id quod est essentialiter ipsa beatitudo, impossibile est quod consistat in actu voluntatis.

Manifestum est enim ex præmissis[10] quod beatitudo est consecutio finis ultimi. Consecutio enim† finis non consistit in ipso actu voluntatis. Voluntas enim fertur in finem et absentem, cum ipsum desiderat; et præsentem, cum in ipso requiescens delectatur. Manifestum est autem quod ipsum desiderium finis non est consecutio finis, sed est motus ad finem. Delectatio autem advenit voluntati ex hoc quod finis est præsens: non autem e converso ex hoc aliquid fit præsens quia voluntas delectatur in ipso. Oportet igitur aliquid aliud esse quam actum voluntatis, per quod fit ipse finis præsens volenti.

Et hoc manifeste apparet circa fines sensibiles. Si enim consequi pecuniam esset per actum voluntatis, statim a principio cupidus consecutus esset pecuniam, quando vult eam habere. Sed a principio quidem est absens ei; consequitur autem ipsam per hoc quod manu ipsam apprehendit, vel aliquo hujusmodi; et tunc jam delectatur in pecunia habita. Sic igitur et circa intelligibilem finem contingit. Nam a principio volumus consequi finem intelligibilem; consequimur autem ipsum per hoc quod fit præsens nobis per actum intellectus; et tunc voluntas delectata conquiescit in fine jam adepto.

Sic igitur essentia beatitudinis in actu intellectus consistit, sed ad voluntatem pertinet delectatio beatitudinem consequens; secundum quod Augustinus dicit,[11] quod beatitudo est *gaudium de veritate*; quia scilicet ipsum gaudium est consummatio beatitudinis.

1. Ad primum ergo dicendum quod pax pertinet ad ultimum hominis

---

*Piana: *esse,* the being of happiness   †Leonine: *autem,* but

[7]*John* 17, 3   [8]art. 2 ad 1 above   [9]1a2æ. 2, 6

[10]1a2æ. 2, 7; 3, 1 & 2   [11]*Confessions* x, 23. PL 32, 793

[b]The distinction between essence and property is applied only by analogy. cf above 1a2æ. 2, 6.

[c]The formal constitutive, which makes it what it is.

[d]See below, 1a2æ. 4, 3, for the holding act of comprehension.

well whenever he wills, for good things make a man blessed, and such a man already has one of them, namely a right good will. Therefore happiness is an activity of will.

ON THE OTHER HAND, our Lord says, *This is eternal life, that they should know thee, the one true God.*[7] Eternal life is our final end, as we have explained,[8] and therefore happiness is knowing God, which is an activity of mind.

REPLY: As we have observed,[9] happiness has two phases, one spells its essence, the other, as it were, an essential property, such as the pleasure which goes with it.[b] Now I say this, that with respect to the crucial stroke,[c] happiness cannot be an act of will.

For it is manifestly clear from our premises[10] that happiness is the laying hold of our ultimate end,[d] and this is not done by the activity of will. For the will is charged with its object whether it be absent, and then desired, or present, and then rested in and enjoyed. Obviously the desiring an end is not the possessing it, but a moving towards it. And while the delighting in an end comes from its presence, the converse does not hold, namely that the presence of the end comes from the will's delights in it. The act, then, which brings about this presence to the lover must be other than an act of will.[e]

To take an illustration from the world of sense. If money could be got by the willing, a needy man[f] would straightway have all he wanted. But he starts by lacking it, and then has to set himself to secure it by the work of his hands or other powers, and then he may come to enjoy its possession. So it is also in the world of intelligence. The will's desire starts for an end, but it is reached by its becoming present to us by an act of mind, and then, when it is already gained, the delight of will rests content with it.

In conclusion, then, an act of mind forms the essence of happiness, while for the will is the delight that follows. Accordingly Augustine speaks of happiness as *joy in the truth*,[11] which joy is the consummation ot happiness.[g]

Hence: 1. Peace is associated with our final end, not that it is the essential

---

[e]The tragic impotence of love alone to secure the presence of its object: 1a2æ. 27, 2; 28, 1, 2 & 6. Vol. 19, ed. E. D'Arcy.

Francis Bacon *On Truth* speaks of the love-making or wooing of truth, the presence of it, and the enjoying of it. The second phase is the point of the debate.
[f]*Cupidus*, greedy, but here, needy and desirous.
[g]Knowing should be taken throughout the argument in its strongest sense, as becoming another, not merely becoming like or conformed to another. cf *De veritate* II, 2.

finem, non quasi essentialiter sit ipsa beatitudo; sed quia antecedenter et consequenter se habet ad ipsam. Antecedenter quidem, inquantum jam sunt remota omnia perturbantia, et impedientia ab ultimo fine. Consequenter vero, inquantum jam homo, adepto ultimo fine, remanet pacatus, suo desiderio quietato.

2. Ad secundum dicendum quod primum objectum voluntatis non est actus ejus sicut nec primum objectum visus est visio, sed visibile. Unde ex hoc ipso quod beatitudo pertinet ad voluntatem tanquam primum objectum ejus, sequitur quod non pertineat ad ipsam tanquam actus ipsius.

3. Ad tertium dicendum quod finem primo apprehendit intellectus quam voluntas: tamen motus ad finem incipit in voluntate. Et ideo voluntati debetur id quod ultimo consequitur consecutionem finis, scilicet delectatio vel fruitio.

4. Ad quartum dicendum quod dilectio præeminet cognitioni in movendo, sed cognitio prævia est dilectioni in attingendo: *non enim diligitur nisi cognitum*, ut dicit Augustinus.[12] Et ideo intelligibilem finem primo attingimus per actionem intellectus, sicut et finem sensibilem primo attingimus per actionem sensus.

5. Ad quintum dicendum quod ille qui habet omnia quæ vult, ex hoc est beatus quod habet ea quæ vult: quod quidem est per aliud quam per actum voluntatis. Sed nihil male velle requiritur ad beatitudinem sicut quædam debita dispositio ad ipsam. Voluntas autem bona ponitur in numero bonorum quæ beatum faciunt, prout est inclinatio quædam in ipsa, sicut motus reducitur ad genus sui termini, ut alteratio ad qualitatem.

articulus 5. utrum beatitudo sit operatio intellectus speculativi, an practici

AD QUINTUM sic proceditur:[1] 1. Videtur quod beatitudo consistat in operatione intellectus practici. Finis enim ultimus cujuslibet creaturæ consistit in assimilatione ad Deum. Sed homo magis assimilatur Deo per intellectum practicum, qui est causa rerum intellectarum, quam per intellectum speculativum, cujus scientia accipitur a rebus. Ergo beatitudo hominis magis consistit in operatione intellectus practici quam speculativi.

2. Præterea, beatitudo est perfectum hominis bonum. Sed intellectus practicus magis ordinatur ad bonum quam speculativus, qui ordinatur ad verum. Unde et secundum perfectionem practici intellectus dicimur boni,

---

[12]*De Trinitate* x, 1. PL 42, 973   [1]cf *In Ethic.* x, *lect.* 10-12. IV *Sent.* 49, 1. 1. iii
[h]2a2æ. 28 & 29.   [i]cf above 1a2æ. 1, 1 ad 2.   [j]cf 2a2æ. 25, 2.
[k]The will a hunting power, as it were, not a capturing power. cf IV *Sent.* 49, 1, 1, ii. CG III, 26.
[l]Intelligible end, or better, an ultimate to be grasped, to avoid any suggestion of purely notional attainment.

constituent of happiness, rather it is a preliminary and a result, the first because it rules out all disturbance together with hindrances to our reaching it, the second because when it is reached and his desire is quieted a man dwells in peace.[h]

2. The prime object of the will is its act of willing, no more than the prime object of sight is the act of seeing.[1] Instead this is the thing to be seen. Likewise the thing to be happy with is the prime object of will, and consequently happiness for will is not its very act of loving.[j]

3. The first grasping of an end is by the mind, not by the will, though the motion towards it starts from the will.[k] Pleasure or enjoyment comes afterwards, when the end is attained, and is a function of will.

4. Love ranks above knowledge as an impulse towards an object, but knowledge is above love in holding it; Augustine says, *None is beloved unless known*.[12] And so we first reach to an intelligible end[l] by activity of mind, as we do a sensible end by an activity of sense.[m]

5. A man is happy in having what he wills, but the actual having is by an act other than one of will. To will nothing amiss is an indispensable precondition.[n] And a good will is numbered among the goods that make a man happy as being a bent to happiness; you take the meaning of a motion under the heading of the term to which it goes, thus alteration refers to quality.[o]

article 5. is happiness an activity of the theoretical or of the practical reason?

THE FIFTH POINT:[1] 1. Of the practical reason it seems.[a] For the ultimate end of any creature lies in becoming like God. Man achieves this likeness mainly through his practical reason, which causes the things it knows, not through his theoretical reason, which draws its knowledge from things. Man's happiness, therefore, is rather a doing and making than a pure knowing.

2. Again, happiness is man's complete good. Now the practical intelligence turns towards good more than does the theoretical intelligence, which turns towards truth. We call men good because of what they do, not

---

[m]The reply is very compressed, for the reference to St Augustine shows only that we must have a notion of what we are about, whereas the full teaching of the article turns on what makes an object really present.
[n]cf below 1a2æ. 4, 4.
[o]Growth and shrinking apply to quantity, alteration, *alloiōsis*, to quality. The *terminus ad quem* denominates the motion: e.g. a turning pale, a flight to Sydney.
[a]The practical and theoretical (speculative) reasons represent distinct functions, not faculties: 1a. 79, 11. The first concerns a truth to be done, the second a truth for itself. The following article will treat of 'speculative' knowledge, and will correct any impression that here it means a spectator-activity.

non autem secundum perfectionem speculativi intellectus, sed secundum eam dicimur scientes vel intelligentes. Ergo beatitudo hominis magis consistit in actu intellectus practici quam speculativi.

3. Præterea, beatitudo est quoddam bonum ipsius hominis. Sed speculativus intellectus occupatur magis circa ea quæ sunt extra hominem: practicus autem intellectus occupatur circa ea quæ sunt ipsius hominis, scilicet circa operationes et passiones ejus. Ergo beatitudo hominis magis consistit in operatione intellectus practici quam intellectus speculativi.

SED CONTRA est quod Augustinus dicit,[2] quod *contemplatio promittitur nobis, actionum omnium finis, atque æterna perfectio gaudiorum.*

RESPONSIO: Dicendum quod beatitudo magis consistit in operatione speculativi intellectus quam practici. Quod patet ex tribus.

Primo quidem ex hoc quod, si beatitudo hominis est operatio, oportet quod sit optima operatio hominis. Optima autem operatio hominis est quæ est optimæ potentiæ respectu optimi objecti. Optima autem potentia est intellectus, cujus optimum objectum est bonum divinum, quod quidem non est objectum practici intellectus, sed speculativi. Unde in tali operatione, scilicet in contemplatione divinorum, maxime consistit beatitudo. Et quia *unusquisque videtur esse id quod est optimum in eo,* ut dicitur in *Ethic.,*[3] ideo talis operatio est maxime propria homini, et maxime delectabilis.

Secundo apparet idem ex hoc quod contemplatio maxime quæritur propter seipsam. Actus autem intellectus practici non quæritur propter seipsum, sed propter actionem. Ipsæ etiam* actiones ordinantur ad aliquem finem. Unde manifestum est quod ultimus finis non potest consistere in vita activa, quæ pertinet ad intellectum practicum.

Tertio idem apparet ex hoc quod in vita contemplativa homo communicat cum superioribus, scilicet cum Deo et angelis, quibus per beatitudinem assimilatur. Sed in his quæ pertinet ad vitam activam, etiam alia animalia cum homine aliqualiter communicant, licet imperfecte.

Et ideo ultima et perfecta beatitudo, quæ expectatur in futura vita, tota principaliter† consistit in contemplatione. Beatitudo autem imperfecta, qualis hic haberi potest, primo quidem et principaliter consistit in contemplatione; secundario vero in operatione practici intellectus ordinantis actiones et passiones humanas, ut dicitur in *Ethic.*[4]

1. Ad primum ergo dicendum quod similitudo prædicta intellectus prac-

---

*Piana: *autem*
†Leonine: omits *principaliter*, and suggests happiness is wholly composed of contemplation
[2]*De Trin.* I, 8. PL 42, 831

74

because of what they think—because of this we call them knowledgeable or intelligent.[b] Hence man's happiness consists in an activity of the practical rather than of the theoretical intelligence.

3. Moreover, happiness is a good for the man himself. Now his theoretical intelligence regards things outside him, whereas his practical intelligence is occupied with what goes on within him, namely with how he acts and is acted upon. Therefore happiness is more for practical than for theoretical understanding.

ON THE OTHER HAND there is Augustine saying that *contemplation is promised us as being the end of every action, the eternal perfection of joys.*[2]

REPLY: The activity happiness is in the theoretical rather than the practical intelligence. This is evident for three reasons.

First, given that happiness is an activity, then it ought to be a man's best activity, that is to say when his highest power is engaged with its highest object. Man's mind is his highest power, and its highest object is divine good, an object for its seeing, not for its doing something in practice. Hence the activity of contemplating the things of God is principal in happiness. And since, as Aristotle puts it,[3] *that strikes each man as himself which is best in him,* such is the activity most proper and congenial to man.

Secondly, the same conclusion appears when we reflect that contemplation above all is sought for its own sake. This is not the case with activity of the practical intellect, which is performed in order to do or make something, and therefore is designed for an end. The ultimate end, then, cannot lie within the active life, which is the field of the practical intelligence.

Thirdly, we draw the same inference because contemplation brings man into converse with the highest beings, namely with God and the angels, and makes him like them in his happiness. Whereas the other animals share, in their own fashion and imperfectly, in the preoccupations of the active life.[c]

Therefore man's last and perfect beatitude, which he expects in the life to come, is wholly centred on contemplation. As for the imperfect beatitude we can have at present, it is primarily and chiefly centred on contemplation, secondarily on the activity of the practical intelligence governing our deeds and feelings, as stated in the *Ethics.*[4]

Hence: 1. The objection fastens on a likeness merely by a parallel,[d]

---

[3]*Ethics* IX, 8 & X. 7. 1169a2 & 1178a2
[4]*Ethics* X, 7 & 8. 1177a12 & 1178a9
[b]Moral good is achieved immediately through practical, not speculative knowledge. cf 1a2æ. 58, 2 & 3.
[c]The active and contemplative lives compared, 2a2æ. 182, Vol. 46, ed. J. Aumann.
[d]Analogy of proportion, 1a. 14, 16.

tici ad Deum est secundum proportionalitatem; quia scilicet se habet ad suum cognitum sicut Deus ad suum. Sed assimilatio intellectus speculativi ad Deum est secundum unionem vel informationem, quæ est multo major assimilatio.

Et tamen dici potest quod, respectu principalis cogniti quod est sua essentia, non habet Deus practicam cognitionem, sed speculativam tantum.

2. Ad secundum dicendum quod intellectus practicus ordinatur ad bonum quod est extra ipsum, sed intellectus speculativus habet bonum in seipso, scilicet contemplationem veritatis. Et si illud bonum sit perfectum, ex eo totus homo perficitur et fit bonus, quod quidem intellectus practicus non habet sed ad illud ordinat.

3. Ad tertium dicendum quod ratio illa procederet, si ipsemet homo esset ultimus finis suus: tunc enim consideratio et ordinatio actuum et passionum ejus esset ejus beatitudo. Sed quia ultimus hominis finis est aliquod bonum extrinsecum, scilicet Deus, ad quem per operationem intellectus speculativi attingimus, ideo magis beatitudo hominis in operatione intellectus speculativi consistit, quam in operatione intellectus practici.

articulus 6. utrum beatitudo consistat in consideratione scientiarum speculativarum

AD SEXTUM sic proceditur:[1] 1. Videtur quod beatitudo hominis consistat in consideratione speculativarum scientiarum. Philosophus enim dicit in *Ethic.*[2] quod *felicitas est operatio secundum perfectam virtutem.* Et distinguens virtutes, non ponit speculativas nisi tres, *scientiam, sapientiam* et *intellectum;*[3] quæ omnes pertinet ad considerationem scientiarum speculativarum. Ergo ultima hominis beatitudo in consideratione scientiarum speculativarum consistit.

2. Præterea, illud videtur esse ultima hominis beatitudo, quod naturaliter desideratur ab omnibus propter seipsum. Sed hujusmodi est consideratio speculativarum scientiarum: quia, ut dicitur in *Meta.,*[4] *omnes homines natura scire desiderant*; et post pauca subditur quod speculativæ scientiæ propter seipsas quæruntur. Ergo in consideratione scientiarum speculativarum consistit beatitudo.

3. Præterea, beatitudo est ultima hominis perfectio. Unumquodque autem perficitur secundum quod reducitur de potentia in actum. Intellectus autem humanus reducitur in actum per considerationem scientiarum

[1]cf *CG* III, 48. *In Ethic.* X, *lect.* 12. *Compend. Theol.* 104
[2]*Ethics* I, 13. 1102a5
[3]*Ethics* VI, 7. 1141a19. cf 1139b16
[4]*Metaphysics* I, 1. 980a21. Later 982a14, 28
[e]See art. 8 below. God himself quickens the mind as its object.

namely that the relation of our practical reason to the things it knows is rather like that of God's mind to things. The being made like to God, however, of the mind in contemplating is closer than this, for it is united with and shaped by him.[e]

It may be pointed out, all the same, that God's knowledge is contemplative, not practical, with regard to its principal object, namely his own essence.[f]

2. As practical the mind bears on a good outside itself, but as contemplative it holds a good within itself, namely the truth contemplated. And if that good be the complete good, then the whole man is thereby fulfilled and good. The practical mind does not hold, though it may plan for such perfection.

3. It would be a telling argument were man himself his own ultimate end;[g] then studying and planning his own acts and emotions would be his happiness. As it is, however, his final end is a good outside himself, and this is God, whom he reaches through activity of the contemplative mind. Consequently his happiness lies here rather than in activity of the practical mind.

article 6. does happiness consist in dwelling on the theoretical sciences?

THE SIXTH POINT:[1] 1. It seems so.[a] Aristotle says that felicity means acting according to perfect virtue.[2] And in dividing the virtues, for theory he names just these three, *demonstrated knowledge, wisdom, and insight*,[3] all which involve the study of the theoretical sciences. It is here, then, that happiness is found.

2. Further, that appears to be man's ultimate happiness which is naturally desired by all for its own sake. Such is the interest in theoretical science; it is remarked in the *Metaphysics* that *by nature all men desire to know*,[4] and, a little later on, that the theoretical sciences are sought for their own sake. Therefore they provide man's ultimate happiness.

3. Besides, happiness is man's crowning perfection, and a thing is per-

---

[f]cf 1a. 14, 2 & 5. Vol. 4, ed. T. Gornall.

[g]It is true in so far as humanism is true.

[a]Speculative intellect and theoretical reason are not happy terms if they suggest merely the rôle of speculating about an object, or theorizing. They apply to the mind also as contemplative, and even that is a weak term for the mind which can hold its object, love-blended in the Gifts of the Holy Ghost, and is capable of seeing God face to face. cf 1a2æ. 68–70. Also Vol. 1, Appendix 10, *The Dialectic of Love in the Summa.*

To meditate, *con/sidero*, perhaps to look at the stars, *sidera*. The present article criticizes Avempace and others, also the idea of a philosopher's heaven of seeing just the meanings of things. cf *CG* III, 41–48. *Compendium theologiæ* 104.

speculativarum. Ergo videtur quod in hujusmodi consideratione ultima hominis beatitudo consistat.

SED CONTRA est quod dicitur *Jerem.*,[5] *Non glorietur sapiens in sapientia sua*; et loquitur de sapientia speculativarum scientiarum. Non ergo consistit in harum consideratione ultima hominis beatitudo.

RESPONSIO: Dicendum quod, sicut supra dictum est,[6] duplex est hominis beatitudo, una perfecta, et alia imperfecta. Oportet autem intelligere perfectam beatitudinem, quæ attingit ad veram beatitudinis rationem; beatitudinem autem imperfectam, quæ non attingit, sed participat quandam particularem beatitudinis similitudinem. Sicut perfecta prudentia invenitur in homine, apud quem est ratio rerum agibilium: imperfecta autem prudentia est in quibusdam animalibus brutis, in quibus sunt quidam particulares instinctus ad quædam opera similia operibus prudentiæ.

Perfecta igitur beatitudo in consideratione scientiarum speculativarum essentialiter consistere non potest. Ad cujus evidentiam, considerandum est quod consideratio speculativæ scientiæ non se extendit ultra virtutem principiorum illius scientiæ, quia in principiis scientiæ virtualiter tota scientia continetur. Prima autem principia scientiarum speculativarum sunt per sensum accepta; ut patet per Philosophum in principio *Meta.* et in fine *Poster.*[7] Unde tota consideratio scientiarum speculativarum non potest ultra extendi quam sensibilium cognitio ducere potest. In cognitione autem sensibilium non potest consistere ultima hominis beatitudo, quæ est ultima ejus perfectio.

Non enim aliquid perficitur ab aliquo inferiori, nisi secundum quod in inferiori est aliqua participatio superioris. Manifestum est autem quod forma lapidis, vel cujuslibet rei sensibilis, est inferior homine. Unde per formam lapidis non perficitur intellectus inquantum est talis forma, sed inquantum in ea participatur aliqua similitudo alicujus quod est supra intellectum humanum, scilicet lumen intelligibile, vel aliquid hujusmodi.

Omne autem quod est per aliud reducitur ad id quod est per se. Unde oportet quod ultima perfectio hominis sit per cognitionem alicujus rei quæ sit supra intellectum humanum. Ostensum est autem[8] quod per sensibilia non potest deveniri in cognitionem substantiarum separatarum, quæ sunt supra intellectum humanum. Unde relinquitur quod ultima hominis beatitudo non possit esse in consideratione speculativarum scientiarum.

---

[5]*Jeremiah* 9, 23
[6]art. 2 ad 4 above
[7]*Metaphysics* I, I. 980b29. *Posterior Analytics* II, 15. 100a6
[8]Ia. 88, 2
[b]Or the data on which they work. The argument is about the deductive sciences.

fected by being raised from potentiality to actuality. And the human mind is actualized by mirroring the truths of science, and this is final happiness.

ON THE OTHER HAND there is *Jeremiah, Let not the wise man glory in his wisdom,*[5] and the warning refers to theoretical knowledge, where, accordingly, final happiness is not to be found.

REPLY: We have noticed[6] that there are two stages in happiness, complete and incomplete. In the first the true meaning of happiness in the fullest sense is realized, in the second happiness is shared in by some particular likeness. To draw an analogy: full practical wisdom or prudence is discovered in a person who has sound judgment about how things should be done, while a partial reflection of this is exhibited by some animals whose particular instinctive manifestations adapt them to tasks similar to those which tax human ingenuity.

Now of its nature complete happiness cannot consist in dwelling on the theoretical sciences. For remember, their study does not extend beyond the premises on which they are based,[b] for the body of a science is virtually contained in its principles. Now the first principles of the theoretical sciences are received through the senses; this is brought out at the opening of the *Metaphysics* and the close of the *Posterior Analytics*.[7] Consequently the study of the speculative sciences cannot range to where sense-objects cannot lead, and in knowing them man's full happiness, which is his final final perfection, cannot consist.

For a thing is not bettered by something lower than itself unless this also in some way shares in something higher.[c] For instance the form of a stone or of a thing of sense is clearly lower than man, and consequently the form of stone enhances the mind, not as being physically stony, but as sharing some likeness with something above the human mind, namely an intelligible light or the equivalent.[d]

Now whatever is derivative should be traced back to that which is of itself; hence man's ultimate perfection has to be resolved into knowing something above the human mind. We have already shown[8] that just through things of sense we cannot rise to a direct knowledge of bodiless substance above our understanding. In consequence we are left to infer that our ultimate happiness is not in our theoretical study of the material world.

---

[c]Obviously the postman is better for warming himself at the kitchen-fire, but he is not simply better as a man unless the physical warmth be part of a higher social situation.
[d]The *intellectus agens, nous poiētikos,* 1a. 79, 3. Or better, the mind's light as strengthened by revelation, 2a2æ. 173, 2.

Sed sicut in formis sensibilibus participatur aliqua similitudo superiorum substantiarum, ita consideratio scientiarum speculativarum est quædam participatio veræ et perfectæ beatitudinis.

1. Ad primum ergo dicendum quod Philosophus loquitur in *Ethic.* de felicitate imperfecta qualiter in hac vita haberi potest, ut supra dictum est.[9]

2. Ad secundum dicendum quod naturaliter desideratur non solum perfecta beatitudo, sed etiam qualiscumque similitudo vel participatio ipsius.

3. Ad tertium dicendum quod per considerationem scientiarum speculativarum reducitur intellectus noster aliquo modo in actum, non autem in ultimum et completum.

articulus 7. *utrum beatitudo consistat in cognitione substantiarum separatarum, scilicet angelorum*

AD SEPTIMUM sic proceditur:[1] 1. Videtur quod beatitudo hominis consistat in cognitione substantiarum separatarum, idest angelorum. Dicit enim Gregorius in quadam homilia,[2] *Nihil prodest interesse festis hominum, si non contingat interesse festis angelorum*; per quod finalem beatitudinem designat. Sed festis angelorum interesse possumus per eorum contemplationem. Ergo videtur quod in contemplatione angelorum ultima hominis beatitudo consistat.

2. Præterea, ultima perfectio uniuscujusque rei est ut conjungatur suo principio: unde et circulus dicitur esse figura perfecta, quia habet idem principium et finem. Sed principium cognitionis humanæ est ab ipsis angelis, per quos homines illuminantur, ut dicit Dionysius.[3] Ergo perfectio humani intellectus est in contemplatione angelorum.

3. Præterea, unaquæque natura perfecta est quando conjungitur superiori naturæ: sicut ultima perfectio corporis est ut conjungatur naturæ spirituali. Sed supra intellectum humanum ordine naturæ sunt angeli. Ergo ultima perfectio intellectus humani est ut conjungatur per contemplationem ipsis angelis.

SED CONTRA est quod dicitur *Jerem.*,[4] *In hoc glorietur qui gloriatur, scire et nosse me.* Ergo ultima hominis gloria vel beatitudo non consistit nisi in cognitione Dei.

RESPONSIO: Dicendum quod, sicut dictum est,[5] perfecta hominis beatitudo non consistit in eo quod est perfectio intellectus secundum alicujus participationem, sed in eo quod est per essentiam tale. Manifestum est autem

---

[9]*Ethics* I, 10. 1101a20. Above art. 2 ad 4
[1]cf 1a. 64, 1 ad 1. *CG* III, 44. *In De Trin.* VI, 4 ad 3
[2]*In Evang.* II, 26. PL 76, 1202

Nevertheless, forms in the material world do reflect some likeness of higher substances, and therefore by dwelling on them disinterestedly there is a sort of anticipation of true and complete happiness.[e]

Hence: 1. As we have already mentioned, in this passage[9] Aristotle is discussing the partial happiness we can possess in this life.

2. By nature we desire, not only perfect happiness, but every likeness or snatch of it.

3. Pure scientific thought raises the mind to some sort of actuality, but not to final and complete actuality.

article 7. does happiness consist in our knowing bodiless substances, namely angels?

THE SEVENTH POINT:[1] 1. So it seems.[a] A homily by Gregory[b] tells us that *it avails little to take part in the feasts of men unless we also take part in those of angels*, by which he means our final happiness.[2] And we are in their company by contemplating them, and this is our final happiness.

2. Besides, a thing reaches its final perfection by rejoining its origins; a circle is called a perfect figure because its end and beginning coincide. But human knowledge flows from an angelic source: Dionysius teaches that men are enlightened through angels.[3] Therefore man is happy by joining with and contemplating the angels.

3. Further, a nature is perfected by conjunction with a higher; thus the final completion of body is to be united to soul. Now angels are ranked above the human mind in the hierarchy of nature. Accordingly to be joined to them through contemplation is its perfection.

ON THE OTHER HAND there is *Jeremiah*,[4] *In this let him glory who glories, that he understands and knows me.* Therefore man's final glory or beatitude consists only in knowing God.

REPLY: As we have stated,[5] man's complete happiness lies in an interest of his mind essentially so of itself, not with one which is communicated to a thing from elsewhere. There is no doubt that the fulfilment of a power

---

[3]*De cælesti hierarchia* 4. PG 3, 180
[4]*Jeremiah* 9, 24   [5]art. 6
[e]True, i.e. not just seeming, *apparens*; complete, i.e. not imperfect.
[a]St Thomas now talks more explicitly as a Christian theologian. The article criticized emanationist theories of the Neo-Platonist and Arabian philosophers: the descent of the One through the Many, the creation of corruptible bodies by spiritual substances lower than God, the illuminism by which we return to these spiritual substances. A full documentation will be found in Ramirez, op. cit. See also *Angels*, by K. Foster. 1a. 50–64. Vol. 9. 1968.
[b]St Gregory the Great (c. 540–604). Pope Gregory I.

quod unumquodque intantum est perfectio alicujus potentiæ inquantum ad ipsum pertinet ratio proprii objecti illius potentiæ. Proprium autem objectum intellectus est verum. Quidquid ergo habet veritatem participatam, contemplatum non facit intellectum perfectum ultima perfectione. Cum autem eadem sit dispositio rerum in esse sicut in veritate, ut dicitur in *Meta.*,[6] quæcumque sunt entia per participationem sunt vera per participationem. Angeli autem habent esse participatum: quia solius Dei suum esse est sua essentia, ut in *Primo* ostensum est.[7] Unde relinquitur quod solus Deus sit veritas per essentiam, et quod ejus contemplatio faciat perfecte beatum.

Aliqualem autem beatitudinem imperfectam nihil prohibet attendi in contemplatione angelorum; et etiam altiorem quam in consideratione scientiarum speculativarum.

1. Ad primum ergo dicendum quod festis angelorum intererimus non solum contemplantes angelos, sed simul cum ipsis, Deum.

2. Ad secundum dicendum quod, secundum illos qui ponunt animas humanas esse ab angelis creatas satis conveniens videtur quod beatitudo hominis sit in contemplatione angelorum, quasi in conjunctione ad suum principium.[8] Sed hoc est erroneum, ut in *Primo* dictum est.[9] Unde ultima perfectio intellectus humani est per conjunctionem ad Deum, qui est primum principium et creationis animæ et illuminationis ejus. Angelus autem illuminat tanquam minister, ut in *Primo* habitum est.[10] Unde suo ministerio adjuvat hominem ut ad beatitudinem perveniat, non autem est humanæ beatitudinis objectum.

3. Ad tertium dicendum quod attingi superiorem naturam ab inferiori contingit dupliciter. Uno modo, secundum gradum potentiæ participantis: et sic ultima perfectio hominis erit in hoc quod homo attinget ad contemplandum sicut angeli contemplantur. Alio modo, sicut objectum attingitur a potentia: et hoc modo ultima perfectio cujuslibet potentiæ est ut attingat ad id in quo plene invenitur ratio sui objecti.

articulus 8. utrum beatitudo hominis sit in visione divinæ essentiæ

AD OCTAVUM sic proceditur:[1] 1. Videtur quod beatitudo hominis non sit in visione ipsius divinæ essentiæ. Dicit enim Dionysius,[2] quod per id quod est supremum intellectus homo Deo conjungitur sicut omnino ignoto. Sed id quod videtur per essentiam non est omnino ignotum. Ergo ultima

---

[6]*Metaphysics* 11, 1. 993b30   [7]Ia. 44, 1. cf Ia. 3, 4; 7, 1 ad 3; 2
[8]*Liber de causis* 3   [9]Ia. 90. 3   [10]Ia. 111, 2 ad 2
[1]cf Ia. 12. 1. *De veritate* VIII. 1. *In Matt.* 5. *In Joann.* 1, *lect.* 11. *Quodl.* x, 8. 1.
Compend. Theol. 104, 106; 11, 9
[2]*De mystica theol.* 1. PG 3, 1001
[c]e.g. Avicenna (d. 1037) and Algazel (d. *c.* 1111).

comes from an object which possesses on its own the shaping interest to which it responds. This object for the intellect is simply being true. And so the mind is not finally fulfilled in contemplating what is derivatively true. Now since the condition of things as being real and as being true is identical, according to the *Metaphysics*,[6] whatever is derivatively real is also derivatively true. Angels have derivative existence, for with God alone is his existence his essence, as we have seen in the *Prima Pars*.[7] It follows that God alone is essential truth of himself: only by contemplating him is man in perfect bliss.

All the same there is no reason to deny some measure of happiness to our contemplation of angels, an even higher happiness than attends our study of the theoretical sciences.

Hence: 1. We enter into the feasts of angels by contemplating them, not apart, but together seen in the presence of God.

2. It seems well enough according to those[c] who maintain that human souls are created by angels, that our happiness should lie in contemplating them, as it were, by a returning to our origins.[8] However, their position is mistaken, as we have shown in the *Prima Pars*.[9] Hence the human mind's final perfection is by coming to union with God, who is the first cause both of the soul's being created and enlightened. The angels shed light as ministers of God, as we have explained,[10] and so their ministry helps men to come through to happiness, but they are not its object.[d]

3. A lower may reach a higher nature in two ways. First, according to the same manner of sharing: thus man's final perfection will be to attain to contemplation such as angels enjoy. Second, in kind, according as a power reaches its object, and thus the ultimate perfection of any power is to attain that in which its shaping interest is fully realized.

article 8. is man's happiness the vision of God's very essence?

THE EIGHTH POINT:[1] 1. It seems not.[a] For Dionysius teaches that the height of understanding is for man to be conjoined to God as the wholly unknown.[2] Could anything be further from seeing an essence?

---

[d]Again, the importance of object. And in the following reply.

[a]All the foregoing discussions have been preliminary to this specifically Christian teaching, anticipated in 1a. 12, 1. Vol. 3. cf Introduction. The treatment there was more epistemological; now the topic appears as the most important of the prolegomena to morality. The beatific vision and love of God are not themselves deliberate and moral acts, or human acts as they have been defined above, 1a2æ. 1, 2.

The present and subsequent discussions show St Thomas ranging well beyond Aristotle, to whom he has seemed committed, (too committed, some think), and holding that men do not really belong to this world, though he is still at pains to make it reasonable and gracious. cf Appendix 5.

intellectus perfectio, seu beatitudo, non consistit in hoc quod Deus per essentiam videtur.

2. Præterea, altioris naturæ altior est perfectio. Sed hæc est perfectio divini intellectus propria ut suam essentiam videat. Ergo ultima perfectio intellectus humani ad hoc non pertingit, sed infra subsistit.

SED CONTRA est quod dicitur 1 *Joan.*,[3] *Cum apparuerit, similes ei erimus, et videbimus eum sicuti ipse est.*

RESPONSIO: Dicendum quod ultima et perfecta beatitudo non potest esse nisi in visione divinæ essentiæ. Ad cujus evidentiam, duo consideranda sunt. Primo quidem, quod homo non est perfecte beatus quandiu restat sibi aliquid desiderandum et quærendum. Secundum est, quod uniuscujusque potentiæ perfectio attenditur secundum rationem sui objecti. Objectum autem intellectus est *quod quid est*, idest essentia rei, ut dicitur in III *De Anima.*[4] Unde intantum procedit perfectio intellectus inquantum cognoscit essentiam alicujus rei.

Si ergo intellectus aliquis cognoscat essentiam alicujus effectus per quam non possit cognosci essentia causæ, ut scilicet sciatur de causa *quid est*; non dicitur intellectus attingere ad causam simpliciter, quamvis per effectum cognoscere possit de causa *an sit.* Et ideo remanet naturaliter homini desiderium, cum cognoscit effectum, et scit eum habere causam, ut etiam sciat de causa *quid est.* Et illud desiderium est admirationis, et causat inquisitionem, ut dicitur in principio *Meta.*[5] Puta si aliquis cognoscens eclipsim solis, considerat quod ex aliqua causa procedit, de qua, quia nescit quid sit, admiratur, et admirando inquirit. Nec ista inquisitio quiescit quousque perveniat ad cognoscendum essentiam causæ.

Si igitur intellectus humanus, cognoscens essentiam alicujus effectus creati, non cognoscat de Deo nisi *an est*, nondum perfectio ejus attingit simpliciter ad causam primam, sed remanet ei adhuc naturale desiderium inquirendi causam. Unde nondum est perfecte beatus. Ad perfectam igitur beatitudinem requiritur quod intellectus pertingat ad ipsam essentiam primæ causæ. Et sic perfectionem suam habebit per unionem ad Deum

[3]1 *John* 3, 2   [4]*De Anima* III. 6. 430b27   [5]*Metaphysics* I, 2. 982b12; 983a12
[b]cf Kirk, op cit. pp. 10–22, Jewish anticipations; pp. 23–38, pagan anticipations (notably *Phædrus* 229, 230B); pp. 94–110, New Testament teaching.
[c]The full strength of the argument appears only when such terms in the premises as 'knowing what really is' and 'essence' and 'effect' and 'cause' are loaded above their Aristotelean burden, and taken beyond conceptual knowledge to real and immediate union. The importance of objectual presence has already been indicated. 1a. 8, 3: 'God is said to be in a thing in two ways. One, as efficient cause, and thus he is in all things he creates. Two, as object of activity in the thing acting, and this is proper to activities of soul, according as the known is in the knower and the desired

So then at its peak of happiness the mind does not see God by his essence.

2. Moreover, the higher a nature the higher its perfection. Seeing the divine essence is proper to the divine mind. The human mind stands below this, and at full height does not break through to such a vision.

ON THE OTHER HAND we are promised, *When he shall appear, we shall be like him and see him as he is.*[3b]

REPLY: There can be no complete and final happiness for us save in the vision of God. The evidence? Consider first, that man is not perfectly happy so long as something remains for him to desire and seek; and secondly, that a power's full development comes only from its shaping object. Now we agree with the *De Anima*,[4] the object of mind is *what really is*, that is the essence of a thing. And so the mind's expansion into perfection is proportionate to its possession of what really is.

If, then, the essence of an effect is known through which, however, the essence of its cause cannot be known, namely what it really is, then quite simply the mind does not reach to the cause, though it may be able to gather from the effect that a cause is really there. Accordingly when a man knows an effect and also that it has a cause, then the desire still stirs in him to know also what the cause really is. This is part of his constitution, and full of wonder, which, as noticed at the opening of the *Metaphysics*,[5] sets us out to explore. For instance, on seeing a solar eclipse, we reflect that there must be a cause for it, yet because this is not known we start to wonder and so go on to investigate, nor shall we rest until we come to see the cause for what it really is.[c]

Well then, were the human mind, from knowing what the created effects about us were, to have reached the position of knowing no more about God than that he exists,[d] then not yet would it have come to the point of perfection by knowing the first cause unreservedly, and a natural desire to find it would remain. Not yet would a man be in perfect bliss. Complete happiness requires the mind to come through to the essence itself of the first cause. And so it will have its fulfilment by union with God

in the desirer. And in this second way God is in a rational creature specially, who knows him and loves him by act and steady disposition. And because this comes from grace, he is said to be in his friends, *sanctis*, through grace.' cf 1a2æ. 2, 8, note *e*; 3, 1, note *d*.

[d]The theme of 1a. 2–13. Vols. 2 & 3. Notice, however, that by his doctrine of positive causal participation, though checked and qualified by the elimination of imperfections and the heightening of values, *via negationis et eminentiæ*, St Thomas goes beyond the *theologia negativa* of his contemporaries. Vol. 3, Introduction by T. Gilby.

sicut ad objectum, in quo solo beatitudo hominis consistit, ut supra dictum est.[6]

1. Ad primum ergo dicendum quod Dionysius loquitur de cognitione eorum qui sunt in via, tendentes ad beatitudinem.

2. Ad secundum dicendum quod, sicut supra dictum est,[7] finis potest accipi dupliciter. Uno modo, quantum ad rem ipsam quæ desideratur: et hoc modo idem est finis superioris et inferioris naturæ, immo omnium rerum, ut supra dictum est.[8] Alio modo, quantum ad consecutionem hujus rei: et sic diversus est finis superioris et inferioris naturæ, secundum diversam habitudinem ad rem talem. Sic igitur altior est beatitudo Dei suam essentiam intellectu comprehendentis quam hominis vel angeli videntis, et non comprehendentis.

---

[6]art 1 & 7. cf Ia2æ. 2, 8

as its object, for we have already explained[6] that in him alone our happiness lies.[e]

Hence: 1. Dionysius is referring to the knowledge we have as pilgrims to happiness.

2. We have already noted[7] that there are two sides to an end. One is the thing itself which is desired, and we have stated[8] that is one and the same for lower and higher natures, indeed for all things. The other is the actual reaching of it, and in this respect ends are diverse for lower and higher natures according to their various relationships to that one thing. So therefore God's happiness in comprehending his essence is higher than the happiness of men and angels, who see but do not comprehend him.[f]

---

[7]1a2æ. 1, 8
[8]ibid
[e]In the foregoing discussion it is enough to take knowing an 'essence' to mean knowing an object for itself, in its very being and its own evidence: the historical— and later—overtones of the term can be here neglected.
[f]For comprehension, see below 1a2æ. 4, 3.

Quæstio 4. de his quæ ad beatitudinem exiguntur

DEINDE CONSIDERANDUM EST de his quæ exiguntur ad beatitudinem. Et circa hoc quæruntur octo:

1. utrum delectatio requiratur ad beatitudinem;
2. quid sit principalius in beatitudine, utrum delectatio vel visio;
3. utrum requiratur comprehensio;
4. utrum requiratur rectitudo voluntatis;
5. utrum ad beatitudinem hominis requiratur corpus;
6. utrum perfectio corporis;
7. utrum aliqua exteriora bona;
8. utrum requiratur societas amicorum.

articulus 1. utrum delectatio requiratur ad beatitudinem

AD PRIMUM sic proceditur:[1] 1. Videtur quod delectatio non requiratur ad beatitudinem. Dicit enim Augustinus quod *visio est tota merces fidei.*[2] Sed id quod est præmium vel merces virtutis, est beatitudo, ut patet per Philosophum.[3] Ergo nihil aliud requiritur ad beatitudinem nisi sola visio.

2. Præterea, beatitudo est *per se sufficientissimum bonum,* ut Philosophus dicit.[4] Quod autem eget aliquo alio non est per se* sufficiens. Cum igitur essentia beatitudinis in visione Dei consistat, ut ostensum est,[5] videtur quod ad beatitudinem non requiratur delectatio.

3. Præterea, *operationem felicitatis* seu beatitudinis oportet esse *non impeditam,* ut dicitur in *Ethic.*[6] Sed delectatio impedit actionem intellectus: *corrumpit* enim *æstimationem prudentiæ,* ut dicitur in *Ethic.*[7] Ergo delectatio non requiritur ad beatitudinem.

SED CONTRA est quod Augustinus dicit,[8] quod beatitudo est *gaudium de veritate.*

RESPONSIO: Dicendum quod quadrupliciter aliquid requiritur ad aliud. Uno modo, sicut præambulum vel præparatorium ad ipsum: sicut disciplina requiritur ad scientiam. Alio modo, sicut perficiens aliquid: sicut anima requiritur ad vitam corporis. Tertio modo, sicut coadjuvans

---

*Piana: *perfecte*
[1]cf Ia2æ. 3, 4. II *Sent.* 38, 2; IV, 49, 1, ii; 3, 4. iii. *In Ethic.* x. lect. 6. *Compend. theol.* 107, 165
[2]*De Trin.* 1, 8. PL 42, 831

Question 4. the conditions of happiness

WE COME NEXT to the elements required for happiness. Here there are eight points of inquiry:

1. whether happiness requires pleasure;
2. whether delight or vision is the more capital;
3. whether comprehending is a condition of being happy;
4. whether rightness of will is required;
5. and having a body;
6. and a body in full health;
7. and some external goods;
8. and the companionship of friends.[a]

article 1. is pleasure required for happiness?

THE FIRST POINT:[1] 1. It seems not.[b] Augustine tells us that *vision is the entire reward of faith.*[2] And it is clear from Aristotle that happiness is the reward of virtue.[3] Its sole requirement, then, is vision.

2. Moreover, as Aristotle says, *happiness is the most self-sufficient of blessings.*[4] Now that which needs a complement is not enough in itself. The essence of happiness is the vision of God, as we have agreed.[5] It would seem, therefore, that this does not demand delight.

3. Further, the activity of felicity or happiness ought to have the note of not being impeded: thus the *Ethics.*[6] But pleasure hinders the activity of understanding; according to the *Ethics* again,[7] it throws out the reckoning of practical wisdom. And therefore it does not come into happiness.

ON THE OTHER HAND there is Augustine speaking of happiness as *joy in the truth.*[8]

REPLY: One requires another in four manners. First, as a preliminary or preparation, thus science requires discipline. Second, as its completion, thus living body requires soul. Third, as an outside help, thus an

---

[3]*Ethics* I, 9. 1099b16   [4]op cit 7. 1097b8
[5]1a2æ. 3, 8   [6]*Ethics* VII, 13. 1153b16
[7]*Ethics* VI, 5. 1140b12   [8]*Confessions* x, 23. PL 32, 793
[a]The Question falls into two groups of four articles, the first on the elements or components of happiness, the second on its possession.
[b]Pleasure, *delectatio,* is the general term; *voluptas* often refers to sensuous pleasure; joy, *gaudium,* to the higher pleasures; *fruitio* to religious pleasure. The three terms are interchangeable. This article and the next pick up from 1a2æ. 2, 6 above. cf Appendix 3.

extrinsecum: sicut amici requiruntur ad aliquid agendum. Quarto modo, sicut aliquid concomitans: ut si dicamus quod calor requiritur ad ignem. Et hoc modo delectatio requiritur ad beatitudinem. Delectatio enim causatur ex hoc quod appetitus requiescit in bono adepto. Unde, cum beatitudo nihil aliud sit quam adeptio summi boni, non potest esse beatitudo sine delectatione concomitante.

1. Ad primum ergo dicendum quod ex hoc ipso quod merces alicui redditur, voluntas merentis requiescit, quod est delectari. Unde in ipsa ratione mercedis redditæ delectatio includitur.

2. Ad secundum dicendum quod ex ipsa visione Dei causatur delectatio. Unde ille qui Deum videt delectatione indigere non potest.

3. Ad tertium dicendum quod delectatio concomitans operationem intellectus, non impedit ipsam, sed magis eam confortat, ut dicitur in *Ethic.*,[9] ea enim quæ delectabiliter facimus attentius et perseverantius operamur. Delectatio autem extranea impedit operationem: quandoque quidem ex intentionis distractione; quia, sicut dictum est, ad ea in quibus delectamur, magis intenti sumus; et dum uni vehementer intendimus, necesse est quod ab alio intentio retrahatur. Quandoque autem etiam ex contrarietate: sicut delectatio sensus contraria rationi, impedit æstimationem prudentiæ magis quam æstimationem speculativi intellectus.

articulus 2. utrum in beatitudine sit principalius visio quam delectatio

AD SECUNDUM sic proceditur:[1] 1. Videtur quod delectatio sit principalius in beatitudine quam visio. Delectatio enim, ut dicitur in *Ethic.*,[2] *est perfectio operationis.* Sed perfectio est potior perfectibili. Ergo delectatio est potior operatione intellectus, quæ est visio.

2. Præterea, illud propter quod aliquid est appetibile est potius. Sed operationes appetuntur propter delectationem ipsarum: unde et natura operationibus necessariis ad conservationem individui et speciei delectationem apposuit, ut hujusmodi operationes ab animalibus non negligantur. Ergo delectatio est potior in beatitudine quam operatio intellectus, quæ est visio.

3. Præterea, visio respondet fidei, delectatio autem, sive fruitio, caritati. Sed caritas est major fide, ut dicit Apostolus I *ad Cor.*[3] Ergo delectatio, sive fruitio, est potior visione.

---

[9]*Ethics* x, 4. 1174b23
[1]cf In *Ethic.* x. *lect.* 6. *CG* III, 26. II *Sent.* 38, 2 ad 6
[2]*Ethics* x, 4. 1174b23, b31
[3]I *Corinthians* 13, 13
[c]The distinction, if any, between *calor* and *ignis*, may be neglected. One is tempted to translate, 'thus fire requires dryness'.
[d]Delight goes with having an end, not a means. Delight is the immediate resonance

enterprise requires friends. Fourth, as an accompaniment; thus we might say fire requires heat.[c]

It is in this last manner that pleasure is bound up with happiness. For it is caused by the repose of desire in a good that is held. What is beatitude but holding the highest good? And so it cannot exist without accompanying delight.[d]

Hence: 1. The will of the person deserving it rests content with the recompense which is granted, in other words finds delight there. Accordingly the notion of reward includes the pleasure it provides.

2. Delight is caused by the very vision of God, and he who sees God has need for no other.

3. The mind's activity, far from being hindered, is concentrated by the attendant delight; thus the remark in the *Ethics*,[9] that what we do pleasurably we do with more attention and perseverance. Extraneous pleasure can hold up activity, sometimes by distracting us from its purpose, sometimes by setting up a conflict. We are more intent on the things we take pleasure in, and strong counter-attraction can deflect us from what we propose to do. Also a sensuous pleasure contrary to reason blocks the judgment of practical wisdom, more than it does that of theoretical understanding.[e]

article 2. is delight or vision more capital in happiness?

THE SECOND POINT:[1] 1. Delight, so it would seem. For delight, as noted in the *Ethics*,[2] is the fulfilment of activity. To be fulfilled is more important than to be capable of being fulfilled. So then delight is more important than the mind's act of vision.

2. Again, that on account of which something is desirable is the more potent of the two. Now activities are desired on account of the pleasures they provide, which is why nature attaches pleasures to activities necessary for the preservation of the individual and the race; otherwise animals would neglect them. Therefore pleasure in happiness is more potent than vision.[a]

3. Besides, vision answers to faith, delight or enjoyment to charity. Now charity is higher than faith: this is St Paul's teaching in I *Corinthians*.[3] Correspondingly, delight or enjoyment is greater than vision.

---

of holding a good, and intelligent delight in an action is a fair test of its rightness, 1a2æ. 34, 4.
[e]Sensuous pleasure as particularized can be divorced from the *ratio finis*, and can trouble virtue. See below art. 2 ad 2.
[a]The first two objections are reputedly from Eudoxus of Cnidus, who lived about 366 B.C. His works are lost.

SED CONTRA, causa est potior effectu. Sed visio est causa delectationis. Ergo visio est potior quam delectatio.

RESPONSIO: Dicendum quod istam quæstionem movet Philosophus in *Ethic.*[4] et eam insolutam dimittit. Sed si quis diligenter consideret, ex necessitate oportet quod operatio intellectus, quæ est visio, sit potior delectatione.

Delectatio enim consistit in quadam quietatione voluntatis. Quod autem voluntas in aliquo quietetur, non est nisi propter bonitatem ejus in quo quietatur. Si ergo voluntas quietatur in aliqua operatione, ex bonitate operationis procedit quietatio voluntatis. Nec voluntas quærit bonum propter quietationem: sic enim ipse actus voluntatis esset finis, quod est contra præmissa.[5] Sed ideo quærit quod quietetur in operatione, quia operatio est bonum ejus. Unde manifestum est quod principalius bonum est ipsa operatio in qua quietatur voluntas quam quietatio voluntatis in ipso.

1. Ad primum ergo dicendum quod, sicut Philosophus ibidem dicit,[6] *delectatio perficit operationem sicut decor juventutem,* qui est ad juventutem consequens. Unde delectatio est quædam perfectio concomitans visionem; non sicut perfectio faciens visionem esse in sua specie perfectam.

2. Ad secundum dicendum quod apprehensio sensitiva non attingit ad communem rationem boni, sed ad aliquod bonum particulare quod est delectabile. Et ideo secundum appetitum sensitivum, qui est in animalibus, operationes quæruntur propter delectationem. Sed intellectus apprehendit universalem rationem boni, ad cujus consecutionem sequitur delectatio. Unde principalius intendit bonum quam delectationem. Et inde est quod divinus intellectus, qui est institutor naturæ, delectationes apposuit propter operationes. Non est autem aliquid æstimandum simpliciter secundum ordinem sensitivi appetitus, sed magis secundum ordinem appetitus intellectivi.

3. Ad tertium dicendum quod caritas non quærit bonum dilectum propter delectationem: sed hoc est ei consequens, ut delectetur in bono

---

[4]*Ethics* x, 4. 1175a18   [5]Ia2æ. 1, 1 ad 2; 3, 4   [6]*Ethics* x, 4. 1174b31
[b]Whether life is for joy, or joy for life.
[c]Acting for pleasure is queried less on moral than on psychological grounds.
[d]The question of right and wrong in the pleasure-causing act revolves round the object causing it, not the pleasure itself; Ia2æ. 34, 1 & 2.
[e]*Communis ratio boni.* One is tempted to translate this as an abstraction, the common form of goodness, but at the risk of missing the causal participation of good things in the *summum bonum*, the subsisting good.
[f]That is, in pleasurable actions. For animals can do painful things for needs they do not reason about; e.g. earwigs in defence of their young. Then there are mysterious drives, e.g. the mass migration of lemmings into the sea.

ON THE OTHER HAND, a cause is more capital than an effect, and vision is the cause of delight, and consequently more capital.

REPLY: Aristotle raises this question[b] in the *Ethics*[4] and leaves it unresolved. But look into it carefully, and you cannot but conclude that happiness turns on the mind's act of vision, not on the delight.[c]

Delight consists in a certain repose of the will, and this comes only because of the goodness of the thing which contents it. If, therefore, the will is at rest though actively loving, then this is because of the goodness in its loving. It is not that the will seeks good for the sake of its resting satisfied, for that would mean that the will's own activity was its end, and we have established the contrary.[5] Instead it seeks to find rest in its activity, because its activity means a good for it. Clearly, therefore, the capital point is the activity in which the will finds rest, and not the actual resting because of it.[d]

Hence: 1. In the same passage Aristotle draws an analogy:[6] delight is the bloom of activity, as beauty is that of youth. Beauty is a consequence of youth, and delight is a certain perfection attendant on vision, not one forming its nature.

2. Sense-perception does not reach to the good which pervades all things,[e] but to some particular good which is pleasurable. And so by their sensitive appetites animals pursue activity for the sake of pleasure,[f] though intelligence perceives the universal meaning of the good, and it is from the holding of good that pleasure arises: hence in the intention the good itself is more capital than the pleasure.[g] For the rest, the divine mind, the author of nature, joins pleasures to natural operations.[h] Purpose should be appreciated in the pattern of intelligent appetite, not just as it appears in that of sensitive appetite.

3. Charity does not seek the beloved for the sake of delight, although that follows the finding. Consequently delight does not correspond to

---

[g]And it is more capital also in the thing, to be good is its being—*ens* and *bonum* are convertible—whereas to give pleasure is consequential. And this appears in a special manner with chosen good: II *Sent.* 17, 2 ad 2.

[h]*Et inde est*, very freely translated to safeguard the antithetical argument.

The thought that pleasure is, as it were, the bait for necessary activity appears in *CG* III, 26. A parallel argument is also applied to pain: how necessary it is, for otherwise you would never have an angry appendix out. But as to the question, Is pleasure for action or action for pleasure? Cajetan observes, *in loc.*, that looked at in isolation, both are desirable in themselves, but looked at in relation, as composing one sensible object, the distinction is pointless. Notice that the question concerns acting for pleasure on the sense-level, where there is no perception of value and an end as such, *honestum* and *ratio finis*. It is only by reflection that we conclude that delight is owing to worth.

adepto quod amat. Et sic delectatio non respondet ei ut finis, sed magis visio, per quam primo finis fit ei præsens.

articulus 3. *utrum ad beatitudinem requiratur comprehensio*

AD TERTIUM sic proceditur:[1] 1. Videtur quod ad beatitudinem non requiratur comprehensio. Dicit enim Augustinus,[2] *Attingere mente Deum magna est beatitudo, comprehendere autem est impossibile.* Ergo sine comprehensione est beatitudo.

2. Præterea, beatitudo est perfectio hominis secundum intellectivam partem, in qua non sunt aliæ potentiæ quam intellectus et voluntas, ut in *Primo* dictum est.[3] Sed intellectus sufficienter perficitur per visionem Dei, voluntas autem per delectationem in ipso. Ergo non requiritur comprehensio tanquam aliquod tertium.

3. Præterea, beatitudo in operatione consistit. Operationes autem determinantur secundum objecta. Objecta autem generalia sunt duo, verum et bonum: verum correspondet visioni, et bonum correspondet delectationi. Ergo non requiritur comprehensio quasi aliquod tertium.

SED CONTRA est quod Apostolus dicit,[4] *Sic currite ut comprehendatis.* Sed spiritualis cursus terminatur ad beatitudinem: unde ipse dicit,[5] *Bonum certamen certavi, cursum consummavi, fidem servavi; in reliquo reposita est mihi corona justitæ.* Ergo comprehensio requiritur ad beatitudinem.

RESPONSIO: Dicendum quod, cum beatitudo consistat in consecutione ultimi finis, ea quæ requiruntur ad beatitudinem sunt consideranda ex ipso ordine hominis ad finem. Ad finem autem intelligibilem ordinatur homo partim quidem per intellectum, partim autem per voluntatem. Per intellectum quidem, inquantum in intellectu præexistit aliqua cognitio finis imperfecta. Per voluntatem autem, primo quidem per amorem, qui est primus motus voluntatis in aliquid; secundo autem, per realem habitudinem amantis ad amatum, quæ quidem potest esse triplex.

Quandoque enim amatum est præsens amanti: et tunc jam non quæritur. Quandoque autem non est præsens, sed impossibile est ipsum adipisci: et tunc etiam non quæritur. Quandoque autem possibile est ipsum adipisci, sed est elevatum supra facultatem adipiscentis, ita ut statim haberi non possit: et hæc est habitudo sperantis ad speratum, quæ sola habitudo facit finis inquisitionem.

---

[1] cf 1a. 12, 7 ad 1. I *Sent.* 1, 1, 1; IV, 49, 4, 5, 1 ad 3
[2] *Serm. ad popul. cxvii*, 3. PL 38, 663   [3] 1a, 79
[4] I *Corinthians* 9, 24   [5] II *Timothy* 4, 7
[a] Comprehension, *comprehensio*: the term comes from the Vulgate, I *Corinthians* 9, 24 (*katalambanō*, to lay hold of), and answers to the virtue of hope, the grasping

charity as its aim, which rather is the vision in which directly and immediately the beloved is present.

article 3. does happiness call for comprehension?

THE THIRD POINT:[1] 1. It would seem not.[a] Augustine says, *For the mind to reach God is great happiness, but to comprehend him is impossible.*[2] Accordingly happiness is without comprehension.

2. Moreover, happiness is fulfilment of man's intellective part, where, as we have seen in the *Prima Pars*,[3] there are no powers other than his mind and will. Now the mind is sufficiently fulfilled by the vision of God, and the will by joy in him. Therefore comprehension is not required as a sort of third.

3. Again, happiness is an activity. The object determines what kind of activity is engaged. The objects of human activity in general are two, namely the true and the good, the first corresponds to vision, the second to delight. There is no need to introduce comprehension as a further third.

ON THE OTHER HAND St Paul bids us, *So run that you may grasp.*[4] And the finish of the spiritual race is happiness; *I have fought the good fight, I have run my course, I have kept the faith; as to the rest there is laid up for me the crown of justice.*[5] Therefore comprehension is part of happiness.

REPLY: Since happiness consists in gaining our last end, its requirements are to be marked in terms of man's relationship to it. He is related to a supra-sensible end partly by mind, partly by will. As for the mind, it has some incomplete knowledge of the end before happiness is reached. As for the will, love is basic, namely, the initial motion of the lover to the thing loved, and secondly a real relation of the lover to the thing loved.

Now there can be three situations for this relation. Sometimes the beloved is really present to the lover, and then is no longer sought. Sometimes the beloved is not present and is quite out of reach, and then also is not sought. Sometimes, though above the lover so as not to be straightway possessed, the beloved may yet be reached. Such is the situation of hope, and it is there only that the love-relation sets us questing for the end.[b]

---

of what is striven for. It does not mean exhaustive knowledge. So the blessed are called *comprehensores*, whereas we are still *viatores*, wayfarers or pilgrims. The terms are found in St Bernard, and are amply treated by the authors, notably John of St Thomas and the Salmanticenses. The article may be read as a dutiful tribute to a hallowed term.
[b]Hopefulness as a feeling, 1a2æ. 40. Hope as a theological virtue, 2a2æ. 17-22.

Et istis tribus respondent aliqua in ipsa beatitudine. Nam perfecta cognitio finis respondet imperfectæ; præsentia vero ipsius finis respondet habitudini spei; sed delectatio in fine jam præsenti* consequitur dilectionem, ut supra dictum est.[6] Et ideo necesse est ad beatitudinem ista tria concurrere: scilicet visionem, quæ est cognitio perfecta intelligibilis finis; comprehensionem, quæ importat præsentiam finis; delectationem, vel fruitionem, quæ importat quietationem rei amantis in amato.

1. Ad primum ergo dicendum quod comprehensio dicitur dupliciter. Uno modo, inclusio comprehensi in comprehendente: et sic omne quod comprehenditur a finito est finitum. Unde hoc modo Deus non potest comprehendi ab aliquo intellectu creato. Alio modo comprehensio nihil aliud nominat quam tentionem alicujus rei jam præsentialiter habitæ: sicut aliquis consequens aliquem dicitur eum comprehendere quando tenet eum. Et hoc modo comprehensio requiritur ad beatitudinem.

2. Ad secundum dicendum quod, sicut ad voluntatem pertinet spes et amor, quia ejusdem est amare aliquid et tendere in illud non habitum, ita etiam ad voluntatem pertinet et comprehensio et delectatio, quia ejusdem est habere aliquid et quiescere in illo.

3. Ad tertium dicendum quod comprehensio non est aliqua operatio præter visionem, sed est quædam habitudo ad finem jam habitum. Unde etiam ipsa visio, vel res visa secundum quod præsentialiter adest, est objectum comprehensionis.

articulus 4. utrum ad beatitudinem requiratur rectitudo voluntatis

AD QUARTUM sic proceditur:[1] 1. Videtur quod rectitudo voluntatis non requiratur ad beatitudinem. Beatitudo enim essentialiter consistit in operatione intellectus, ut dictum est.[2] Sed ad perfectam intellectus operationem non requiritur rectitudo voluntatis, per quam homines mundi dicuntur: dicit enim Augustinus,[3] *Non approbo quod in oratione dixi, Deus qui non nisi mundos verum scire voluisti. Responderi enim potest multos etiam non mundos multa scire vera.* Ergo rectitudo voluntatis non requiritur ad beatitudinem.

2. Præterea, prius non dependet a posteriori. Sed operatio intellectus est

---

*Piana: *in præsentia*
[6]art. 2 ad 3
[1]cf Ia2æ. 5, 7. *CG* IV, 92. *Compend. Theol.* 166
[2]Ia2æ. 3, 4
[3]*Retractations* I, 4. PL 32, 589
[c]cf Ia2æ. 28, 1 & 2.
[d]Comprehension, remarks Cajetan *in loc.*, does not add another activity to that of vision; it is a relation resulting in the will from the vision in the mind. The will is

There is a correspondence in happiness to these three conditions of mind and will. Complete knowledge of the end is the response to incomplete knowledge, its real presence to the longing of hope, and delight in its possession, as we have said,[6] follows from loving choice of it. All three must combine in integral happiness, namely vision, the complete knowledge of an end by the mind, comprehension, which implies its presence, and delight or joy, which implies the resting of the lover with the beloved.[c]

Hence: 1. Comprehension has two meanings. First, the containing of one in another; and thus all finite being comprehends itself finite. In this sense God cannot be comprehended by a created mind. Second it means, no more than the holding of an object present and possessed, thus a person running after is said to lay hold of him when he catches him. In this sense comprehension is necessary for happiness.[d]

2. As loving and hoping are both functions of the will, for the same power loves a good and tends to it when not yet possessed, so also are comprehending and delighting, since it is the same power that possesses a thing and is at rest with it.

3. Comprehension is not an activity apart from vision, but a relationship to an end already possessed. Consequently the seeing or the thing seen as really present is the single object of comprehension.

article 4. does happiness require rightness of will?

THE FOURTH POINT:[1] 1. Apparently not.[a] We have agreed that activity of mind constitutes happiness.[2] Now this activity does not depend on rightness of will, or purity of heart, as it is called, in order to be complete. Augustine retracts his words in a prayer which began, *O God who didst will none but the clean of heart to know the truth. For it can be retorted that many who are not such know many truths.*[3] Therefore happiness does not call for rightness of will.

2. Moreover, what comes first does not depend on what comes after.

---

one term of this relation, the other is the real and immediately known presence of God.

Notice again the distinction between finiteness of entity and infiniteness of object: cf above 1a2æ, 2, 8 ad 3.

[a]Two points are raised. First, that happiness requires a morally good predisposition. cf below 1a2æ. 5, 7. Second, that it sets up a condition excluding moral fault, or of impeccability. cf below 1a2æ. 5, 4.

Beatitude itself is a post-moral condition. The stonemason was not altogether off the mark when he carved on the gravestone that the departed died confident in a life of blissful immorality, though non-morality would have been more accurate.

Even in a completed human act the final stages, *usus activus* and *quies*, come after its morality has been constituted. But cf 1a2æ. 20, 4 & 5.

prior quam operatio voluntatis. Ergo beatitudo, quæ est perfecta operatio intellectus, non dependet a rectitudine voluntatis.

3. Præterea, quod ordinatur ad aliquid tanquam ad finem non est necessarium adepto jam fine: sicut navis postquam pervenitur ad portum. Sed rectitudo voluntatis, quæ est per virtutem, ordinatur ad beatitudinem tanquam ad finem. Ergo, adepta beatitudine, non est necessaria rectitudo voluntatis.

SED CONTRA est quod dicitur *Matt.*,[4] *Beati mundo corde, quoniam ipsi Deum videbunt.* Et *Hebr.*,[5] *Pacem sequimini cum omnibus, et sanctimoniam, sine qua nemo videbit Deum.*

RESPONSIO: Dicendum quod rectitudo voluntatis requiritur ad beatitudinem et antecedenter et concomitanter.

Antecedenter quidem, quia rectitudo voluntatis est per debitum ordinem ad finem ultimum. Finis autem comparatur ad id quod ordinatur ad finem sicut forma ad materiam. Unde sicut materia non potest consequi formam, nisi sit debito modo disposita ad ipsam, ita nihil consequitur finem nisi sit debito modo ordinatum ad ipsum. Et ideo nullus potest ad beatitudinem pervenire nisi habeat rectitudinem voluntatis.

Concomitanter autem, quia, sicut dictum est,[6] beatitudo ultima consistit in visione divinæ essentiæ, quæ est ipsa essentia bonitatis. Et ita voluntas videntis Dei essentiam ex necessitate amat quidquid amat, sub ordine ad Deum, sicut voluntas non videntis Dei essentiam ex necessitate amat quidquid amat sub communi ratione boni quam novit. Et hoc ipsum est quod facit voluntatem rectam. Unde manifestum est quod beatitudo non potest esse sine recta voluntate.

1. Ad primum ergo dicendum quod Augustinus loquitur de cognitione veri quod non est ipsa essentia bonitatis.

2. Ad secundum dicendum quod omnis actus voluntatis præceditur* ab aliquo actu intellectus: aliquis tamen actus voluntatis est prior quam aliquis actus intellectus. Voluntas enim tendit in finalem actum intellectus, qui est beatitudo. Et ideo recta inclinatio voluntatis præexigitur ad beatitudinem, sicut rectus motus sagittæ ad percussionem signi.

---

*Piana: *procedit*, proceeds from
[4]*Matthew* 5, 8   [5]*Hebrews* 12, 14   [6]Ia2æ. 3, 8
[b]In the act of willing form (object) and end coincide. cf Ia2æ. 8, 2.
[c]The act of loving God seen face to face is voluntary, but it is not deliberate, nor therefore a moral or human act as we have defined the term. cf above Ia2æ. I, I. Any holding back of love will be out of the question; the majority teaching is that there will be no 'indifference' *quoad exercitium*, or what is called the liberty of contradiction, of acting or not acting. Moreover no quasi-ultimate alternatives will be

Activity of mind comes before activity of will. And so happiness, which spells a fully active mind, does not depend on an upright will.

3. Besides, a means to an end ceases to be necessary when the end has been reached; a ship is no longer on course when she has come to port. Now rightness of will, which is through virtue, is a means to an end, namely happiness, and, therefore, is no longer required when this has been achieved.

ON THE OTHER HAND we are told, *Blessed are the clean of heart for they shall see God.*[4] And again, *Let all follow peace and holy living, without which no man shall see God.*[5]

REPLY: A right good will is required, both beforehand and during happiness.

The will is rightful when duly bent on its ultimate end, which end is to intermediate purposes as form to matter.[b] Now as material cannot be shaped unless it be duly prepared, so likewise nothing gains its end unless it be well adapted to it. The inference is that nobody can come through to happiness without a right good will, which, therefore, is an antecedent condition.

It is also an attendant condition of final happiness, which, as we have stated,[6] consists in the vision of the divine essence, which is goodness pure and unalloyed. And so the will of a person who sees God face to face must needs love whatsoever he loves within the embrace of God's goodness;[c] to draw a parallel, even now the will of a person not seeing God must needs love whatsoever he does love within the common notion of goodness known to him.[d] So is the will set straight, and final happiness cannot exist manifestly without this rightness.

Hence: 1. Augustine is there speaking of the knowledge of particular truths, not involving an appreciation of the very nature of goodness.[e]

2. Every act of will is preceded by some act of mind, yet some acts of will precede some acts of mind. The will tends to that final act of mind which is happiness, and accordingly it has to be rightly bent if final happiness is to be reached—so also an arrow has to be accurately flighted to hit the target.

---

offered, and here there will be no 'indifference' *quoad specificationem,* or what is called the liberty of contrariety, of acting thus or thus. cf 1a2æ. 10, 2. Also below, 1a2æ. 5, 4.
[d]Only a faint parallel, for though everybody, even in sinning, must needs will within the frame of goodness in general, his will is not thereby put right.
[e]A man may have a shrewd judgment about what is good within a particular system of reference while yet lacking direction to and sympathy with the good of his final and complete end. cf 1a2æ. 59, 5.

3. Ad tertium dicendum quod non omne quod ordinatur ad finem cessat adveniente fine, sed id tantum quod se habet in ratione imperfectionis, ut motus. Unde instrumenta motus non sunt necessaria postquam pervenitur ad finem, sed debitus ordo ad finem est necessarius.

articulus 5. utrum ad beatitudinem hominis requiratur corpus

AD QUINTUM sic proceditur:[1] 1. Videtur quod ad beatitudinem requiratur corpus. Perfectio enim virtutis et gratiæ præsupponit perfectionem naturæ. Sed beatitudo est perfectio virtutis et gratiæ. Anima autem sine corpore non habet perfectionem naturæ: cum sit pars naturaliter humanæ naturæ, omnis autem pars est imperfecta a suo toto separata. Ergo anima sine corpore non potest esse beata.

2. Præterea, beatitudo est operatio quædam perfecta, ut supra dictum est.[2] Sed operatio perfecta sequitur esse perfectum: quia nihil operatur nisi secundum quod est ens in actu. Cum ergo anima non habeat esse perfectum quando est a corpore separata, sicut nec aliqua pars quando separata est a toto, videtur quod anima sine corpore non possit esse beata.

3. Præterea, beatitudo est perfectio hominis. Sed anima sine corpore non est homo. Ergo beatitudo non potest esse in anima sine corpore.

4. Præterea, secundum Philosophum,[3] *felicitatis operatio*, in qua consistit beatitudo, est *non impedita*. Sed operatio animæ separatæ est impedita: quia, ut dicit Augustinus,[4] *inest ei naturalis quidam appetitus corpus administrandi, quo appetitu retardatur quodammodo ne tota intentione pergat in illud summum cælum*, idest in visionem essentiæ divinæ. Ergo anima sine corpore non potest esse beata.

5. Præterea, beatitudo est sufficiens bonum et quietat desiderium. Sed hoc non convenit animæ separatæ: quia adhuc appetit corporis unionem, ut Augustinus dicit.[5] Ergo anima separata a corpore non est beata.

6. Præterea, homo in beatitudine est angelis æqualis. Sed anima sine corpore non æquatur angelis, ut Augustinus dicit.[6] Ergo non est beata.

SED CONTRA est quod dicitur *Apoc.*,[7] *Beata mortui qui in Domino moriuntur*.

RESPONSIO: Dicendum quod duplex est beatitudo, una imperfecta, quæ habetur in hac vita, et alia perfecta, quæ in Dei visione consistit. Manifestum est autem quod ad beatitudinem hujus vitæ de necessitate requiritur

---

[1]cf 3a. 15, 10. *CG* IV, 79 & 91. *De potentia* v, 10. *Compend. Theol.* 151
[2]Ia2æ. 3, 2 & 5   [3]*Ethics* VII, 13. 1153b16
[4]*Super Genes. ad litt.* XII, 35. PL 34, 483
[5]ibid   .   [6]ibid
[7]*Revelations* 14, 13

3. Not every part of what is for an end is scrapped when the end is reached, but that part only which has the interim and provisional reality of getting there.[1] So, for instance, the vehicle for a journey is no longer necessary once you have arrived, yet you still have to be adapted to your welcome.

article 5. does our body come into our happiness?

THE FIFTH POINT:[1] 1. It would seem so. The completion of virtue and grace, which is happiness, is based on the completion of human nature. Is not this lacking in soul without body? The soul, after all, is but part of human nature, and any part is incomplete outside its whole. Therefore soul without body cannot be happy.

2. Again, we have agreed that happiness is acting completely,[2] and this follows from existing completely, for nothing is active except in so far as it is an actual being. Since the soul lacks complete existence when isolated from the body, as does any portion apart from the whole, it would appear that it is not open to beatitude in that condition.

3. Then also, happiness is fulfilment for a human being. Now a soul without a body is not a human being. Therefore happiness cannot lie in a soul without a body.

4. To continue, according to Aristotle,[3] *the activity of felicity*, in which happiness consists, *is unhindered*. But the activity of a disembodied soul is cramped, for, as Augustine writes,[4] *In it there is a natural appetite for governing the body, with the result that it is held back, so to speak, from pressing with all its forces to high heaven.* Therefore soul without body cannot be happy.

5. Further, happiness is blessing enough to content all desire. How can it be the lot of a disembodied soul, which, as Augustine remarks, *still craves to be united with body*.[5] How can it be completely happy?

6. Besides, man ranks with the angels in bliss. But according to Augustine a disembodied soul does not rank with the angels,[6] and therefore is not in bliss.

ON THE OTHER HAND there is the text from *Revelations*,[7] *Blessed are the dead who die in the Lord.*

REPLY: Happiness has two phases, one incomplete, and possible in this life, the other completed and subsisting in the vision of God. As for the first, the body is clearly needed, for such happiness comes through activity of mind,

---

[1]Motion ceases when the term is reached, yet the term holds all the actual reality of the motion. cf reflections on the *prima via*, 1a. 2, 3. Vol. 1.

corpus. Est enim beatitudo hujus vitæ operatio intellectus, vel speculativi vel practici. Operatio autem intellectus in hac vita non potest esse sine phantasmate, quod non est nisi in organo corporeo, ut in *Primo* habitum est.[8] Et sic beatitudo quæ in hac vita haberi potest, dependet quodammodo ex corpore.

Sed circa beatitudinem perfectam, quæ in Dei visione consistit, aliqui posuerunt quod non potest animæ advenire sine corpore existenti; dicentes quod animæ sanctorum a corporibus separatæ ad illam beatitudinem non perveniunt usque ad diem judicii, quando corpora resument. Quod quidem apparet esse falsum et auctoritate, et ratione.

Auctoritate quidem, quia Apostolus dicit, II *ad Cor.,*[9] *Quandiu sumus in corpore, peregrinamur a Domino*; et quæ sit ratio peregrinationis ostendit, subdens, *Per fidem enim ambulamus, et non per speciem.* Ex quo apparet quod quandiu aliquis ambulat per fidem et non per speciem, carens visione divinæ essentiæ, nondum est Deo præsens. Animæ autem sanctorum a corporibus separatæ, sunt Deo præsentes: unde subditur, *Audemus autem, et bonam voluntatem habemus peregrinari a corpore, et præsentes esse ad Dominum.* Unde manifestum est quod animæ sanctorum separatæ a corporibus ambulant per speciem, Dei essentiam videntes, in quo est vera beatitudo.

Hoc etiam per rationem apparet. Nam intellectus ad suam operationem non indiget corpore nisi propter phantasmata, in quibus veritatem intelligibilem contuetur, ut in *Primo* dictum est.[10] Manifestum est autem quod divina essentia per phantasmata videri non potest, ut in *Primo*[11] ostensum est. Unde, cum in visione divinæ essentiæ perfecta hominis beatitudo consistat, non dependet beatitudo perfecta hominis a corpore. Unde sine corpore potest anima esse beata.

Sed sciendum quod ad perfectionem alicujus rei dupliciter aliquid pertinet. Uno modo, ad constituendam essentiam rei; sicut anima requiritur ad perfectionem hominis. Alio modo requiritur ad perfectionem rei quod pertinet ad bene esse ejus; sicut pulchritudo corporis et velocitas ingenii pertinet ad perfectionem hominis.

Quamvis ergo corpus primo modo ad perfectionem beatitudinis humanæ

---

[8]1a. 84, 6 & 7   [9]II *Corinthians* 5, 6, 8   [10]1a. 84, 7   [11]1a. 12, 3
[a]*CG* III, 91 is more precise and refers to the *opinio quorumdam Græcorum.* The Greek tradition that the beatific vision is delayed until the resurrection of the body, represented by Origen, Justin, Clement of Alexandria, Gregory Nazianzen, is found in Latin theology with Lactantius, Hilary, Ambrose, Bernard. John XXII also entertained a private opinion on the matter, on which account he was challenged by the English Dominican, Thomas Waleys. cf T. Käppeli, *Le procès contre Thomas Waleys*, Rome, 1936.
The question was settled for Latin theologians by the Apostolic Constitution of Benedict XII, *Benedictus Deus*, 1336, which speaks of the blessed souls in heaven

theoretical and practical, which cannot be performed without imagination, and this, as we have shown in the *Prima Pars*,[8] works in a bodily organ. And so the happiness open to us at present depends to some extent on the body.

As for the second, some[a] have maintained that it cannot come to the soul existing outside the body, and that the souls of the saints do not attain the vision of God until Judgment Day, when they will receive back their bodies. They are mistaken, however, as appears in the light both of authority and of reason.[b]

First there is the teaching of St Paul. *While we are in the body we are absent from the Lord*, he says,[9] and then points out why God seems so distant; *For we walk by faith and not by sight*. From which it appears that so long as we are wayfarers lacking the vision of the divine essence we are not yet present before God. The souls of the saints, however, while still apart from their bodies, are present before God; and so St Paul continues, *We are confident and have a good will to fare forth from the body and to be present before the Lord*. Hence, it is evident that the souls of the saints, separated from their bodies, walk by sight in the vision of God's essence, which is true happiness.

Secondly, the confirmatory rational evidence.[c] The mind does not need the body for its activity except as providing images in which intelligible truths are viewed, as we have explained in the *Prima Pars*.[10] Obviously the divine essence cannot be seen through such images; we dealt with this point also in the *Prima Pars*.[11] Accordingly, since complete happiness is the vision of the divine essence, it does not hinge on the body, and the soul can be happy without it.

Note, however, that something may be part of a thing's perfection in two ways. First, as constituting its nature; thus soul is part of man's perfection. Secondly, as required for its full development; thus good looks and swift wit are parts of his perfection.

Now the body enters into happiness in the second way, not in the first. For since a thing's activity depends on its nature, the more perfect its

---

seeing God in a vision *intuitiva et etiam faciali, nulla mediante creatura*. Denz. 530. Vol. 3 of this series, Introduction.

[b]That is, by an appeal to divine Revelation, the source of *sacra doctrina*, and to theological science itself, 1a. 1. Vol. 1.

[c]Though not unduly exercised as a Christian theologian, St Thomas has to strain to give a purely rational account of the lot of a disembodied soul (1a. 89), because of his acceptance of man's psychophysical unity (1a. 76). The soul is the single substantial form of the body, and its understanding and willing are so bound up with sense and feeling that it is difficult to see how it can operate apart from the body. The same embarrassment appears in this and the following article, and the same tendency to tap Neo-Platonist, rather than Aristotelean, sources.

non pertineat, pertinet tamen secundo modo. Cum enim operatio dependeat ex natura rei, quando anima perfectior erit in sua natura tanto perfectius habebit suam propriam operationem, in qua felicitas consistit. Unde Augustinus, cum quæsivisset,[12] *Utrum spiritibus defunctorum sine corporibus possit summa illa beatitudo præberi,* respondet quod *non sic possunt videre incommutabilem substantiam, ut sancti angeli vident; sive alia latentiore causa, sive ideo quia est in eis naturalis quidam appetitus corpus administrandi.*

1. Ad primum ergo dicendum quod beatitudo est perfectio animæ ex parte intellectus, secundum quem anima transcendit corporis organa: non autem secundum quod est forma naturalis corporis. Et ideo illa naturæ perfectio manet secundum quam ei beatitudo debetur, licet non maneat illa naturæ perfectio secundum quam est corporis forma.

2. Ad secundum dicendum quod anima aliter se habet ad esse quam aliæ partes. Nam esse totius non est alicujus suarum partium: unde vel pars omnino desinit esse, destructo toto, sicut partes animalis destructo animali; vel, si remanent, habent aliud esse in actu, sicut pars lineæ habet aliud esse quam tota linea. Sed animæ humanæ remanet esse compositi post corporis destructionem.

Et hoc ideo, quia idem est esse formæ et materiæ, et hoc est esse compositi. Anima autem subsistit in suo esse, ut in *Primo* ostensum est.[13] Unde relinquitur quod post separationem a corpore perfectum esse habeat, unde et perfectam operationem habere potest; licet non habeat perfectam naturam speciei.

3. Ad tertium dicendum quod beatitudo est hominis secundum intellectum, et ideo, remanente intellectu, potest inesse ei beatitudo. Sicut dentes Æthiopis possunt esse albi, etiam post evulsionem, secundum quos Æthiops dicitur albus.

4. Ad quartum dicendum quod dupliciter aliquid impeditur ab alio. Uno modo per modum contrarietatis, sicut frigus impedit actionem caloris: et tale impedimentum operationis repugnat felicitati. Alio modo per modum cujusdam defectus, quia scilicet res impedita non habet quidquid ad omnimodam sui perfectionem requiritur: et tale impedimentum operationis non repugnat felicitati, sed omnimodæ perfectioni ipsius. Et sic separatio a corpore dicitur animam retardare, ne tota intentione tendat in visionem divinæ essentiæ. Appetit enim anima sic frui Deo, quod etiam ipsa fruitio derivetur ad corpus per redundantium, sicut est possibile. Et ideo quamdiu ipsa fruitur Deo sine corpore, appetitus ejus sic quiescit in eo

---

[12]*Super Genes. ad litt.* XII, 35. PL 34, 483   [13]Ia. 75, 2
[d]St Augustine suspects that the human soul, since it is made for the body and holds an intermediate position between spirit and sense, might be somehow unequal to full happiness when separated from the body. A deficiency in depth is suggested, IV *Sent.* 49, 1, 4, i.

condition so much the more perfectly will the soul enjoy its characteristic activity, in which happiness lies. Accordingly, after inquiring *whether sovereign happiness can be granted to the spirits of the dead*, Augustine answers that *they cannot see the eternal substance as the holy angels do, either for some hidden reason or because they naturally yearn to work with the body*.[12d]

Hence: 1. Happiness is the perfection of soul on the part of the mind which transcends the organs of body; it is not the perfection of soul precisely as the natural form of the body.[e] A disembodied soul keeps enough natural completeness to be equal to happiness, although the natural completeness of actually being the form of body has departed.

2. The relationship in which soul stands to existence is not that of other parts of a composite thing. The existence of the whole is not that of any one of these parts; when the whole is destroyed they cease to be, like living organs when an animal is killed, or when they remain it is with another actual existence, as when quantities are broken up.[f] In the case of man, however, the existence of the composite thing, namely the man, continues in the soul after the dissolution of the body.

And for this reason. The existence of matter and form in a thing is identical, namely the existence of the composite. Now, as we have shown in the *Prima Pars*,[13] the soul subsists in its existing. We are left to infer that when parted from the body the soul can exist completely, and therefore act completely, although its specific nature is not entire.[g]

3. Happiness is a man's in respect of his mind, so that happiness can still be his, somewhat as an Ethiopian's teeth, in respect of which he is said to be white, can stay white even after they have been extracted.[h]

4. One holds up another in two ways. First, as a contrary, thus cold resists the action of heat: such an obstacle to activity is opposed to felicity. Secondly, in the manner of a deficiency, as when the thing arrested is not ready at every point: this is not opposed to its happiness, but to its completion on every count. And thus its separation from the body is said to retard the soul from pressing on with all its might to the sight of God, in the sense that it still wants its joy to overflow into the body, as is possible. And therefore so long as the soul enjoys God without its partner, its desire,

---

[e]The difficulty is faced in 1a. 89, 1. Vol. 12, ed. P. R. Durbin.

[f]Literal translation: 'A part of a line has another *esse* than the whole line.' The example illustrates the argument; there is no need to flog the question of the existence of such entities.

[g]A disembodied soul is said to be complete with respect to substance, not to specific nature, *ratione substantialitatis*, not *ratione speciei*. cf 1a. 75, 2 & 6.

[h]An arch scholastic joke? In fact a stock example of *per accidens* predication.

quod habet, quod tamen adhuc ad participationem ejus vellet suum corpus pertingere.

5. Ad quintum dicendum quod desiderium animæ separatæ totaliter quiescit ex parte appetibilis, quia scilicet habet id quod suo appetitui sufficit. Sed non totaliter requiescit ex parte appetentis, quia illud bonum non possidet secundum omnem modum quo possidere vellet. Et ideo, corpore resumpto, beatitudo crescit non intensive, sed extensive.

6. Ad sextum dicendum quod id quod ibidem dicitur, quod *spiritus defunctorum non sic vident Deum sicut angeli*,[14] non est intelligendum secundum inæqualitatem quantitatis: quia etiam modo aliquæ animæ beatorum sunt assumptæ ad superiores ordines angelorum, clarius videntes Deum quam inferiores angeli. Sed intelligitur secundum inæqualitatem proportionis: quia angeli, etiam infimi, habent omnem perfectionem beatitudinis quam sunt habituri, non autem animæ separatæ sanctorum.

articulus 6. utrum ad beatitudinem requiratur aliqua perfectio corporis

AD SEXTUM sic proceditur:[1] 1. Videtur quod perfectio corporis non requiratur at beatitudinem hominis perfectam. Perfectio enim corporis est quoddam corporale bonum. Sed supra ostensum est[2] quod beatitudo non consistit in corporalibus bonis. Ergo ad beatitudinem hominis non requiritur aliqua perfecta dispositio corporis.

2. Præterea, beatitudo hominis consistit in visione divinæ essentiæ, ut ostensum est.[3] Sed ad hanc operationem nihil exhibet corpus, ut dictum est.[4] Ergo nulla dispositio corporis requiritur ad beatitudinem.

3. Præterea, quanto intellectus est magis abstractus a corpore tanto perfectius intelligit. Sed beatitudo consistit in perfectissima operatione intellectus. Ergo oportet omnibus modis animam esse abstractam a corpore. Nullo ergo modo requiritur aliqua dispositio corporis ad beatitudinem.

SED CONTRA, præmium virtutis est beatitudo: unde dicitur *Joan.*,[5] *Beati eritis, si feceritis ea.* Sed sanctis repromittitur pro præmio non solum visio Dei et delectatio, sed etiam corporis bona dispositio: dicitur enim *Isaiæ*,[6] *Videbitis, et gaudebit cor vestrum, et ossa vestra quasi herba germinabunt.* Ergo bona dispositio corporis requiritur ad beatitudinem.

RESPONSIO: Dicendum quod, si loquamur de beatitudine hominis qualis in hac vita potest haberi, manifestum est quod ad eam ex necessitate requiritur bona dispositio corporis. Consistit enim hæc beatitudo, secundum Philosophum,[7] *in operatione virtutis perfectæ.* Manifestum est autem quod per

---

[14]Augustine *loc. cit*   [1]cf 3a. 15, 10. IV *Sent.* 49, 4, 5, ii
[2]1a2æ. 2, 5   [3]1a2æ. 3, 8   [4] art. 5

though at rest with what it has, still longs for the body to enter in and share.

5. Desire in a disembodied soul is wholly at rest on the part of the object loved, for it possesses what contents it. Yet not on the part of the subject desiring, for the good is not possessed in every manner that can be wished for. Hence when the body is reassumed happiness will grow, not in depth but in extent.[1]

6. The statement, *that the spirits of the dead do not see God as the angels do*,[14] is to be read, not according to an inequality of amount, for even now some blessed souls are raised to the higher orders of angels and see God more clearly than do the lower orders, but according to an inequality of proportion, for angels, even the lowest, have every perfection of happiness they ever will have, whereas this is not the case with the blessed souls of the departed.[j]

article 6. does happiness require some perfection of body?

THE SIXTH POINT:[1] 1. Apparently not.[a] For perfection of body is a bodily good, and we have decided that happiness is not centred there.[2] And consequently does not require some perfect disposition of body.

2. Moreover, we have agreed that man's happiness is seeing the divine essence,[3] an activity to which the body contributes nothing.[4] Hence no quality of body is needed for happiness.

3. Further, the more detached it is from body the better a mind understands. Happiness is the best activity of mind, and therefore requires complete detachment of soul in every way. Consequently no disposition of body is needed at all.

ON THE OTHER HAND, happiness is the reward of virtue; *You shall be blessed if you do these things.*[5] Now the saints are promised, not only the sight of God and joy with him, but also health of body: thus in *Isaiah*, *You shall see and your heart shall rejoice, and your bones will be clothed like grass.*[6]

REPLY: If we are speaking of the happiness open to us in this life, then manifestly health of body is postulated. For such happiness lies, as Aristotle says,[7] *in the activity of full virtue*, and certainly ill-health can put a stop to this altogether.

---

[5]*John* 13, 17   [6]*Isaiah* 66, 14   [7]*Ethics* I, 13. 1102a5
[1]A retractation of IV *Sent.* 49, 1, 4, i. For intensive and extensive growth. cf 1a2æ. 52, 1–2; 53, 2. Vol. 22, ed. A. Kenny.
[j]cf 1a. 93, 3. Vol. 13, ed. E. Hill.
[a]This article takes a tack against the preceding article.

invaletudinem corporis, in omni operatione virtutis homo impediri potest.

Sed si loquamur de beatitudine perfecta, sic quidam posuerunt quod non requiritur ad beatitudinem aliqua corporis dispositio: immo requiritur ad eam ut omnino anima sit a corpore separata. Unde Augustinus[8] introducit verba Porphyrii dicentis quod *ad hoc quod beata sit anima, omne corpus fugiendum est.*

Sed hoc est inconveniens. Cum enim naturale sit animæ corpori uniri, non potest esse quod perfectio animæ naturalem ejus perfectionem excludat.

Et ideo dicendum est quod ad beatitudinem omnibus modis perfectam, requiritur perfecta dispositio corporis et antecedenter et consequenter. Antecedenter quidem, quia, ut Augustinus dicit,[9] *Si tale sit corpus, cujus sit difficilis et gravis administratio, sicut caro quæ corrumpitur et aggravat animam, avertitur mens ab illa visione summi cæli.* Unde concludit quod *cum hoc corpus jam non erit animale, sed spirituale, tunc angelis adæquabitur, et erit ei ad gloriam quod sarcinæ fuit.* Consequenter vero, quia ex beatitudine animæ fiet redundantia ad corpus, ut et ipsum sua perfectione potiatur. Unde Augustinus dicit,[10] *Tam potenti natura Deus fecit animam, ut ex ejus plenissima beatitudine redundet in inferiorem naturam incorruptionis vigor.*

1. Ad primum ergo dicendum quod in corporali bono non consistit beatitudo sicut in objecto beatitudinis, sed corporale bonum potest facere ad aliquem beatitudinis decorem vel perfectionem.

2. Ad secundum dicendum quod, etsi corpus nihil conferat ad illam operationem intellectus qua Dei essentia videtur, tamen posset ab hac impedire. Et ideo requiritur perfectio corporis, ut non impediat elevationem mentis.

3. Ad tertium dicendum quod ad perfectam operationem intellectus requiritur quidem abstractio ab hoc corruptibili corpore, quod aggravat animam; non autem a corpore spirituali, quod erit totaliter spiritui subjectum, de quo in *Tertia Parte* hujus operis dicetur.[11]

articulus 7. utrum ad beatitudinem requirantur aliqua exteriora bona

AD SEPTIMUM sic proceditur:[1] 1. Videtur quod ad beatitudinem requirantur etiam exteriora bona. Quod enim in præmium sanctis promittitur, ad beatitudinem pertinet. Sed sanctis repromittuntur exteriora bona, sicut cibus

[8]*De civit. Dei* XXII, 26. PL 41, 794   [9]*Super Genes. ad litt.* XII. 35. PL 34, 483
[10]*Epist.* CXVIII, 3. *Ad Dioscurum.* PL 33, 439   [11]*Supplementum* 82
[1]cf 2a2æ. 186, 3 ad 4. 3a. 15, 10 ad 2
[b]So falling into an occupational hazard for mystical writers.
[c]Porphyry (b. 233), a Palestinian. A disciple and editor of Plotinus. His treatise against the Christian religion was publicly destroyed by order of the Emperor Theodosius.

But if we are speaking of complete happiness, then it may be recalled how some have maintained that no disposition of body is called for; indeed they go further and hold that the soul should be quite detached from the body.[b] Augustine cites Porphyry,[c] *for the soul to be happy it should be severed from everything corporeal.*[8]

How odd this is. For since it is natural for the soul to be united to the body how is it credible that the perfection of the one should exclude the perfection of the other?

Let us declare, then, that happiness complete and entire requires the well-being of the body, both before and during its activity. It is an antecedent condition because, and we quote Augustine,[9] *if the body be such that its governance is difficult and burdensome, like unto the flesh which sickens and weighs upon the soul, then the mind is turned away from that far vision in high heaven.* He concludes that *when the body will no longer be animal but spiritual, then it will match the angels, and that will be glory which erstwhile was a carcass.* Bodily well-being, then, is a consequent condition, for happiness of soul overflows into body, which drinks of the fulness of soul.[d] Hence Augustine says,[10] *God made soul of so potent a nature that from its brimming happiness the strength of incorruption flows into lower nature.*

Hence: 1. Happiness is not centred on bodily good as its object, but can be endowed with a certain glow and beauty by it.

2. Even though the body contributes nothing to that activity of mind which sees God's essence, it could prove a drag. And therefore its perfection is required so as not to encumber the mind's ascent.

3. Complete activity of mind calls for a certain detachment from this corruptible body which burdens the soul, but not from the immortal body which will be completely responsive to spirit,[e] a topic we shall discuss in *Tertia Pars.*[11]

article 7. does happiness require external goods?

THE SEVENTH POINT:[1] 1. So it seems. All that is promised the saints is part of happiness. External goods are included, such as food and drink, riches and a kingdom. Thus the Gospel texts: *That you might eat and drink at my*

---

[d]The complete possession of body by spirit, cf *CG* IV, 86. For the four conditions of the glorified body, invulnerability, *impassibilitas,* lightsomeness, *subtilitas,* radiance, *claritas,* and lissomeness, *agilitas,* see *Supplementum* 82–85. For the dowries, *dotes,* of the blessed, op cit 95. For the condition of original rightness in which human nature was created, cf Vol. 26 of this series, ed. T. C. O'Brien.

[e]St Thomas's reading of the Pauline contrast between the spiritual and the animal body. He died before he could finish the *Tertia Pars;* the reference is to its supplement, compiled from his commentary on the *Sentences.*

et potus, divitiæ et regnum: dicitur enim *Luc.*,[2] *Ut edatis et bibatis super mensam meam in regno meo*; et *Matt.*,[3] *Thesaurizate vobis thesauros in cælo*; et *Matt.*,[4] *Venite, benedicti Patris mei, possidete regnum.* Ergo ad beatitudinem requiruntur exteriora bona.

2. Præterea, secundum Boëtium,[5] beatitudo est *status omnium bonorum aggregatione perfectus.* Sed exteriora sunt aliqua hominis bona, licet minima, ut Augustinus dicit.[6] Ergo ipsa etiam requiruntur ad beatitudinem.

3. Præterea, Dominus, *Matt.*[7] dicit, *Merces vestra multa est in cælis.* Sed esse in cælis significat esse in loco. Ergo saltem locus exterior requiritur ad beatitudinem.

SED CONTRA est quod dicitur in *Psalmo,*[8] *Quid enim mihi est in cælo? Et a te quid volui super terram?* Quasi dicat, Nihil aliud volo nisi hoc quod sequitur, *Mihi adhærere Deo bonum est.* Ergo nihil aliud exterius ad beatitudinem requiritur.

RESPONSIO: Dicendum quod ad beatitudinem imperfectam, qualis in hac vita potest haberi, requiruntur exteriora bona, non quasi de essentia beatitudinis existentia, sed quasi instrumentaliter deservientia beatitudini, quæ consistit in operatione virtutis, ut dicitur in *Ethic.*[9] Indiget enim homo in hac vita necessariis corporis tam ad operationem virtutis contemplativæ quam etiam ad operationem virtutis activæ, ad quam etiam plura alia requiruntur, quibus exerceat opera activæ virtutis.

Sed ad beatitudinem perfectam, quæ in visione Dei consistit, nullo modo hujusmodi bona requiruntur. Cujus ratio est quia omnia hujusmodi bona exteriora vel requiruntur ad sustentationem animalis corporis; vel requiruntur ad aliquas operationes quas per animale corpus exercemus, quæ humanæ vitæ conveniunt. Illa autem perfecta beatitudo quæ in visione Dei consistit, vel erit in anima sine corpore, vel erit in anima corpori unita non jam animali, sed spirituali. Et ideo nullo modo hujusmodi exteriora bona requiruntur ad illam beatitudinem, cum ordinentur ad vitam animalem.

Et quia in hac magis accedit ad similitudinem illius perfectæ beatitudinis felicitas contemplativa quam activa, utpote etiam Deo similior, ut ex dictis patet,[10] ideo minus indiget hujusmodi bonis corporis, ut dicitur in *Ethic.*[11]

1. Ad primum ergo dicendum quod omnes illæ corporales promissiones quæ in sacra Scriptura continentur sunt metaphorice intelligendæ, secundum quod in Scripturis solent spiritualia per corporalia designari, *ut ex his quæ novimus, ad desiderandum incognita consurgamus,* sicut Gregorius dicit in quadam homilia.[12] Sicut per cibum et potum intelligitur delectatio

---

[2]*Luke* 22, 30   [3]*Matthew* 6, 20   [4]*Matthew* 25, 34   [5]*De consol.* III, 2. PL 63, 724

table in my kingdom.[2] *Lay up to yourselves treasure in heaven.*[3] *Come, ye blessed of my Father, possess the kingdom.*[4] External goods, then, are part of happiness.

2. Moreover, Boethius describes happiness as a state made complete by the accumulation of all goods.[5] Augustine notes[6] that among human blessings, although the least, come possessions.[a] And so they come into happiness.

3. Further, our Lord told his disciples, *Your reward is very great in heaven.*[7] To be in heaven is to be in a place. Therefore to have a place, which after all is outside us, is an element in happiness.

ON THE OTHER HAND there is the *Psalm,*[8] *For what have I in heaven? And what besides thee do I desire on earth?* As though to say, I desire nothing but what follows, *For me to cleave to God is good.* And so no external possessions are needed for happiness.

REPLY: External goods are required for the imperfect happiness open to us in this life, not that they lie at the heart of happiness, yet they are tools to serve happiness which lies, says Aristotle,[9] in the activity of virtue. Ownership of them is required in order to lead a life of contemplative virtue, and of active virtue as well, particularly the last, which calls for many more.

Nowise are they needed for the perfect happiness of seeing God. We need them now to support our animal bodies or to exercise the physical functions proper to our condition. Perfect happiness, however, is for a soul without a body or a soul united to a body which is no longer animal but spiritual.

And in this life as we draw nearer to it by the felicity of the contemplative life rather than of the active life, and grow more like God, as we have stated,[10] so do we become less dependent, as noted in the *Ethics,*[11] on these external bodily goods.[b]

Hence: 1. All material promises of this sort, recorded in holy Scripture, are to be taken metaphorically, in accordance with its style of symbolizing spiritual by earthly realities,[c] so that, as a homily by Gregory puts it,[12] *from the things known to us we may be lifted up to things unknown.* Food and drink signify the delight of beatitude; riches, the abundance with which we

---

[6]*De lib. arbit.* II, 19. PL 32, 1267   [7]*Matthew* 5, 12
[8]*Psalms* 72, 25 & 28   [9]*Ethics* I, 13. 1102a5
[10]1a2æ. 3, 5 ad 1   [11]*Ethics* X, 8. 1178b1   [12]*In Evang.* II, 11. PL 76, 1114
[a]e.g. a horse, a dog, a boat, a garden of one's own.
[b]The argument is consistent and severe; the replies to the objections are less unbending.   [c]cf 1a, 1, 9. Vol. I.

beatitudinis, per divitias sufficientia qua homini sufficiet Deus, per regnum exaltatio hominis usque ad conjunctionem cum Deo.

2. Ad secundum dicendum quod bona ista deservientia animali vitæ non competunt vitæ spirituali in qua beatitudo perfecta consistit. Et tamen erit in illa beatitudine omnium bonorum congregatio, quia quidquid boni invenitur in istis totum habebitur in summo fonte bonorum.

3. Ad tertium dicendum quod, secundum Augustinum,[13] merces sanctorum non dicitur esse in corporeis cælis; sed per cælos intelligitur altitudo spiritualium bonorum. Nihilominus tamen locus corporeus, scilicet cælum empyreum, aderit beatis, non propter necessitatem beatitudinis, sed secundum quandam congruentiam et decorem.

articulus 8. *utrum ad beatitudinem requiratur societas amicorum*

AD OCTAVUM sic proceditur: 1. Videtur quod amici sint necessarii ad beatitudinem. Futura enim beatitudo in Scripturis frequenter nomine *gloriæ* designatur. Sed gloria consistit in hoc quod bonum hominis ad notitiam multorum deducitur. Ergo ad beatitudinem requiritur societas amicorum.

2. Præterea, Boëtius dicit quod *nullius boni sine consortio jucunda est possessio.*[1] Sed ad beatitudinem requiritur delectatio. Ergo etiam requiritur societas amicorum.

3. Præterea, caritas in beatitudine perficitur. Sed caritas se extendit ad dilectionem Dei et proximi. Ergo videtur quod ad beatitudinem requiratur societas amicorum.

SED CONTRA est quod dicitur Sap.,[2] *Venerunt mihi omnia bona pariter cum illa*, scilicet cum divina sapientia, quæ consistit in contemplatione Dei. Et sic ad beatitudinem nihil aliud requiritur.

RESPONSIO: Dicendum quod, si loquamur de felicitate præsentis vitæ, sicut Philosophus dicit,[3] felix indiget amicis, non quidem propter utilitatem, cum sit sibi sufficiens; nec propter delectationem, quia habet in seipso delectationem perfectam in operatione virtutis; sed propter bonam operationem, ut scilicet eis benefaciat, et ut eos inspiciens benefacere delectetur, et ut etiam ab eis in benefaciendo adjuvetur. Indiget enim homo ad bene operandum auxilio amicorum, tam in operibus vitæ activæ quam in operibus vitæ contemplativæ.

---

[13]*De serm. Dom. in monte* I, 5. PL 34, 1237   [1]Seneca, *Ad Lucilium epist.* 6
[2]*Wisdom* 7, 11   [3]*Ethics* IX, 9. 1169b22
[a]The empyrean heaven, the sphere of fire or highest heaven. 'Go soar with Plato to th' empyreal sphere.' Pope. Since bodies must have some sort of location the

are satisfied by God; the kingdom, the dignity to which we are raised by union with God.

2. The temporal possessions serving our animal life do not belong to the life of the spirit in which perfect happiness is found. Nevertheless all these benefits will be gathered there, for whatever good they manifest is contained in the high fount whence all and each of them flow.

3. According to Augustine,[13] the rewards of the saints are not laid up in the physical heavens, for by heaven is understood the height of spiritual good. Nevertheless the blessed will dwell in space, and the empyrean heaven will be appointed for them, not because beatitude demands it, but because it is fitting and handsome.[d]

article 8. does happiness call for the companionship of friends?

THE EIGHTH POINT: 1. It seems that friends are needed for happiness.[a] For often the Scriptures give to future happiness the name of glory, and this consists in a man's worth being recognized by many. Therefore happiness is necessarily social.

2. Besides, Boethius[b] remarks[1] that no possession of good is joyful without companionship. And happiness requires joy. And therefore companionship.

3. Again, charity, which is crowned by happiness, goes out to God and our neighbour. Happiness, then, demands the companionship of friends.

ON THE OTHER HAND, in *Wisdom*[2] it is written, *All good things come to me in her train*, that is, they come with divine wisdom which consists in contemplating God. And this is enough for beatitude.

REPLY: If we speak of present-life happiness and agree with Aristotle,[3] then the happy man must have friends. It is not that he makes use of them, since he is self-contained, or because he finds them pleasant, since he finds his pleasure in the activity of virtue, but that he needs them in order that he may act well, namely that he may do them good, that he may take delight in seeing them do good, and also that they may help him in his good works, for he needs their support in both the active and the contemplative life.

---

medievals thought of the empyreum as suitable for the blessed, yet they were well aware that they were going mainly on the authority of Strabo and the Venerable Bede. cf 1a. 66, 3. Vol. 10, ed. W. A. Wallace.

[a]The reader may well feel that this article marks a relapse into a primness of the *Nicomachean Ethics*. However a more generous ideal will reappear with the communication of the faithful in God's friendship, 2a2æ. 23, 1 & 5; 25, 1 & 12.

[b]Seneca, *Nullius boni, sine socio, jucunda possessio est.*

Sed si loquamur de perfecta beatitudine quæ erit in patria, non requiritur societas amicorum de necessitate ad beatitudinem, quia homo habet totam plenitudinem suæ perfectionis in Deo. Sed ad bene esse beatitudinis facit societas amicorum. Unde Augustinus dicit[4] quod *creatura spiritualis, ad hoc quod beata sit, non nisi intrinsecus adjuvatur æternitate, veritate, caritate Creatoris. Extrinsecus vero, si adjuvari dicenda est, fortasse hoc solo adjuvatur, quod invicem vident, et de sua societate gaudent in Deo.*

1. Ad primum ergo dicendum quod gloria quæ est essentialis beatitudini est quam habet homo non apud hominem, sed apud Deum.

2. Ad secundum dicendum quod verbum illud intelligitur, quando in eo bono quod habetur non est plena sufficientia. Quod in proposito dici non potest; quia omnis boni sufficientiam habet homo in Deo.

3. Ad tertium dicendum quod perfectio caritatis est essentialis beatitudini quantum ad dilectionem Dei, non autem quantum ad dilectionem proximi. Unde si esset una sola anima fruens Deo beata esset, non habens proximum quem diligeret. Sed supposito proximo, sequitur dilectio ejus ex perfecta dilectione Dei. Unde quasi concomitanter se habet amicitia ad beatitudinem perfectam.

---

[4] *Super Genes. ad litt.* VIII, 25. PL 34, 391

If, however, we speak of perfect happiness in our heavenly home, then companionship with other human beings is not strictly necessary, since a man is wholly and completely fulfilled in God. Nevertheless friends add a well-being to happiness. And so Augustine reflects[4] that *spiritual creatures receive no other interior aid to happiness than the eternity, truth, and friendship of the Creator. And if they can be said to be helped from without, perhaps it is only because they see one another, and rejoice in God at their companionship together.*

Hence: 1. Glory before God, not before man, is essential happiness.

2. The passage cited refers to a condition when the blessings present are not entirely sufficient. It is not relevant to the present inquiry, for a man has a sufficiency of every good in God.

3. The flowering of charity into beatitude essentially corresponds to our loving choice of God, not of our neighbour.[c] Were there but one single soul enjoying God it would be happy though without a neighbour to love. But granted neighbours, our loving choice of them results from our full loving of God. Consequently these friendships go along, as it were, with perfect happiness.

---

[c]*Dilectio*, late Latin from *diligo*, hence *diligens*. The principal act of charity, 2a2æ. 27

Quæstio 5. de adeptione beatitudinis

DEINDE CONSIDERANDUM EST de ipsa adeptione beatitudinis. Et circa hoc quæruntur octo:

1. utrum homo possit consequi beatitudinem;
2. utrum unus homo possit esse alio beatior;
3. utrum aliquis possit esse in hac vita beatus;
4. utrum beatitudo habita possit amitti;
5. utrum homo per sua naturalia possit acquirere beatitudinem;
6. utrum homo consequatur beatitudinem per actionem alicujus superioris creaturæ;
7. utrum requirantur opera hominis aliqua ad hoc quod homo beatitudinem consequatur a Deo.
8. utrum omnis homo appetat beatitudinem.

articulus 1. *utrum homo possit consequi beatitudinem*

AD PRIMUM sic proceditur:[1] 1. Videtur quod homo beatitudinem adipisci non possit. Sicut enim natura rationalis est supra sensibilem ita natura intellectualis est supra rationalem ut patet per Dionysium in multis locis.[2] Sed bruta animalia, quæ habent naturam sensibilem tantum, non possunt pervenire ad finem rationalis naturæ. Ergo nec homo, qui est rationalis naturæ, potest pervenire ad finem intellectualis naturæ, qui est beatitudo.

2. Prætera, beatitudo vera consistit in visione Dei, qui* est veritas pura. Sed homini est connaturale ut veritatem intueatur in rebus materialibus: unde *species intelligibiles in phantasmatibus intelligit*, ut dicitur in *De Anima*.[3] Ergo non potest ad beatitudinem pervenire.

3. Præterea, beatitudo consistit in adeptione summi boni. Sed aliquis non potest pervenire ad summum, nisi transcendat media. Cum igitur inter Deum et naturam humanam media sit natura angelica, quam homo transcendere non potest; videtur quod non possit beatitudinem adipisci.

SED CONTRA est quod dicitur in *Psalmo*,[4] *Beatus homo quem tu erudieris, Domine.*

RESPONSIO: Dicendum quod beatitudo nominat adeptionem perfecti boni. Quicumque ergo est capax perfecti boni potest ad beatitudinem pervenire. Quod autem homo perfecti boni sit capax ex hoc apparet, quia et ejus intellectus apprehendere† potest universale et perfectum bonum, et ejus

---

*Piana: *quæ*, referring to the vision   †Piana: *comprehendere*, to comprehend
[1]cf CG III, 25

Question 5. gaining happiness

UNDER THIS HEADING there are eight points for inquiry:

1. whether a human being can attain happiness;
2. whether one can be happier than another;
3. whether anybody can be happy in this life;
4. whether happiness once gained can be lost;
5. whether a man can acquire happiness from his natural resources;
6. whether he reaches happiness from being acted on by some higher creature;
7. whether he must do something himself in order to gain happiness from God;
8. whether everybody desires happiness.

article 1. can a human being attain happiness?

THE FIRST POINT:[1] 1. It seems that happiness is beyond us. For as rational is above sentient nature, so is intellectual above rational nature: Dionysius draws the analogy in many places.[2] The beasts with their sentient nature cannot reach the development of rational nature. No more can men, with their rational nature, reach the final stage of intellectual nature, which is beatitude.

2. Moreover, true happiness consists in seeing God who is pure truth. Now human nature is adapted to seeing truth embodied in material things; the *De Anima* says that we form intelligible meanings in images of sense.[3] And so we cannot arrive at true happiness.

3. Further, happiness means scaling the peak of good, and this means climbing the intermediate stages. Since we cannot climb above angelic nature, which is midway between God and human nature, it would seem that we cannot gain the summit of happiness.

ON THE OTHER HAND there is the verse of the *Psalms*, *Happy the man whom thou, O Lord, shalt instruct.*[4]

REPLY: Happiness means gaining perfect good. Now whoever has the capacity for this good can be brought to bliss. That man has the capacity appears from the fact that his mind can apprehend good which is universal

---

[2]*De div. nom.* 4. PG 3, 693. cf 696, 856, 868
[3]*De Anima* III, 7. 431b2
[4]*Psalms* 93, 12

voluntas appetere illud. Et ideo homo potest beatitudinem adipisci. Apparet etiam idem ex hoc quod homo est capax visionis divinæ essentiæ, sicut in *Primo*[5] habitum est; in qua quidem visione perfectam hominis beatitudinem consistere diximus.[6]

1. Ad primum ergo dicendum quod aliter excedit natura rationalis sensitivam, et aliter intellectualis rationalem. Natura enim rationalis excedit sensitivam quantum ad cognitionis objectum; quia sensus nullo modo potest cognoscere universale, cujus ratio est cognoscitiva. Sed intellectualis natura excedit rationalem quantum ad modum cognoscendi eandem intelligibilem veritatem.

Nam intellectualis natura statim apprehendit veritatem, ad quam rationalis natura per inquisitionem rationis pertingit, ut patet ex his quæ in *Primo* dicta sum.[7] Et ideo ad id quod intellectus apprehendit, ratio per quendam motum pertingit. Unde rationalis natura consequi potest beatitudinem, quæ est perfectio intellectualis naturæ, tamen alio modo quam angeli. Nam angeli consecuti sunt eam statim post principium suæ conditionis;* homines autem per tempus ad ipsam perveniunt. Sed natura sensitiva ad hunc finem nullo modo pertingere potest.

2. Ad secundum dicendum quod homini, secundum statum præsentis vitæ, est connaturalis modus cognoscendi veritatem intelligibilem per phantasmata. Sed post hujus vitæ statum, habet alium modum connaturalem, ut in *Primo* dictum est.[8]

3. Ad tertium dicendum quod homo non potest transcendere angelos gradu naturæ, ut scilicet naturaliter sit eis superior. Potest tamen eos transcendere per operationem intellectus, dum intelligit aliquid super angelos esse quod homines beatificat; quod cum perfecte consequetur perfecte beatus erit.

---

*Piana: *cognitionis*, of their knowledge

[5] 1a. 12, 1
[6] 1a2ae. 3, 8
[7] 1a. 58, 3; 79, 8
[8] 1a. 84, 7; 89, 1

[a]The question has already been broached, 1a2æ, 3, 8. But how can a desire welling up from man's nature really reach to the supernatural? A long-felt difficulty, and the controversies surrounding it have been touched off anew in recent years. cf H. de Lubac, *Le surnaturel*, Paris, 1946. But see Appendix 5.

Some guide-lines may be quickly stated. First, a Christian theologian is dealing with the happiness promised us by God in the historic plan of Providence: natural beatitude is for him an academic question. Second, the present article proposes to show only the possibility of the divine vision for us, not the fact, from natural desire. Third, the term 'natural' has at least two meanings; one refers to the constitution of

and unrestricted and his will can desire it. Therefore he is open to receive it.

Moreover, we have shown in the *Prima Pars*[5] that he is able to see the divine essence, in which, as we have defined,[6] his complete happiness lies.[a]

Hence: 1. While rational exceeds sentient nature as intellectual exceeds rational nature, the grounds of comparison shift when we come to the present question. Rational surpasses sentient nature with respect to the object it can reach, for reason can know the universal, which sense cannot know at all. Whereas intellectual surpasses rational nature with respect to the mode of knowing, but not to the object.[b] Let me explain.

We have shown in the *Prima Pars*[7] how an intellectual nature lights on a truth straightway which a rational nature has to approach by reasoning about it. For one there is insight, for the other a discourse. And so a rational being can reach the happiness which is the perfection of a pure intelligence, though the manner is not the same. For angels gain it immediately after their beginning in nature and grace, whereas men come through to it in time.[c] In no way, however, can sentient nature arrive at this goal.

2. Under the conditions of the present life the connatural mode for the human perception of intelligible truth is through images of sense. After this life another mode of knowing, which we have examined in the *Prima Pars*,[8] will be connatural.

3. In the hierarchy of beings men cannot surpass the angels, who by nature are of higher order. Yet a man can pass beyond them in his knowing, as when he understands there is a being above them who can make him blessed and when quite possessed will give complete bliss.

---

a thing at the level of its species, the other to the principle of movement from within. Thus the life of grace is supernatural to man according to the first meaning, but not according to the second. But cf Vol. 1 of this series, Appendix 8, *Natural and Supernatural.*

The capacity of human nature to be acted on by grace and to receive the beatific vision is known as obediential potentiality. See 2a2æ. 2, 3; 3a. 11, 1; and Glossary.
[b]The proper object of the human mind in its present state is said to be the essences of material things, in other words to know what's what in the world about us. cf 1a. 85 & 86. But this present proper object does not constitute the adequate object of the mind.

Note again the stress on the object of an act, not on its category according to created reality, or mode of knowing. cf 1a2æ. 2, 8, note *e*; 3, 1, note *d*.
[c]For the angels there was one dramatic test. cf 1a. 62, 5; 63, 4 & 5. Vol. 9, ed. K. Foster. St Thomas recognizes the restlessness of the human will, its 'vertibility', and is accordingly not inclined to be crisis-minded. 'Divine justice does not treat men who still have their course to run as though they had finished.' *Compend. Theol.* 145.

articulus 2. utrum unus homo possit esse beatior altero

AD SECUNDUM sic proceditur:[1] 1. Videtur quod unus homo alio non possit esse beatior. Beatitudo enim est *præmium virtutis*, ut Philosophus dicit.[2] Sed pro operibus virtutum omnibus æqualis merces redditur: dicitur enim *Matt.*,[3] quod omnes qui operati sunt in vinea, *acceperunt singulos denarios; quia*, ut dicit Gregorius,[4] *æqualem æternæ vitæ retributionem sortiti sunt.* Ergo unus non erit alio beatior.

2. Præterea, beatitudo est summum bonum. Sed summo non potest esse aliquid majus. Ergo beatitudine unius hominis non potest esse alia major beatitudo.

3. Præterea, beatitudo, cum sit perfectum et sufficiens bonum desiderium hominis quietat. Sed non quietatur desiderium, si aliquod bonum deest quod suppleri possit: si autem nihil deest quod suppleri possit, non poterit esse aliquid aliud majus bonum. Ergo vel homo non est beatus, vel si est beatus non potest alia major beatitudo esse.

SED CONTRA est quod dicitur *Joann.*,[5] *In domo Patris mei mansiones multæ sunt*; per quas, ut Augustinus dicit,[6] *diversæ meritorum dignitates intelliguntur in vita æterna.* Dignitas autem vitæ æternæ, quæ pro merito datur, est ipsa beatitudo. Ergo sunt diversi gradus beatitudinis, et non omnium est æqualis beatitudo.

RESPONSIO: Dicendum quod, sicut supra dictum est,[7] in ratione beatitudinis duo includuntur, scilicet ipse finis ultimus, qui est summum bonum, et adeptio vel fruitio ipsius boni. Quantum igitur ad ipsum bonum quod est beatitudinis objectum et causa, non potest esse una beatitudo alia major: quia non est nisi unum summum bonum, scilicet Deus, cujus fruitione homines sunt beati. Sed quantum ad adeptionem hujusmodi boni vel fruitionem, potest aliquis alio esse beatior; quia quanto magis hoc bono fruitur tanto beatior est. Contingit autem aliquem perfectius frui Deo quam alium, ex eo quod est melius dispositus vel ordinatus ad ejus fruitionem. Et secundum hoc potest aliquis alio beatior esse.

1. Ad primum ergo dicendum quod unitas denarii significat unitatem beatitudinis ex parte objecti. Sed diversitas mansionum significat diversitatem beatitudinis secundum diversum gradum fruitionis.

2. Ad secundum dicendum quod beatitudo dicitur esse summum bonum, inquantum est summi boni perfecta possessio sive fruitio.

3. Ad tertium dicendum quod nulli beato deest aliquod bonum desiderandum: cum habeat ipsum bonum infinitum, quod est *bonum omnis*

---

[1]cf Ia2æ. 1, 7. *In Matt.* 20. *In Joann.* 14, *lect.* 1. *In* I *Cor.* 3, *lect.* 2. IV *Sent.* 49, 1, 4, ii

article 2. can one be happier than another?

THE SECOND POINT:[1] 1. It would seem not. According to Aristotle, happiness is *the reward of virtue*,[2] and for the works of virtue the recompense is equal. Recall the parable of the labourers in the vineyard *who received every man a penny*,[3] which, comments Gregory,[4] *signifies an equal return in eternal life*. Consequently, one man will not be happier than another.

2. Besides, beatitude is the highest good. And what can be higher than the highest? Therefore the beatitude of one cannot be higher than that of another.

3. Further, since it is complete and sufficient good, happiness brings man's desires to rest. This it would not do if some available good were still wanting: if nothing were wanting then, of course, there could be no other greater good. Either, then, a man is not happy, or if he is, then no other could be happier than he is.

ON THE OTHER HAND there is the Gospel saying, *In my Father's house there are many mansions*,[5] which for Augustine[6] signifies *the various dignities of merit in eternal life*. The worth of eternal life, granted in reward, lies in the happiness itself, and this, therefore, admits of various degrees, and is not equal in every case.

REPLY: We have explained how there are two sides to happiness, the objective ultimate end, which is the sovereign good, and the gaining and enjoying of it by the subject.[7] As for the first, the object and the cause of happiness, there is no variation in blessedness, for there is but one supreme good, namely God, and men are in bliss by their joy with him. As for the second, one can be more blessed than another, for the deeper his joy the more blessed he is. And in point of fact his joy can be deeper because he is more open and adapted to receive it.[a]

Hence: 1. The one penny symbolizes the unity of happiness with regard to its object, the many mansions its diversity with regard to the various degrees of enjoyment in its subjects.

2. Happiness is called the supreme good as being the complete possession or enjoyment of that.

3. None of the blessed wants for any good he can desire, since each has

---

[2]*Ethics* I, 9. 1099b16   [3]*Matthew* 20, 10   [4]*In Evang.* I, 19. PL 76, 1156
[5]*John* 14, 2   [6]*In Joann.* LXVII. *super* 14, 2. PL 35, 1812   [7]1a2æ. 1, 8; 2, 7
[a]The underlying philosophy here is of the greater and less, *magis et minus*, in analogical values. For the intensification of dispositions, see 1a2æ. 52, 1: they increase by a deepening possession by their subject, not by addition, by *intensionem* rather than by *extensionem*. Also 1a2æ. 66, 1. The deeper the power of loving, the greater the capacity for happiness, 2a2æ. 24, 4–6.

boni, ut Augustinus dicit.[8] Sed dicitur aliquis alio beatior, ex diversa ejusdem boni participatione. Additio autem aliorum bonorum non auget beatitudinem: unde Augustinus dicit,[9] *Qui te et alia novit, non propter illa beatior, sed propter te solum beatus*.

articulus 3. utrum aliquis in hac vita possit esse beatus

AD TERTIUM sic proceditur:[1] 1. Videtur quod beatitudo possit in hac vita haberi. Dicitur enim in *Psalmo*,[2] *Beati immaculati in via, qui ambulant in lege Domini*. Hoc autem in hac vita contingit. Ergo aliquis in hac vita potest esse beatus.

2. Præterea, imperfecta participatio summi boni non adimit rationem beatitudinis, alioquin unus non esset alio beatior. Sed in hac vita homines possunt participare summum bonum, cognoscendo et amando Deum, licet imperfecte. Ergo homo in hac vita potest esse beatus.

3. Præterea, quod a pluribus dicitur non potest totaliter falsum esse: videtur enim esse naturale quod in pluribus est; natura autem non totaliter deficit. Sed plures ponunt beatitudinem in hac vita, ut patet per illud *Psalmi*,[3] *Beatum dixerunt populum cui hæc sunt*, scilicet præsentis vitæ bona. Ergo aliquis in hac vita potest esse beatus.

SED CONTRA est quod dicitur *Job*,[4] *Homo natus de muliere, brevi vivens tempore, repletus multis miseriis*. Sed beatitudo excludit miseriam. Ergo homo in hac vita non potest esse beatus.

RESPONSIO: Dicendum quod aliqualis beatitudinis participatio in hac vita haberi potest: perfecta autem et vera beatitudo non potest haberi in hac vita. Et hoc quidem considerari potest dupliciter.

Primo quidem, ex ipsa communi beatitudinis ratione. Nam beatitudo, cum sit perfectum et sufficiens bonum, omne malum excludit, et omne desiderium implet. In hac autem vita non potest omne malum excludi. Multis enim malis præsens vita subjacet quæ vitari non possunt; et ignorantiæ ex parte intellectus, et inordinatæ affectioni ex parte appetitus, et multiplicibus poenalitatibus ex parte corporis; ut Augustinus diligenter prosequitur.[5] Similiter etiam desiderium boni in hac vita satiari non potest. Naturaliter enim homo desiderat permanentiam ejus boni quod habet. Bona autem præsentis vitæ transitoria sunt, cum et ipsa vita transeat, quam naturaliter desideramus, et eam perpetuo permanere vellemus, quia

---

[8]*Enarrat. in Psalm.* 114, 3. PL 37, 1741
[9]*Confessions* v, 4. PL 32, 708
[1]cf *CG* III, 48. *In Ethic.* I, lect. 10 & 16. IV *Sent.* 43, I, i; 49, I, I, iv.

the infinite good itself, which, in Augustine's phrase,[8] is *the good of every good*. But we call one more blessed than another from the degree of his sharing in this good. There is no question here of his receiving an additional good,[b] since this does not increase perfect happiness; Augustine declares,[9] *He who knows thee and other things as well is not the happier because of them, but is happy solely because of thee.*

article 3. can anybody in this life find bliss?

THE THIRD POINT:[1] 1. It seems possible. There is the verse from the *Psalms*,[2] *Blessed are the undefiled in the way, who walk in the law of the Lord.* They are met with in this life, where, accordingly, a man can be happy.

2. Moreover, a partial sharing in sheer good does not derogate from the notion of happiness, otherwise you could not use it as a standard of reference and speak of one being happier than another. Yet in this life we can share in the supreme good, by knowing and loving God, if imperfectly. Therefore we can be happy now.

3. Further, a view widely entertained cannot be an entire illusion, indeed the majority view seems to represent the natural course of things, for nature is not altogether ineffective.[a] And how many men place their happiness in this world, of whom the *Psalm* speaks,[3] *They have called the people blessed that hath these things*, namely the good things of the present life. Surely somebody can be happy in this world.

ON THE OTHER HAND there is *Job* saying,[4] *Man born of woman living for a short time is filled with many miseries.* But happiness drives out misery. And so man cannot be happy in this life.

REPLY: Some share of happiness can be reached now, but not true and complete happiness. Let us consider first what happiness means, and second, where in reality it lies.

The general notion of happiness, of goodness perfect and sufficient, implies that every ill is banished and every desire fulfilled. Neither is possible in this life. We are subject to many unavoidable ills. Augustine carefully sets them out:[5] ignorance in our mind, inordinate loves in our affections, and pains exacted of our body. Nor can our desire for good be satisfied. By nature we crave for security, yet how transitory are our blessings: life itself fades away, although our nature is always to hold on to

---

[2]*Psalms* 118, 1   [3]*Psalms* 143, 15   [4]*Job* 14, 1   [5]*De civ. Dei* XIX, 4. PL 41, 628
[b]For the medieval speculation about the accidental rewards of heaven, see *Supplementum* 96, *De aureolis.*
[a]The 'natural' is here taken as the normal: a statistical reading.

123

naturaliter homo refugit mortem. Unde impossibile est quod in hac vita vera beatitudo habeatur.

Secundo, si consideretur id in quo specialiter beatitudo consistit, scilicet visio divinæ essentiæ, quæ non potest homini provenire in hac vita, ut in *Primo* ostensum est.[6] Ex quibus manifeste apparet quod non potest aliquis in hac vita veram et perfectam beatitudinem adipisci.

1. Ad primum ergo dicendum quod beati dicuntur aliqui in hac vita, vel propter spem beatitudinis adipiscendæ in futura vita, secundum illud *Rom.*,[7] *Spe salvi facti sumus*: vel propter aliquam participationem beatitudinis, secundum aliqualem summi boni fruitionem.

2. Ad secundum dicendum quod participatio beatitudinis potest esse imperfecta dupliciter. Uno modo, ex parte ipsius objecti beatitudinis, quod quidem secundum sui essentiam non videtur. Et talis imperfectio tollit rationem veræ beatitudinis. Alio modo potest esse imperfecta ex parte ipsius participantis, qui quidem ad ipsum objectum beatitudinis secundum seipsum attingit, scilicet Deum, sed imperfecte, per respectum ad modum quo Deus seipso fruitur. Et talis imperfectio non tollit veram rationem beatitudinis: quia, cum beatitudo sit operatio quædam, ut supra dictum est,[8] vera ratio beatitudinis, consideratur ex objecto, quod dat speciem actui, non autem ex subjecto.

3. Ad tertium dicendum quod homines reputant in hac vita esse aliquam beatitudinem propter aliquam similitudinem veræ beatitudinis. Et sic non ex toto in sua æstimatione deficiunt.

articulus 4. *utrum beatitudo habita possit amitti*

AD QUARTUM sic proceditur:[1] 1. Videtur quod beatitudo possit amitti. Beatitudo enim est perfectio quædam. Sed omnis perfectio inest perfectibili secundum modum ipsius. Cum igitur homo secundum suam naturam sit mutabilis, videtur quod beatitudo mutabiliter ab homine participetur. Et ita videtur quod homo beatitudinem possit amittere.

2. Præterea, beatitudo consistit in actione intellectus, qui subjacet voluntati. Sed voluntas se habet ad opposita. Ergo videtur quod possit desistere ab operatione qua homo beatificatur: et ita homo desinet esse beatus.

3. Præterea, principio respondet finis. Sed beatitudo hominis habet principium: quia homo non semper fuit beatus. Ergo videtur quod habeat finem.

SED CONTRA est quod dicitur *Matt.*[2] de justis, quod *ibunt in vitam æternam*;

---

[6]Ia. 12, 2   [7]*Romans* 8, 24   [8]Ia2æ. 3, 2
[1]cf Ia. 64, 2; 94, 1. *CG* III, 62. I *Sent.* 7, 3, 2; IV, 49, 1, 1, iv. *In Joann.* 10, *lect.* 5. *Compend. Theol.* 166; II, 9

it, and shrink from death. Hence the possession of true happiness is not possible in this life.

Next, to consider where happiness lies, namely in the vision of God face to face. And this, as we have shown in the *Prima Pars*,[6] men cannot reach it in this life. And so, on both counts, it is manifest that none of us can gain true and complete happiness now.

Hence: 1. Men are called blessed in this life either because of their hope of gaining happiness in the future life—*By hope we are saved*[7]—or because of some snatch of happiness anticipating our joy in the supreme good.

2. Shared happiness can be incomplete on two sides. First, on that of the object itself of happiness: not seeing as it really is implies an incompleteness incompatible with true happiness. Second, on that of the sharer, who may indeed attain the very object of happiness, namely God himself, yet not of the manner of God's joy in himself. Such a non-completeness is not incompatible with true beatitude, for it is an activity, as we have already said,[8] and consequently its true nature is decided by the object which shapes it, not by the subject.[b]

3. Men are persuaded that some happiness can be found in the world now because of the reflections about us of true beatitude. Nor are they entirely out in their reckoning.

article 4. *once gained can happiness be lost?*

THE FOURTH POINT:[1] 1. It seems so.[a] For happiness is a quality of perfection, and a perfection endows its subject in the style of that subject. Since man's nature is mutable, it seems that he is not charged with happiness except mutably. Therefore he can lose it.

2. Moreover, happiness is an act of the mind which is subject to the will. Now the will can switch between opposites, and accordingly can desist from the activity which makes us happy. Therefore we can cease to be happy.

3. Besides, where there is a start there is a stop. But there is a start to happiness, for man was not always happy. It would seem, then, that it comes to a stop.[b]

ON THE OTHER HAND the Gospel says of the just that *they will go into life*

---

[2]*Matthew* 25, 46
[b]Again the subject-object antithesis. cf Foreword note *a*.
[a]Cajetan, *in loc*, observes that the inquiry is about the complete security or *inamissibilitas* of happiness, not its perpetuity. The first is a matter of immutability, the second of duration. cf 1a. 9 & 10 respectively.
[b]Happiness a creature of time, and all that begins in time ends in time.

quæ, ut dictum est,[3] est beatitudo sanctorum. Quod autem est æternum, non deficit. Ergo beatitudo non potest amitti.

RESPONSIO: Dicendum quod, si loquamur de beatitudinem imperfecta qualis in hac vita potest haberi, sic potest amitti. Et hoc patet in felicitate contemplativa, quæ amittitur vel per oblivionem, puta cum corrumpitur scientia ex aliqua ægritudine; vel etiam per aliquas occupationes quibus totaliter abstrahitur aliquis a contemplatione. Patet etiam idem in felicitate activa: voluntas enim hominis transmutari potest, ut in vitium degeneret a virtute, in cujus actu principaliter consistit felicitas. Si autem virtus remaneat integra, exteriores transmutationes possunt quidem beatitudinem talem perturbare, inquantum impediunt multas operationes virtutum: non tamen possunt eam totaliter auferre, quia adhuc remanet operatio virtutis, dum ipsas adversitates homo laudabiliter sustinet. Et quia beatitudo hujus vitæ amitti potest, quod videtur esse contra rationem beatitudinis; ideo Philosophus dicit[4] aliquos esse in hac vita beatos, non simpliciter, sed *sicut homines*, quorum natura mutationi subjecta est.

Si vero loquamur de beatitudine perfecta quæ expectatur post hanc vitam, sciendum est quod Origenes posuit,[5] quorundam Platonicorum errorem sequens, quod post ultimam beatitudinem homo potest fieri miser. Sed hoc manifeste apparet esse falsum dupliciter.

Primo quidem, ex ipsa communi ratione beatitudinis. Cum enim ipsa beatitudo sit *perfectum bonum et sufficiens*, oportet quod desiderium hominis quietet, et omne malum excludat. Naturaliter autem homo desiderat retinere bonum quod habet, et quod ejus retinendi securitatem obtineat: alioquin necesse est quod timore amittendi, vel dolore de certitudine amissionis, affligatur. Requiritur igitur ad veram beatitudinem quod homo certam habeat opinionem bonum quod habet nunquam se amissurum. Quæ quidem opinio si vera sit, consequens est quod beatitudinem nunquam amittet. Si autem falsa sit, hoc ipsum est quoddam malum, falsam opinionem habere: nam falsum est malum intellectus, sicut verum est bonum ipsius, ut dicitur in *Ethic.*[6] Non igitur jam vere erit beatus, si aliquod malum ei inest.

Secundo idem apparet, si consideretur ratio beatitudinis in specialis. Ostensum est enim supra[7] quod perfecta beatitudo hominis in visione divinæ essentiæ consistit. Est autem impossibile quod aliquis videns divinam essentiam velit eam non videre. Quia omne bonum habitum quo quis carere vult, aut est insufficiens, et quæritur aliquid sufficientius loco ejus, aut habet aliquod incommodum annexum, propter quod in fasti-

---

[3]art. 2 *sed contra*
[4]*Ethics* I, 10. 1101a19

everlasting,[2] which, as we have said,[3] is the beatitude of God's friends. What is eternal never falls away. Beatitude, consequently, cannot be lost.

REPLY: The partial happiness we can obtain now can be lost. This appears alike in contemplative felicity which can fall into oblivion, as when disease attacks consciousness, or it can be displaced by other occupations which can be completely absorbing and distracting. Active felicity, too, which consists mainly in the activity of virtue, can be lost when the will degenerates into vice. And even if virtue remains unimpaired, external changes can upset the happiness of the active life, at least by hindering good deeds, though they cannot take them away completely, since a man displays active virtue when he honourably sustains his adversities. It is because present happiness can be lost, which is incompatible with the nature of perfect happiness, that Aristotle speaks[4] of some men being happy, not downrightly, but *as men are,* whose nature is subject to change.

If, however, we are speaking of the perfect human happiness to which we look forward, then we may recall Origen's[c] view that a man may fall into misery after reaching final beatitude.[5] He was misled by certain Platonists.[d] How mistaken they were may be shown by two arguments, one from the abstract, the other from the concrete.

First, let us take the general notion of happiness, which signifies the complete and sufficient good. This should put our desires at peace and banish all evil. For it is our nature to want to hold on to the good we have and to be assured of keeping it, otherwise the threat or the fear of certain loss would cast us into sadness. Happiness demands the conviction that it will never forsake us. If this conviction is unfounded, this itself is an evil, namely of holding what is not true; to quote the *Ethics,*[6] for mind, the false is the bad as the true is the good. No man will be truly happy who labours under any evil.

Secondly, and to be more specific, we consider the realization of beatitude. It consists, as we have shown,[7] in seeing God just as he is. To gaze on him and to will not to see him is impossible. For a good that is possessed and is nevertheless relinquished is either found insufficient, so that something more satisfying is sought instead, or else has something wearisome about it, so that it becomes distasteful. Now by seeing God just as he is, the soul

---

[5]*Peri Archon.* I, 5 & 6. PG 11, 164 & 167. So read by Jerome, *Ep.* CXXIV, 2. PL 22, 1066. cf Augustine, *De civ. Dei* X, 30. PL 41, 309
[6]*Ethics* VI, 2. 1139a26   [7]1a2æ. 3, 8
[c]Origen (185–c. 254). That there should be an indefinite succession of falls and restorations seems to him a consequence of the endless succession of worlds.
[d]Or better, by certain Gnostics.

dium venit. Visio autem divinæ essentiæ replet animam omnibus bonis, cum conjungat fonti totius bonitatis: unde dicitur in *Psalmo*,[8] *Satiabor cum apparuerit gloria tua*; et *Sap.*,[9] *Venerunt mihi omnia bona pariter cum illa,* scilicet cum contemplatione sapientiæ. Similiter etiam non habet aliquod incommodum adjunctum: quia de contemplatione sapientiæ dicitur *Sap.*,[10] *Non habet amaritudinem conversatio illius,nec tædium convictus ejus.* Sic ergo patet quod propria voluntate beatus non potest beatitudinem deserere.

Similiter etiam non potest eam perdere, Deo subtrahente. Quia, cum subtractio beatitudinis sit quædam pœna, non potest talis subtractio a Deo, justo judice, provenire, nisi pro aliqua culpa: in quam cadere non potest qui Dei essentiam videt, cum ad hanc visionem ex necessitate sequatur rectitudo voluntatis, ut supra ostensum est.[11] Similiter etiam nec aliquod aliud agens potest eam subtrahere. Quia mens Deo conjuncta super omnia alia elevatur; et sic ab hujusmodi conjunctione nullum aliud agens potest ipsam excludere.

Unde inconveniens videtur quod per quasdam alternationes temporum transeat homo de beatitudine ad miseriam, et e converso: quia hujusmodi temporales alternationes esse non possunt, nisi circa ea quæ subjacent tempori et motui.

1. Ad primum ergo dicendum quod beatitudo est perfectio consummata, quæ omnem defectum excludit a beato. Et ideo absque mutabilitate advenit eam habenti, faciente hoc virtute divina, quæ hominem sublevat in participationem æternitatis transcendentis omnem mutationem.

2. Ad secundum dicendum quod voluntas ad opposita se habet in his quæ ad finem ordinantur: sed ad ultimum finem naturali necessitate ordinatur. Quod patet ex hoc, quod homo non potest non velle esse beatus.

3. Ad tertium dicendum quod beatitudo habet principium ex conditione participantis, sed caret fine, propter conditionem boni cujus participatio facit beatum. Unde ab alio est initium beatitudinis; et ab alio est quod caret fine.

articulus 5. utrum homo per sua naturalia possit acquirere beatitudinem

AD QUINTUM sic proceditur:[1] 1. Videtur quod homo per sua naturalia possit beatitudinem consequi. Natura enim non deficit in necessariis. Sed nihil est homini tam necessarium quam id per quod finem ultimum consequitur.

---

[8]*Psalms* 16, 15   [9]*Wisdom* 7, 11   [10]*Wisdom,* 8, 6   [11]Ia2æ. 4, 4
[1]cf Ia. 12, 4; 62, 1. Ia2æ. 62, 1. *CG* III, 52 & 147. III *Sent.* 27, 2, 2; IV, 49, 2, 6
[e]cf the eloquent foreword to *Opusc.* IX. Exposition *De hebdomadibus.*
[f]cf Ia2æ. 31, 2: on the note of eternity in all delight.
[g]Being unable to wish not to be happy, this would be a sufficient conclusion. St Thomas, however, prefers to be more sweeping.

is filled with every good; the vision unites us with the source of all good-ness: accordingly we read in the *Psalms*,[8] *I shall be satisfied with beholding thy form*; and in *Wisdom*,[9] *All good things came to me in her train*, that is, with divine wisdom when contemplated. Nor is any hint conveyed of boredom; *Her conversation hath no bitterness, nor her company any tedious-ness*.[10e] Manifestly nobody could give up such brimming happiness of his own accord.

Moreover it cannot be lost by God's withdrawal, for this would be a sort of penalty which God, our just judge, would not impose except because of fault, and a person who sees him face to face cannot fall, for, as we have seen,[11] rightness of will necessarily results from seeing him. Nor is there any outside agent who can intervene, for when so conjoined with God the mind is raised above all other things, and what force is there that can break the union?

So then it seems not at all credible that man should alternate between beatitude and misery, passing from one to another and back again, for such vicissitudes can affect creatures only of time and change.

Hence: 1. Beatitude is consummate perfection; it rules out every flaw, and thanks to divine power is granted without shadow of change, so that the blessed are lifted up and share in eternity transcending it.[f]

2. Though faced with opposites in decisions concerning objects which are meant for an end, the will has a bent towards the ultimate end from inborn necessity, as is evidenced by human beings being unable not to wish to be happy.[g]

3. Happiness has a beginning from the condition of the subject, but no ending from the condition of the object, and it is this when shared in which makes a person happy. And so there is one principle for beatitude starting off, another for its never coming to a stop.[h]

article 5. can a man come to happiness from his native resources?

THE FIFTH POINT:[1] 1. It would seem that he can.[a] For nature does not fail in necessaries. And what more necessary for a man than that he should find

---

[h]See cross-references in Foreword, note *a*.

[a]Man is not born to be happy: the statement is true if it refers merely to his native endowments, not true if it refers to what he is designed for under Providence. The paradox remains, however, that the last end for which we are born we can reach only through a divine and supernatural gift: Vatican I. Denz. 1786. Appendix 5.

The inquiry is not precisely whether we can deserve happiness, which is dealt with later, 1a2æ. 109, 5 & 114, 2, but whether the activity in which it consists can be exercised by our natural powers. For discussions on the ability of human nature to reach truth and goodness, see 1a2æ. 109, 1–4, 8 & 10.

Ergo hoc naturæ humanæ non deest. Potest igitur homo per sua naturalia beatitudinem consequi.

2. Præterea, homo, cum sit nobilior irrationalibus creaturis, videtur esse sufficientor. Sed irrationales creaturæ per sua naturalia possunt consequi suos fines. Ergo multo magis homo per sua naturalia potest beatitudinem consequi.

3. Præterea, beatitudo est *operatio perfecta*, secundum Philosophum.[2] Ejusdem autem est incipere rem et perficere ipsam. Cum igitur operatio imperfecta, quæ est quasi principium in operationibus humanis, subdatur naturali hominis potestati, qua suorum actuum est dominus; videtur quod per naturalem potentiam possit pertingere ad operationem perfectam, quæ est beatitudo.

SED CONTRA, homo est principium naturaliter actuum suorum per intellectum et voluntatem. Sed ultima beatitudo sanctis præparata excedit intellectum hominis et voluntatem: dicit enim Apostolus,[3] *Oculus non vidit, et auris non audivit, et in cor hominis non ascendit, quæ præparavit Deus diligentibus se.* Ergo homo per sua naturalia non potest beatitudinem consequi.

RESPONSIO: Dicendum quod beatitudo imperfecta quæ in hac vita haberi potest potest ab homine acquiri per sua naturalia, eo modo quo et virtus, in cujus operatione consistit: de quo infra dicetur.[4] Sed beatitudo hominis perfecta, sicut supra dictum est,[5] consistit in visione divinæ essentiæ. Videre autem Deum per essentiam est supra naturam non solum hominis, sed etiam omnis creaturæ, ut in *Primo* ostensum est.[6]

Naturalis enim cognitio cujuslibet creaturæ est secundum modum substantiæ ejus: sicut de intelligentia dicitur in *Libro de causis*,[7] quod *cognoscit ea quæ sunt supra se, et ea quæ sunt infra se, secundum modum substantiæ suæ.* Omnis autem cognitio quæ est secundum modum substantiæ creatæ deficit a visione divinæ essentiæ, quæ in infinitum excedit omnem substantiam creatam.

Unde nec homo, nec aliqua creatura, potest consequi beatitudinem ultimam per sua naturalia.

1. Ad primum ergo dicendum quod, sicut natura non deficit homini in necessariis, quamvis non dederit sibi arma et tegumenta sicut aliis animalibus, quia dedit ei rationem et manus, quibus possit hæc sibi conquirere; ita nec deficit homini in necessariis, quamvis non daret sibi aliquod principium, quo posset beatitudinem consequi; hoc enim erat impossibile. Sed dedit ei liberum arbitrium, quo possit converti ad Deum, qui eum faceret

---

[2]*Ethics* VII, 13. 1153b16

his destiny? Here human nature is not found wanting. The inference is that he can achieve happiness from his native resources.

2. Moreover, man is a higher organism than non-rational creatures, and therefore should be better able to look after himself. Yet they can reach their goals by their natural powers. All the more should man be able to reach happiness of himself under his own power.

3. Aristotle defines happiness as complete activity.[2] Now it is for the same subject to make a start and to come to a finish. Since incomplete activity, which is like the opening in human acts, falls under man's natural ability, since he is master of his own actions, it would seem that the same ability will take him to complete activity, namely happiness.

ON THE OTHER HAND, men themselves are the natural sources of their own activity through mind and will. Yet the final happiness prepared for the saints surpasses both our thinking and our willing. *Eye hath not seen, nor ear heard, neither hath it entered into the heart of man, what things God hath prepared for them that love him.*[3] Such happiness goes beyond our natural reach.

REPLY: The partial happiness we can hold in this life a man can secure for himself, as he can virtue, in the activity of which it consists: we shall discuss this later.[4] But man's complete happiness, as we have found,[5] consists in the vision of the divine essence, and this is beyond the natural stretch of any creature, not merely of man, as we have established in the *Prima Pars*.[6]

The knowing natural to any creature corresponds to what sort of thing[b] it is; the *Liber de causis*[7] says of intelligence that it knows objects above it and below it according to what sort of substance it is. Now all knowing according to a manner of created thing falls short of seeing what God really is, for the divine infinitely surpasses every created nature.

Consequently neither man nor any creature can attain final happiness through their natural resources.[c]

Hence: 1. Nature does not fail man in necessary helps, for though unprovided with armour and weapons like other animals, he is given the ingenuity and powers to make them for himself. Nor does it fail because it provides him with no inborn ability to reach happiness on his own. For he has been endowed with freewill, so that he can be turned to God who can

---

[3] *I Corinthians* 2, 9   [4] 1a2æ. 83
[5] 1a2æ. 3, 8   [6] 1a. 12, 4
[7] *Liber de causis* 7
[b] *substantia, ousia.*
[c] The question of purely natural beatitude is passed over.

beatum. *Quæ enim per amicos possumus, per nos aliqualiter possumus,* ut dicitur in *Ethic.*[8]

2. Ad secundum dicendum quod nobilioris conditionis est natura quæ potest consequi perfectum bonum, licet indigeat exteriori auxilio ad hoc consequendum, quam natura quæ non potest consequi perfectum bonum, sed consequitur quoddam bonum imperfectum, licet ad consecutionem ejus non indigeat exteriori auxilio, ut Philosophus dicit.[9] Sicut melius est dispositus ad sanitatem qui potest consequi perfectam sanitatem, licet hoc sit per auxilium medicinæ quam qui solum potest consequi quandam imperfectam sanitatem sine medicinæ auxilio. Et ideo creatura rationalis, quæ potest consequi perfectum beatitudinis bonum, indigens ad hoc divino auxilio, est perfectior quam creatura irrationalis, quæ hujusmodi boni non est capax, sed quoddam imperfectum bonum consequitur virtute suæ naturæ.

3. Ad tertium dicendum quod, quando imperfectum et perfectum sunt ejusdem speciei, ab eadem virtute causari possunt. Non autem hoc est necesse, si sunt alterius speciei: non enim quidquid potest causare dispositionem materiæ potest ultimam perfectionem conferre. Imperfecta autem operatio, quæ subjacet naturali hominis potestati, non est ejusdem speciei cum operatione illa perfecta quæ est hominis beatitudo: cum operationis species dependeat ex objecto. Unde ratio non sequitur.

articulus 6. utrum homo consequatur beatitudinem per actionem alicujus superioris creaturæ

AD SEXTUM sic proceditur:[1] 1. Videtur quod homo possit fieri beatus per actionem alicujus superioris creaturæ, scilicet angeli. Cum enim duplex ordo inveniatur in rebus, unus partium universi ad invicem, alius totius universi ad bonum quod est extra universum, primus ordo ordinatur ad secundum sicut ad finem, ut dicitur *Meta.,*[2] sicut ordo partium exercitus ad invicem est propter ordinem totius exercitus ad ducem. Sed ordo partium universi ad invicem attenditur secundum quod superiores creaturæ agunt in inferiores, ut in *Primo* dictum est:[3] beatitudo autem consistit in ordine hominis ad bonum quod est extra universum, quod est Deus. Ergo per actionem superioris creaturæ, scilicet angeli, in hominem, homo beatus efficitur.

2. Præterea, quod est in potentia tale potest reduci in actum per id quod est actu tale: sicut quod est potentia calidum fit actu calidum per id quod est actu calidum. Sed homo est in potentia beatus. Ergo potest fieri actu beatus per angelum, qui est actu beatus.

[8]*Ethics* III, 3. 1112b27   [9]*De Cælo* II, 12. 292a22
[1]cf Ia2æ. 3, 7   [2]*Metaphysics* XI, 10. 1075a11

make him happy. To quote the *Ethics*,⁸ *what we can do through our friends can, in a sense, be done through ourselves.*ᵈ

2. Aristotle reasons⁹ that a nature which can attain the perfect good, although it needs outside help, is of a higher condition than a nature which can attain without such recourse only a lesser good: a man is better disposed to health who can be perfectly fit, though with medical aid, than one who has but middling health without it. Likewise it is better to be a rational creature who can reach complete happiness, though needing divine help, than a non-rational creature which is not capable of this happiness, but arrives at some partial good under its own natural power.

3. When the embryonic and fully developed conditions of a thing are the same in kind, then they can be caused by the same cause. Not necessarily, however, when they are different in kind. For not everything that can prepare the material can give the finishing touch. The inchoate activity falling under our natural control is not the same in kind as the culminating activity of happiness. Remember it is its object which shapes the specific character of an activity.ᵉ And so the objection does not hold.

article 6. does man reach happiness because acted on by a higher creature?

THE SIXTH POINT:¹ 1. It would seem that he can become blessed through the action of angels.ᵃ A double order runs through the universe: one makes the pattern of things among themselves, the other sets the whole towards a good beyond. And the second is the purpose of the first, according to the *Metaphysics*,² thus the co-ordination of its various arms is in order that the whole force in the field may execute the plan of the commander. Now, as was agreed in the *Prima Pars*,³ the acting of higher on lower creatures composes the pattern of parts within the universe. Man's beatitude bears on a good outside the universe, namely God. Therefore he reaches happiness under the action of superior or angelic creatures.

2. Moreover, what is potentially positive can be made actually positive by what is actually positive; thus the potentially hot is made actually so by what is actually hot. Man is potentially happy, and can be made actually so by an angel who is actually happy.

---

³1a. 19, 5 ad 2; 48, 1 ad 5; 109, 2

ᵈThe quotation suggests in miniature the world of difference between Aristotle's ideal of friendship and the Christian *agapē*. The answer parries the objection, but does not meet the point, that man is a misfit by his nature if his nature is unable to make him happy.

ᵉAgain the importance of 'object', already noted. cf 1a2æ. 2, 8, note *e*; 3, 8, note *d*; 5, 1, note *b*.

ᵃThe article has in mind the views of Algazel and Averroes, that our happiness depends on a First Intelligence midway between God and man, and corresponds to 1a2æ. 3, 7 above.

3. Præterea, beatitudo consistit in operatione intellectus, ut supra dictum est.[4] Sed angelus potest illuminare intellectum hominis, ut in *Primo* habitum est.[5] Ergo angelus potest facere hominem beatum.

SED CONTRA est quod dicitur in *Psalmo*,[6] *Gratiam et gloriam dabit Dominus.*

RESPONSIO: Dicendum quod, cum omnis creatura naturæ legibus sit subjecta, utpote habens limitatam virtutem et actionem, illud quod excedit naturam creatam non potest fieri virtute alicujus creaturæ. Et ideo si quid fieri oporteat quod sit supra naturam, hoc fit immediate a Deo; sicut suscitatio mortui illuminatio cæci, et cetera hujusmodi. Ostensum est autem[7] quod beatitudo est quoddam bonum excedens naturam creatam. Unde impossibile est quod per actionem alicujus creaturæ conferatur: sed homo beatus fit solo Deo agente, si loquamur de beatitudine perfecta. Si vero loquamur de beatitudine imperfecta, sic eadem ratio est de ipsa et de virtute, in cujus actu consistit.

1. Ad primum ergo dicendum quod plerumque contingit in potentiis activis ordinatis, quod perducere ad ultimum finem pertinet ad supremam potentiam, inferiores vero potentiæ coadjuvant ad consecutionem illius ultimi finis disponendo: sicut ad artem gubernativam, quæ præest navifactivæ, pertinet usus navis, propter quem navis ipsa fit. Sic igitur et in ordine universi, homo quidem adjuvatur ab angelis ad consequendum ultimum finem secundum aliqua præcedentia, quibus disponitur ad ejus consecutionem: sed ipsum ultimum finem consequitur per ipsum primum agentem, qui est Deus.

2. Ad secundum dicendum quod, quando aliqua forma actu existit in aliquo secundum esse perfectum et naturale, potest esse principium actionis in alterum; sicut calidum per calorem calefacit. Sed si forma existit in aliquo imperfecte, et non secundum esse naturale, non potest esse principium communicationis sui ad alterum: sicut intentio coloris quæ est in

---

[4]1a2æ. 3, 4   [5]1a. 111, 1
[6]*Psalms* 83, 12   [7]art. 5 above
[b]Not natural law, which for St Thomas is moral law (cf 1a2æ. 94. Vol. 28, ed. T. Gilby), but a generalization of natural philosophy drawn from the observation of more or less constant sequences.
[c]Miracle: an effect produced from outside the natural order of things, *præter ordinem naturalem rerum*, 1a. 105, 6-8. God alone is the principal cause, though a creature may be an instrumental cause. A miracle is not supernatural in the way that we say sanctifying grace is supernatural, namely a sharing in the divine nature; it is rather a preternatural event wrought by divine power to witness to the divine life shared by men. It is, then, a gracious interposition—though it may shock the sensibilities of a culture remote by region and period from its original *mise-en-scène*—and falls under the heading of the extraordinary graces, *gratiæ gratis datæ*, which are

3. Again, we have agreed that beatitude consists in an activity of intelligence.⁴ And we have seen that an angel can enlighten a man's intelligence.⁵ And therefore render him blessed.

ON THE OTHER HAND we sing, *The Lord will give grace and glory*.⁶

REPLY: Since their abilities and activities are limited, all creatures are bound by the laws of nature,ᵇ and a work exceeding the world in which they live cannot be produced by any power there. And if it comes about, then it is done immediately by God, such as raising the dead to life, giving sight to the blind, and the like.ᶜ We have shown⁷ that happiness is a kind of blessing surpassing the natural scheme of things. Consequently for it to be conferred by any creaturely action is not possible; a man becomes blessed by the agency of God alone. Mind you, we are speaking of perfect bliss, for if we are speaking of partial happiness, which consists in the activity of virtue, then the same rules apply to the acquisition of happiness and of virtue.ᵈ

Hence: 1. Frequently it is the function of the highest power to achieve the final purpose of a working system of active causes, while that of the subordinate causes is to prepare the material; thus the art of admiralty governs the art of naval construction and decides how the ships built for its purpose are to be effectively concentrated. Likewise the order of the universe: angels help men to their ultimate end by bringing them into readiness; all the same, the actual gaining of the ultimate end is from the first cause, who is God.

2. When actually existing in a thing with full and physical being, a form can be the source of action on another, as when a hot thing heats another. But when not so existing in a thing, that is not completely and physically, then a form cannot be the source of such communication, thus the image of colour in the eye cannot paint a thing white.ᵉ Nor, for that matter, can

given *ad utilitatem, pros to sumpheron*, 1 *Corinthians* 12, 7, and without directly sanctifying help to build up the Church, 2a2æ. 171, Introduction.
The *illuminatio cæci*, given as an example in the text, is taken by commentators to refer to a person radically blind, not one suffering, for instance, from a cataract, but in the light of St Thomas's teaching on the degrees of miracle, 1a. 105, 8, their insistence seems superfluous. The point of the argument is to show that the source of man's happiness lies outside the created universe.
ᵈThe cause of virtue, 1a2æ. 63. Vol. 23, ed. D. Hughes.
ᵉ'Image of colour' translates *intentio coloris* and shows the run of the reply, yet misses the suggestiveness of the text. *Intentio* is a strong word, and implies the objectual relationship and presence to which we have alluded in several places. cf Foreword note *a*.
For *lumen gloriæ* see 1a. 12, 5. Vol. 3.

pupilla non potest facere album; neque etiam omnia quæ sunt illuminata aut calefacta possunt alia calefacere et illuminare; sic enim illuminatio et calefactio essent usque ad infinitum. Lumen autem gloriæ, per quod Deus videtur, in Deo quidem est perfecte secundum esse naturale; in qualibet autem creatura est imperfecte, et secundum esse similitudinarium vel participatum. Unde nulla creatura beata potest communicare suam beatitudinem alteri.

3. Ad tertium dicendum quod angelus beatus illuminat intellectum hominis, vel etiam inferioris angeli, quantum ad aliquas rationes divinorum operum non autem quantum ad visionem divinæ essentiæ, ut in *Primo* dictum est.[8] Ad eam enim videndam omnes immediate illuminantur a Deo.

articulus 7. utrum requirantur aliqua opera bona ad hoc quod homo beatitudinem consequatur a Deo

AD SEPTIMUM sic proceditur:[1] 1. Videtur quod non requirantur aliqua opera hominis ad hoc ut beatitudinem consequatur a Deo. Deus enim, cum sit agens infinitæ virtutis, non præexigit in agendo materiam, aut dispositionem materiæ, sed statim potest totum producere. Sed opera hominis, cum non requirantur ad beatitudinem ejus sicut causa efficiens, ut dictum est,[2] non possunt requiri ad eam nisi sicut dispositiones. Ergo Deus, qui dispositiones non præexigit in agendo, beatitudinem sine præcedentibus operibus confert.

2. Præterea, sicut Deus est auctor beatitudinis immediate, ita et naturam immediate instituit. Sed in prima institutione naturæ, produxit creaturas nulla dispositione præcedente vel actione creaturæ; sed statim fecit unumquodque perfectum in sua specie. Ergo videtur quod beatitudinem conferat homini sine aliquibus operationibus præcedentibus.

3. Præterea, Apostolus dicit,[3] beatitudinem hominis esse *cui Deus confert justitiam sine operibus.* Non ergo requiruntur aliqua opera hominis ad beatitudinem consequendam.

SED CONTRA est quod dicitur *Joann.*,[4] *Si hæc scitis, beati eritis si feceritis ea.* Ergo per actionem ad beatitudinem pervenitur.

RESPONSIO: Dicendum quod rectitudo voluntatis, ut supra dictum est,[5] requiritur ab beatitudinem, cum nihil aliud sit quam debitus ordo voluntatis ad ultimum finem; quæ ita exigitur ad consecutionem ultimi finis, sicut debita dispositio materiæ ad consecutionem formæ. Sed ex hoc non

---

[8]Ia. 106, 1   [1]cf IV *Sent.* 49, 1, 3, i   [2]art. 6 above
[3]*Romans* 4, 6   [4]*John* 13, 17   [5]Ia2æ. 4, 4

everything which is lit or warmed give light or heat to others; for if they could the process of lighting or heating would go on indefinitely.[f] The light of glory, however, in which God is seen, is fully his by natural being; it is in creatures in a lesser way as being by likeness and derivation. Hence no blessed creature can communicate its happiness to another.[g]

3. A blessed angel enlightens the intelligence of a man or a lower angel with regard to some meanings in the works of God, not to the face to face vision of him: as we have said in the *Prima Pars*,[8] God himself immediately shines on those who see him.[h]

article 7. are good deeds required in order to gain happiness from God?

THE SEVENTH POINT:[1] 1. Apparently not. Since God is a cause of infinite power, his action requires neither pre-existing nor suitably-disposed material, but can produce the whole effect regardless. Now happiness does not require men's deeds as an efficient cause, on this we have agreed,[2] and so then they can be required only as predispositions. But we have just ruled out the need for predispositions for God to act on, and therefore he grants happiness without preceding good works on our part.

2. Again, as God is the immediate founder of nature, so he is the immediate author of beatitude. When his world was founded he produced creatures without their being prepared or co-operative beforehand: each he made all at once and complete of its kind. Does he not, then, confer happiness on men without preceding good deeds?

3. Besides, St Paul speaks of happiness as for the man *to whom God reputeth righteousness without good works*.[3] These, consequently, are not required in order to attain happiness.[a]

ON THE OTHER HAND the Gospel tells us, *If you know these things, you shall be blessed if you do them.*[4]

REPLY: We have already explained how a right good will is required for beatitude,[5] since it is nothing else than a will properly set on the ultimate end, and is as necessary in order to reach it as the due disposition of material in order to receive a form.[b] However, this does not prove that any

---

[f]The diminution of light and the degradation of thermal energy enter the argument by way of examples, and need not be pressed. The reply seems to be *ad hominem*.
[g]That is, as a principal cause.
[h]cf Ia. 12, 1 & 5.
[a]For the objections cf Ia. 45, 1, 5 & 8. Vol. 8.
[b]For the order of grace, election, predestination, merit, glorification, see Ia. 23, 2, 4 & 5. Vol. 5, ed. T. Gilby.

ostenditur quod aliqua operatio hominis debeat præcedere ejus beatitudinem: posset enim Deus simul facere voluntatem recte tendentem in finem, et finem consequentem; sicut quandoque simul materiam disponit, et inducit formam.

Sed ordo divinæ sapientiæ exigit ne hoc fiat: ut enim dicitur in II *de Cælo*,[6] *eorum quæ nata sunt habere bonum perfectum, aliquid habet ipsum sine motu, aliquid uno motu, aliquid pluribus.* Habere autem perfectum bonum sine motu convenit ei quod naturaliter habet illud. Habere autem beatitudinem naturaliter est solius Dei. Unde solius Dei proprium est quod ad beatitudinem non moveatur per aliquam operationem præcedentem.

Cum autem beatitudo excedat omnem naturam creatam, nulla pura creatura convenienter beatitudinem consequitur absque motu operationis per quam tendit in ipsam. Sed angelus, qui est superior ordine naturæ quam homo, consecutus est eam, ex ordine divinæ supientiæ, uno motu operationis meritioriæ, ut in *Primo* expositum est.[7] Homines autem consequuntur ipsam multis motibus operationum, qui merita dicuntur. Unde etiam, secundum Philosophum,[8] beatitudo est præmium virtuosarum operationum.

1. Ad primum ergo dicendum quod operatio hominis non præexigitur ad consecutionem beatitudinis propter insufficientiam divinæ virtutis beatificantis, sed ut servetur ordo in rebus.

2. Ad secundum dicendum quod primas creaturas statim Deus perfectas produxit, absque aliqua dispositione vel operatione creaturæ præcedente, quia sic instituit prima individua specierum, ut per ea natura propagaretur ad posteros. Et similiter, quia per Christum, qui est Deus et homo, beatitudo erat ad alios derivanda, secundum illud Apostoli,[9] *qui multos filios in gloriam adduxerat*; statim a principio suæ conceptionis, absque aliqua operatione meritoria præcedente, anima ejus fuit beata. Sed hoc est singulare in ipso: nam pueris baptizatis subvenit meritum Christi ad beatitudinem consequendam, licet desint eis merita propria, eo quod per baptismum sunt Christi membra effecti.

3. Ad tertium dicendum quod Apostolus loquitur de beatitudine spei quæ habetur per gratiam justificantem, quæ quidem non datur propter

---

[6]*De Cælo* II, 12. 292a22 [7]1a. 62, 5
[8]*Ethics* I, 9. 1099b16 [9]*Hebrews* 2, 10
[c]Motion, here taken as synonymous with change, and implying potentiality, not as meaning activity. cf 1a. 9, 1 ad 1. Vol. 2. Aristotle, *Metaphysics* XI, 6. 1071b37. Plato, *Timæus* 30A, 34B; *Phædrus* 245C.
[d]cf 1a. 26.
[e]Happiness itself, as we have already observed, is a post-moral condition, and therefore as such not a moral value. Moral values in the strictest meaning of the term would seem to be non-ultimate *honesta* subordinate to the ultimate end, the *summum*

work of man is an indispensable precondition of his happiness, for God could at one stroke make a man whose will was at once rightly set on its end and already possessing it, as sometimes he simultaneously disposes matter and produces its form.

But the order in fact established by divine wisdom does not have it so. The *De Cælo* observes[6] that *of things that have a natural capacity for complete good, one has it without motion, another with one motion, another with many motions.*[c] To possess perfect good without motion is proper to that reality which has it by nature, and to possess happiness by nature is for God alone. Hence it is proper to him alone never to have been in process of becoming happy through activity preceding happiness.[d]

Such happiness surpasses all created nature, and so in the fitting course of things no mere creature gains it without some motion of activity towards it. Superior in nature to man, an angel gains it, according to the economy of divine wisdom, by one meritorious motion: this we have explained in the *Prima Pars*.[7] Man, however, reaches it through many motions of activity, which are called his merits. The conclusion is in line with Aristotle,[8] who thought of happiness as the reward for virtuous acts.[e]

Hence: 1. It is the established course of things, not any limit to divine power, that postulates human deeds as necessary preliminaries to happiness.

2. The original things of creation were produced wholly and immediately by God without creaturely contribution by way of disposition or action; so also he set up the original individuals of a species for them to propagate it to posterity.[f] And likewise, because happiness flows to men from Christ,[g] who is God and man, and, according to *Hebrews*,[9] *has brought many children into glory*, his soul was blessed from the first moment of his conception, without any preceding meritorious activity.[h] But he is unique. Though baptized babies attain bliss through no merits of their own, they draw on his, because Baptism makes them his members.[i]

3. St Paul is speaking of the happiness of hope, bestowed by the grace which makes us pleasing to God, and not owing to preceding good works. For this blessing of hope does not imply the meaning of being the finish of

---

bonum. God's own goodness transcends moral categories. cf Vol. 18, Appendices 3, 5 & 6.
[f]Read in accordance with 1a. 47, 1 (Vol. 8), that God is the immediate cause of the distinctiveness in things, not as taking up any position, for or against, the process of evolution.
[g]cf 3a, 8, *De gratia capitali Christi*.
[h]cf 3a. 7, 1, 9, 11 & 13; 9, 2.
[i]cf 3a. 68, 9.

opera præcedentia. Non enim habet rationem termini motus, ut beatitudo, sed magis est principium motus quo ad beatitudinem tenditur.

articulus 8. *utrum omnis homo appetat beatitudinem*

AD OCTAVUM sic proceditur:[1] 1. Videtur quod non omnes appetant beatitudinem. Nullus enim potest appetere quod ignorat: cum bonum apprehensum sit objectum appetitus, ut dicitur in III *De Anima*.[2] Sed multi nesciunt quid sit beatitudo: quod, sicut Augustinus dicit,[3] patet ex hoc, quod *quidam posuerunt beatitudinem in voluptate corporis, quidam in virtute animi, quidam in aliis rebus*. Non ergo omnes beatitudinem appetunt.

2. Præterea, essentia beatitudinis est visio essentiæ divinæ, ut dictum est.[4] Sed aliqui opinantur hoc esse impossibile, quod Deus per essentiam ab homine videatur: unde hoc non appetunt. Ergo non omnes homines appetunt beatitudinem.

3. Præterea, Augustinus dicit,[5] quod *beatus est qui habet omnia quæ vult, et nihil male vult*. Sed non omnes hoc volunt: quidam enim male aliqua volunt, et tamen volunt illa se velle. Non ergo omnes volunt beatitudinem.

SED CONTRA est quod Augustinus dicit,[6] *Si minus* dixisset, 'Omnes beati esse vultis, miseri esse non vultis', dixisset aliquid quod nullus in sua non cognosceret voluntate*. Quilibet ergo vult esse beatus.

RESPONSIO: Dicendum quod beatitudo dupliciter potest considerari. Uno modo, secundum communem rationem beatitudinis. Et sic necesse est quod omnis homo beatitudinem velit. Ratio autem beatitudinis communis est ut sit bonum perfectum, sicut dictum est.[7] Cum autem bonum sit objectum voluntatis, perfectum bonum est alicujus quod totaliter ejus voluntati satisfacit. Unde appetere beatitudinem nihil aliud est quam appetere ut voluntas satietur. Quod quilibet vult.

Alio modo possumus loqui de beatitudine secundum specialem rationem quantum ad id in quo beatitudo consistit. Et sic non omnes cognoscunt beatitudinem, quia nesciunt cui rei communis ratio beatitudinis conveniat. Et per consequens, quantum ad hoc, non omnes eam volunt.

1. Unde patet responsio ad primum.

2. Ad secundum dicendum quod, cum voluntas sequatur apprehensionem intellectus seu rationis, sicut contingit quod aliquid est idem secundum rem quod tamen est diversum secundum rationis considerationem,

---

*Piana: *unus*, if one says.

[1]IV *Sent*. 49, 1, 3, i   [2]*De Anima* III, 10. 433a27; b12
[3]*De Trin*. XIII, 4. PL 42, 1018   [4]Ia2æ. 3, 8
[5]*De Trin*. XIII, 5. PL 42, 1020   [6]ibid. 3. PL 42, 1018   [7]art 4 ad 2

motion, which happiness is, but rather of being the start of the motion towards happiness.[j]

article 8. does every human being desire happiness?

THE EIGHTH POINT:[1] 1. It seems not.[a] For who can want what he does not know about? The object of human desire is good perceived, as stated in the *De Anima*.[2] Now many do not know what happiness is; Augustine observes[3] that *some put it in pleasures of body, some in virtue of soul and others elsewhere*. Not all, therefore, desire happiness.

2. Further, we have agreed[4] that the vision of God constitutes happiness. Some, however, reckon this quite beyond the bounds of possibility.[b] And consequently do not long for it.

3. Besides, Augustine says that *blessed is he who has all he wills, and wills for nothing amiss*.[5] Not all have that sort of will. For some will amiss, and are quite determined about it. Therefore all do not will happiness.

ON THE OTHER HAND there is Augustine,[6] *If the compère says from the stage, You all want to be happy, and do not want to be miserable, his words echo what none of the audience fails to find in his heart*. Everyone, in fact, desires to be happy.

REPLY: Beatitude can be considered in the abstract and in the concrete. Take it in its general meaning, then everybody is bound to wish for happiness. For it signifies, as we have said,[7] complete goodness. Since the good is the object of the will, the perfect good is that which satisfies it altogether. To desire to be happy is nothing else than to wish for this satisfaction. And each and everyone wishes it.

Take it, however, to point to where happiness lies, then all do not recognize it, for they are ignorant about the object which gathers all good together. And so in this sense not everybody wills happiness.

Hence: 1. The answer is clear.

2. Willing follows perceiving by intelligence or reason. And accordingly, just as a thing which is single in reality may be split into parts in our

---

[j]Hope, theological virtue, 2a2æ. 17–22. Vol. 33, ed. W. Hill.

[a]As in the other four Questions, the final article brings the topic to a head.

[b]Allegedly Amaury, or Almaric of Bène (near Chartres), professor |at Paris, d. 1207. The 'Amaurians' or 'Amauricians' laid themselves open to the charge of pantheism and were censured. Amaury seems to have taken up the Eruigenian doctrine of theophanies, and denied the beatific vision. cf the first of the theses condemned at Paris. Denifle, *Cartularium*, 123 (I, 170). C. Capelle, *Autour du décret de 1210*. Paris, 1932.

ita contingit quod aliquid est idem secundum rem et tamen uno modo appetitur, alio modo non appetitur. Beatitudo ergo potest considerari sub ratione finalis boni et perfecti, quæ est communis ratio beatitudinis: et sic naturaliter et ex necessitate voluntas in illud tendit, ut dictum est.[8] Potest etiam considerari secundum alias speciales considerationes, vel ex parte ipsius operationis, vel ex parte potentiæ operativæ, vel ex parte objecti: et sic non ex necessitate voluntas tendit in ipsam.

3. Ad tertium dicendum quod ista definitio beatitudinis quam quidam posuerunt,[9] *Beatus est qui habet omnia quæ vult*, vel, *cui omnia optata succedunt*, quodam modo intellecta est bona et sufficiens; alio vero modo est imperfecta. Si enim intelligatur simpliciter de omnibus quæ vult homo naturali appetitu, sic verum est quod qui habet omnia quæ vult est beatus: nihil enim satiat naturalem hominis appetitum nisi bonum perfectum, quod est beatitudo. Si vero intelligatur de his quæ homo vult secundum apprehensionem rationis, sic habere quædam quæ homo vult non pertinet ad beatitudinem, sed magis ad miseriam, inquantum hujusmodi habita impediunt hominem ne habeat quæcumque naturaliter vult: sicut etiam ratio accipit ut vera interdum quæ impediunt a cognitione veritatis. Et secundum hanc considerationem, Augustinus addidit ad perfectionem beatitudinis, quod *nihil mali velit*. Quamvis primum posset sufficere, si recte intelligeretur, scilicet quod *beatus est qui habet omnia quæ vult*.

---

[8]art. 3 & 4 above
[9]Following Augustine *De Trin.* III, 5. PL 42, 1020. Thus Peter Lombard, *Sent.* IV, 49, I

thinking about it, so also it may be wanted under one aspect and not wanted under another.[c] Happiness, therefore, can be considered *qua* final and perfect good—its general meaning—and to this, as we have noticed,[8] the will tends by nature and of necessity. Yet it can also be considered in some particular respect, for instance, in terms of the act of willing, or of the active power engaged, or of what the object involves, and to this the will does not tend of necessity.

3. Blessed is the man who has all he wills, or, as sometimes put, whose choices succeed—this description of happiness[9d] is well enough in one sense, but not in another. If you take it to refer to wishes that spring from his nature, then it is true that one who has all he wants is happy, for nothing but the perfect good, which is beatitude, satisfies the desires of human nature. If you take it to refer to all that strike him as his wants, then to have some of them will not be his happiness, but rather the reverse: in fact they will stop him from getting what his nature wants. There is a parallel here with the reason, which on occasion thinks things are true which in fact are barriers to knowing the truth. That is why Augustine adds the qualification that no touch of evil[e] is willed. Though, as we have admitted, the unqualified statement is well enough if rightly understood.

---

[c]Thus I might wish to love God with my whole heart, and yet at the same time feel disinclined to make the effort entailed. Though he is the universal good, he is not yet seen as such. Following a hidden God means taking particular and sometimes unattractive courses. cf 1a2æ. 10, 2; 75, 2.

[d]Adopted by Peter Lombard, *Sentences* IV, 49. 1.

[e]*Nihil male* in objection, *nihil mali* in reply.

Appendix 1

ACTING FOR A PURPOSE
(1a2æ. 1, 1 & 2)

'No wise fish,' said the Mock Turtle, 'would go anywhere without a porpoise.'
'Wouldn't it really?' said Alice in a tone of great surprise.
'Of course not,' said the Mock Turtle, 'why, if a fish came to *me* and told me
he was going on a journey, I should say, "With what porpoise?" '
'Don't you mean "purpose"?' said Alice.
'I mean what I say,' replied the Mock Turtle in an offended tone.

END SO DOMINATES the *Secunda Pars* of the *Summa* that it should be read to
say what it means. For the term can be taken in various senses; for a finish—
the end of life is death, for a term to a continuum—the end of the line, or for
a conclusion or completion—the end of a work. None of these, however, is
the main sense for moral theology, where it means the goal or aim of a human
act. It is well to keep this restriction in mind, so that more general problems
relating to teleology in the field of natural and metaphysical philosophy may
be left out of properly ethical discussions. All the same, since moral theory is
a subordinate science, and therefore must assume its principles from elsewhere,[1] in the present case from the positions of anthropological theology
established in the *Prima Pars*, some recapitulation will be useful, all the more
because the present volume and the one following are about the precondi-
tions of morality rather than about morality itself, though some moral questions already cast their shadow before.

Wherever a thing or event is not self-explanatory and, if we are prepared
to make the effort, we look at it first, as it were, in isolation and then cast
about for the 'outside' principles on which it depends. These are its causes.
We may not succeed in discovering what they are, but only that they are.[2]
The final cause, end, *finis*, indicates the answer to 'why?', the efficient cause,
agens, that to 'whence?' or 'how?' And since on ultimate analysis the action
of the efficient cause is for some reason, which reason is the end it intends
('reason' and 'intention' should not be particularized in human terms, nor
should 'appetite' or 'love', if we are to avoid the Pathetic Fallacy), this aim
is regarded as the first of the causes, that is to say, in the order of intention,
for in the order of execution it comes last.

The efficient cause, then, does not work, or set in motion, except by intention of the end.[3] Being an end is being a good; the two coincide, and there
is only a notional distinction between them: the end is what sets desire in
motion, the good what is desirable.[4] Now it is a cardinal principle in St

---

[1]cf Vol. 18, Appendices 2–7   [2]cf 1a. 2, 1 & 2
[3]1a2æ. 1, 2   [4]1a. 5, 4. *In Ethic.* I, 5. *lect.* 9

Thomas's dialectic of love,[5] though easily neglected because of his insistence on intelligibility, and particularly on right reason in moral matters, that the apprehension of an end, or its mental-volitional condition *in esse intentionali*, is only a condition of its causality. The reason why it causes is its real being, *in esse naturali*. In other words we are not moved by thinking it, but by the thing through thinking it. You want real health, real science, a real bath, says Cajetan,[6] not just the thought of them.

The two statements are not inconsistent, that the end is the first of the causes because it comes first in intention, and that its causality consists in its being objectively real and good. Natural theology breaks out of the circle of creaturely attractions: God is the ultimate final cause of all things whatsoever,[7] and all ends and all goods—both genuine and sham, says St Thomas, pre-exist in him.[8] This is to look back. Then also, to look forward, we should observe the Aristotelean canon that the nature of anything is its complete development, *hē phusis telos estin*.[9]

The end, then, which brings human acts into play and shapes their character is not just an ideal projection, but a real thing, if we may so speak of the subsistent goodness of God.[10] We seek it for itself, and for its sake, *gratia cujus, heneka*, we seek other things as well. Other things—here we are brought to the contrast between means and ends, which, as customarily stated, is too simplified to render St Thomas's thought. He regards pure means as utilities, *bona utilia*, desired for no other reason than that they serve something else, and therefore not what the real drama of our choices is about. He prefers to speak of *ea quæ sunt ad finem*, the things which are towards an end, leaving it implied that although subordinate they are goods and therefore ends in themselves.

The question engages his whole pluralist metaphysics.[11] There are real beings distinct from the subsistent being of God, real secondary principal causes distinct from the First Cause, and real ends distinct from the ultimate end. Indeed it is not too much to say that there are no means to God in the difficulties of loving him, but only things that are from him and should be for him, for the moral problem lies in our taking of lesser goods: if we choose them for what they really are as creatures, then all is well, but not if we take them as ultimate ends and substitutes for God.[12] Accordingly to look at the whole of life, God alone is our ultimate end, but within his Providence there are other non-ultimate ends, noble and delightful in themselves. In any one particular frame of reference, for instance the political life of one country, we may of course set up an ultimate, for instance the national good, and subordinate all relevant issues to that.

---

[5]Vol. 1, Appendix 10
[7]1a. 44, 4
[9]cf *De partibus animalium* I, I. 639b14
[11]cf 1a. 45 & 47. Vol. 8

[6]Commentary on 1a. 5, 4
[8]1a. 4, 2
[10]cf 1a. 3, 2–5

[12]cf the analysis of the interior causes of sin, 1a2æ. 75–78. Vol. 25, ed. J. Fearon.

Moral science itself may set up such ends in its particular systems of reference. They are called moral objects,[13] and are treated as the proximate determinants of kinds of moral activity. They provide indispensable 'fixes', but not such as to stop the movement for a moral theology which follows the trajectory of Aristotle's thought on teleology and of St Augustine's on beatitude, and which comes to rest only with the living God.

[13]Vol. 18, Appendices 10 & 11

Appendix 2

ACTING FOR HAPPINESS
(1a2æ. 2–3)

A CERTAIN UTILITARIAN TEMPER, already evident in the present discourse, will be more pronounced when the discourse moves to morals.[1] The content of human activity is not regarded as a sort of enshrined value, self-evident and independent of context; its movement, which rises from the grounds of physical and human nature and reaches out to ends beyond, needs to be tested by looking both backward and forward, backward to the data of psychology and forward to the condition called human happiness, which for the Christian theologian is defined by the promise of divine Revelation. The purpose of this note is not to compare ethical doctrines as such, but to indicate a pre-moral principle, running throughout this treatise, which should qualify the opening observation.

Utilitarianism, which holds that an action is right in proportion to the benefits it effects, covers the noblest altruism as well as the lowest self-seeking; it need not be criticized for its practice in the field of morals, nor even there precisely for its theory. The contrast with St Thomas's position lies elsewhere, in an underlying philosophy and theology about the nature of happiness. Admittedly this is certainly a human benefit, indeed it is a man's own highest blessing, a good-for-him: so far there is agreement. All utilitarian theories are teleological, and so are all eudemonian theories. Nevertheless it does not follow that the two are identical.

For whereas utilitarians describe happiness as a condition of the human subject or subjects without pressing a subject-object analysis to conclusions in metaphysics or dogmatic theology, largely perhaps because of their surrounding climate of thought, St Thomas, though accepting these subjective and perfecting conditions, and in fact finding the activity of happiness, *beatitudo formalis*, among them, treats them as responses to an object, *beatitudo objectiva*, which object in perfect happiness is God.

At once there is a difference of tone, and one not confined to the issue between anthropocentric and theocentric moralism. It is not that the second is more improving than the first, but that it allows for more of a fling, an extravagance, a rapture. There is God, and he is to be loved just because he is God, and sometimes with a recklessness a somewhat pursy moralist may find hard to approve. Gallantry apart, however, this motion of love of God above all, the *summum bonum* and culmination of all desire, runs throughout the universe; St Thomas sees it in every motion of appetite, rational, sensitive, blind.[2] And it is caught up into new dimensions of grace so that he is

---

[1] 1a2æ. 18–21. Vol. 18   [2] 1a2æ. 109, 3

loved for himself regardless of benefit, *ut in ipso sistat, non ut ex eo aliquid nobis proveniat*.[3] Thus is the eudemonianism of Aristotle transmuted by the thought of St Augustine and presented in the *Summa* as a preparation for the Gospel law of love.

Notice, however, that this love of God sheerly for himself is not the 'pure' love inculcated by some late seventeenth-century mystics. It is not the pursuit of self-forgetfulness, and does not depend on an introspective 'purifying' of motives. It is not altruism—the word has no meaning in this divine situation where charity or friendship nourishes hope or desire for God as good for us. Taught by theology that he is not one among many things,[4] and therefore not to be isolated even as the best of them, it is not God alone whom we love, but God above all. Who and what is thereby excluded when we love God who so loved his world? Nothing save sin.

---

[3] 2a2æ. 23, 6
[4] Ia. 3, 5. Vol. 2

Appendix 3

ACTING FOR PLEASURE

(1a2æ. 2, 6; 4, 1 & 2)

ARE THINGS GOOD because they are pleasant, or pleasant because they are good? The question introduces opposed ethical theories, one that 'right' is an absolute value, and 'ought' an object of direct intuition, seen like a form out of matter, and to be followed without regard to context or consequences; the other that it is a practical and relative value, conditional on the happiness it produces, which happiness is stated in terms of pleasure. Between such extremes of formalism and utilitarianism St Thomas holds to a *via media*: on one side he sees morality as subordinate to wider and deeper blessings, on the other he sees that its object is not a function of the self.[1] Our present inquiry is about the last point. Is our happiness the same as our pleasure?

It is likely that he would not have admitted William James's criticism of hedonism: to say that, because actions are accompanied by pleasure or pain, these therefore are the motives is like arguing that because an ocean liner consumes coal on its passage, the purpose therefore of the voyage is to consume coal. Nevertheless he agrees with the 'platitude' of the *Phædo* and the *Nicomachean Ethics* that happiness is man's chief good, and with the analysis that pleasure is not its constituent, but its accompaniment and complement. This is to speak of pleasure as such, which carries the note of having attained an end, not as experienced on a purely sensuous level, for there it can appear as a kind of bait in order that certain necessary actions relative to food and sex should be performed;[2] in this respect pleasure is diminished to a condition of a means or utility, *bonum utile*.

This consideration, however, is not proper to the human appreciation of pleasure, so we leave it aside and stay on the note of its being an ultimate which requires no further justification. It marks a period, and is of itself, *secundum se* (though not, of course, because of other factors, *per aliud et quasi per accidens*) timeless and reflects the *quies* of eternity.[3] Hence our motion towards a pleasure is our motion towards an end. St Thomas warns us against separating the two,[4] which seems to be done both by hedonists who would idolize pleasure as a main object of action distinct from its grounds and by formalists who would dismiss it as an experience irrelevant to doing your duty.

Accepting, then, that pleasure is part of an end, it remains for us to determine in what sense we can say that human acts are on account of it, *propter delectationem*. 'On account of' may be the equivalent of 'for the sake of', *gratia cujus, heneka*, and signify purpose, in which case, since pleasure has no purpose other than itself, it is final, and human actions are for it and not for

---

[1]1a2æ. 2, 7   [2]1a2æ. 4, 2 ad 2   [3]1a2æ. 31, 2   [4]1a2æ. 2, 6 ad 1 & 3

anything beyond. 'On account of' may also be the equivalent of 'because of' or 'owing to', and signify the grounds on which pleasure is true and real, or, as St Thomas says, its formal cause and efficient cause, namely its shaping and making principles.[5] In this case the meaning and existence of pleasure derive from a real good which is itself not constituted by our taking pleasure in it, and it is this, not the pleasure, which is the object of action. It is called *beatitudo objectiva*, and our happiness, *beatitudo subjectiva*, is formed by our attaining it. Whether this last consists in a holding act of mind or an enjoying act of will is another question,[6] also whether in pleasure itself cognition or appetition is predominant.[7]

In brief, a good as a real being of true worth, *bonum honestum*, is the form and cause of its affording delight, *bonum delectabile*. It will be noticed that the criticism of hedonism is psychological, not moral. On the level of intelligence men simply do not act 'owing to' the pleasure they will derive, and those who think they do are confusing pleasure in idea and idea of pleasure. To take the debate into ethics is largely a waste of time. No serious writer will defend mere self-indulgence, and certainly preoccupation with pleasure, as with health, can defeat its own end and produce a sort of hypochondria; for the rest it is largely a matter outside morals whether or not you are apt to look gift horses in the mouth or to have feelings of guilt when you are enjoying yourself. As for St Thomas, though quite severe about our sensitive appetites, he is not at all disposed to agree that pleasure needs any excuse; on the contrary he holds that when charged with intelligence it offers a good test for judging between moral right or wrong.[8]

---

[5] ibid ad I
[6] cf Appendix 4. Also Ia2æ. 4, 3
[7] cf Ia2æ. II, I
[8] Ia2æ. 34, 4

Appendix 4

MIND AND HEART IN HAPPINESS

(1a2æ. 3, 4)

THE CONTRAST between the intellectualism of Dominican and the voluntarism of Franciscan theologians is sufficiently hackneyed; the terms themselves are too thin to do justice to the richness of the mystical teaching released by the debates, and somewhat misleading if one side suggests cold thinking and the other warm feeling. Both had their hard reasoners who were also men of devotion, and nobody could call the theology of Duns Scotus merely or even mainly affective. The issue was not whether knowing was better than loving, but which gave the decisive stroke in the activity of happiness.

As for the first, the *Summa* repeatedly gives the primacy in this life to loving, above all to charity. St Paul had said as much, *These three, and the greatest of these is charity.*[1] One reason was to be found in comparison of the movements of cognition and appetition respectively. The first is incoming, and so the object is limited according to the condition of the subject; the second is outgoing and reaches to the object without such reserve.[2] The analysis, of course, is much more delicate than will appear from this rough simplification. Hence, so ran one conclusion, our knowing a thing below us was better than our loving it, but the converse held true with a thing above us; the comparison was not a moral one, nor did it mark exclusions, but laid the proper emphasis. Consequently, loving God with our whole heart was higher than having true thoughts about him, for in love we go to the object, whereas in knowledge the object comes to us, and in this life we can love him directly though he is hidden to our knowledge in the darkness of faith. That love could take over where knowledge had to leave off was a principle enough to prompt a copious literature of affective and mystical theology,[3] of which some of the classical treatises centre on the love-knowledge inspired by the Gifts of the Holy Ghost.[4]

So far there is little if any dispute among the great realist Scholastics. Disagreement begins with the present inquiry. Now notice that St Thomas is not here engaged with relative nobilities, but with human happiness. It lies in our union with the *Summum Bonum*, which is God. Are not those who cleave to him with their whole hearts already united to him? Yet are they completely happy? What is it, then, in us which marks the difference between being perfectly in love with God and in being perfectly happy with

---

[1] I *Corinthians* 13, 13
[2] 1a. 5, 1; 16, 1, 3, 4. 1a2æ. 22.2. *De veritate* XXII, 4 ad 1. And passim
[3] Vol. I, Appendix 10, *The Dialectic of Love in the Summa*
[4] 1a2æ. 68 & 2a2æ. 45. For the doctrine of the Gifts of the Holy Ghost see especially the commentaries of John of St Thomas

God? And so he looks for it in an activity which holds the real presence of God. There is no need to paraphrase his dry words about the impotence of love alone to hold the beloved;[5] they record the tragic experience of lovers, that and the strain for the impossible, to have the other expressed and to express themselves only in the language of love. But love is the same in absence and in presence: such is its grandeur, yet also its misery. Consequently he turns to the activity of knowing, which of its nature is one of holding its object. Yet complete happiness cannot lie in holding merely its representation[6] or by expressing merely its notional meaning.[7] He has already considered how God's own essence can immediately flood the mind and be known without intervening concepts.[8] He concludes, therefore, that the dominant is an act of knowledge, and he appeals for confirmation to the Johannine teaching that we shall see God himself.[9] The act is not arrested, as it were, at knowing, for it sets up at once a 'comprehension' in the beatific love of the will.[10]

The setting of the debate may seem strange to those who frame man's true happiness according to contemporary personalism and hold that it consists in a perfect dialogue between God and man in the *I-Thou* relationship of sacred Scripture, in which 'to see' or vision means to live in conscious personal union with divine, angelic, and human persons.[11] It may well be that this is enough for the simple Gospel message, and that there is no need to answer questions which are not raised. But some questions are quite properly raised, among them the present question, and they are not just for a period, but perennial. Moreover they deserve an answer, which should be given with a frank acknowledgment of the limitations of our knowledge. This will be found in St Thomas—it has already appeared in our second paragraph—and, it may be added, the preoccupations of the old mystical theologians are not so very remote and their terminology not so very quaint, for they still bear directly on the critical study of the aesthetic experience.

For the rest, the steady emphasis on mind and reason runs throughout the *Summa*. From the *Verbum spirans Amorem*[12] it descends to the word made in wisdom and freedom,[13] and continues through the right reason in human action,[14] the rôle of prudence among the moral virtues,[15] the note of reasonableness in law,[16] until at last it reaches its end, and divinity flows into it with the beatific vision.

---

[5]1a2æ. 3, 4. The examination is pursued in 1a2æ. 28, 1 & 2
[6]1a. 12, 2. Vol. 3   [7]1a2æ. 3, 7
[8]1a. 12, 1–11
[9]*John* 17, 3. I *John* 3, 2
[10]1a2æ. 4, 3
[11]R. Troisfontaines. 'Le ciel.' *Nouvelle revue théologique.* 1960. pp. 225–46
[12]1a. 34, 1 & 2
[13]1a. 34, 3
[14]1a2æ, 58, 4
[15]2a2æ, 47, 7. Also 1a2æ. 65, 1
[16]1a2æ. 90, 1

Appendix 5

THE VISION OF GOD

(1a2æ. 3, 8)

THE ARTICLE, the centre-piece of the treatise, has been already anticipated in the *Prima Pars*, which has considered the possibility and nature of divine vision;[1] it will be gone over again in discussing the heights of mystical experience.[2] Here it is treated as constituting man's own happiness, yet it also raises the question of no natural desire being pointless, a wish-fulfilment dialectic that has proved a vexed problem from the period of Trent to that of Modernism and still continues as theologians increasingly criticize past presentations of the two-layer workings of nature and grace.[3] Consequently some mapping will be useful.

The problem briefly is about the paradox in traditional teaching, and the reconciliation of two positions. First, that man has been created by God in his nature and natural powers, not as a heartless joke, but with some natural expectancy of such development that he will reach to his fulfilment or happiness. Second, that this end can be reached only by the pure gift of grace quite beyond his deserving by any natural efforts of his own. It is objected that either man has from within himself some claim or 'exigence' to such happiness, in which case heaven is not wholly a gift or, as they say, gratuitous, or he has not, in which case it is wholly out of the range of nature, and the argument for it from natural desire is quite off the mark; moreover the giving of grace will look like an imposition, benign maybe, but quite foreign to human nature.

The paradox itself seems to belong to the teaching of the Church, yet the various attempts at elucidation which have been made need be given no more weight than their authors and their evidences will carry. It may also be noticed that the debate can be conducted without reference to complications introduced by questions of sin, original or actual. It considers man in a state of pure human nature, such as he has never been under the historical conditions under God's saving Providence. Nevertheless the abstraction is legitimate so long as it is recognized as such.[4] *Agitur de puncto insertionis*, declares Garrigou-Lagrange, *ordinis supernaturalis in ordinem naturalem*: a latinist

---

[1] 1a. 12. Vol. 3   [2] 2a2æ. 175, 1 & 3
[3] cf Vol. 1, Appendix 8, *Natural and Supernatural*
[4] So long also as the *homo in puris naturalibus* is not made so really separate from the *homo in gratia* that two streams of human activity are separated in the present treatise, one of the Aristotelean man going to *eudaimonia*, the other of the Christian-ized man going to glory. It seems that this is not altogether avoided by Ramirez, op cit, when he considers Question 1 as providing the philosophical groundwork, and Questions 2–5 the theological build-up.

may wince, but the characteristic phrase has its heuristic pungency, and shows what is really at issue in the confrontation of grace and nature, that is, when nature is accorded a real standing.

For, it may be noticed, the currents that flow along the right and left banks of Christian thought, and have sometimes broken them down offer fairly plain sailing. One side makes too little of nature, as though all it could do, that is, when it was not considered as utterly depraved, was to send out a wavering and idle wish for happiness from God. The other side makes too much, as though it were quite sufficient in itself to reach to natural happiness, to which grace and glory are, as it were, supplementary.[5] The problem arises for theologians who keep to midstream, and accordingly must respect the curves of either bank. Let us look briefly at what St Thomas says, and then at how he has been interpreted.[6]

His texts fall into two antithetical groups. That he was conscious of a contradiction but let it ride is quite uncharacteristic of him; that he changed his mind is ruled out by their chronology for they come from all periods of his writing career. They are to be held together, and their coherence explored. The first group teach that by our nature the desire for the vision of God is so strong that unless it is reached complete happiness is not complete.[7] The second that by our nature the mind is not even able to conceive of the possibility of this vision and consequently the will is not able to desire it.[8]

How to reconcile this seeming opposition, of an object of a desire from within human nature which at the same time is an object utterly beyond its ken? Let us look at some of the commentators.

We start with Cajetan (1469–1534), rarely the man to shirk untying the

---

[5]The opposites are commonly contrasted as Jansenism and Pelagianism. The first is a species of Augustinianism, though this is too versatile a term to stand for a rigid generic school. Accepting the total depravity of human nature, Luther, Baius, and Jansenius regarded natural desire as a figment. St Augustine's idea of human nature, born from his own experiences and meditations on the Scriptures, was not, unlike St Thomas's, strongly marked by the metaphysics of nature; man was made in a paradisal state, and his lapse from it left a hollow, which is to some extent filled, now that he is redeemed, by an aspiration to God himself. Man is single throughout his history, and not sectioned into the parts of nature and of grace. The insights of post-Blondelian theologians, that man is not closed in by his nature, have led some to comprehend the natural in the supernatural, and, not rarely, in perfect consonance with St Thomas.

[6]The matter is summarized by A. Motte, *Bulletin thomiste*, 1932, pp. 653–75. This appendix also gratefully acknowledges its borrowings from the ms. lecture notes, *Cours de théologie morale*, Toulouse, 1961, by M. M. Labourdette.

[7]The first group is represented in the present text, 1a2æ. 3, 8. It states a position maturely reflected on; e.g. 1a. 12, 1; *CG* III, 25–51; *Compendium theologiæ* 104.

[8]For the second group, see *De veritate* XXII, 7; 1a. 62, 2, on the vision of God beyond natural desire. *De veritate* XIV, 2; 1a2æ. 62, 1 & 3; III *Sent.* 23, 1, 4, iii, on the need for the theological virtues to relate our mind and will directly to God. *De malo* V, 3; II *Sent.* 33, 2, 2, on Limbo or natural happiness.

most tangled of knots. This, however, he simply cuts. The desire in question does not spring from human nature in some hypothetical state, but as it really is in men as they have always been, *supposita Revelatione'*, overshadowed for weal or woe with God's saving favour. He fixes on no abstract pattern to find a want which should be met, but on the efficient cause, God's generosity working through human history and matching a desire his freedom has implanted. Usually he is critical of the Scotists, but there are points of un-expressed sympathy with them here which are significant, and which relate him to modern theologians who refuse to detach man from his historical setting.

Dominic Soto, a younger contemporary (1494–1560), a theologian with a varied background, in his *De natura et gratia*, a work addressed to the Council of Trent, gives a hint that proves congenial to our generation which has learnt to respect drives more or less unconscious, or at least wholly indeliberate. The desire which wells up from within human nature for God is a *pondus naturæ*, Keat's load of immortality, and literally the *appetitus naturalis* which is the blind craving for fulfilments unmediated by consciousness, in contrast to the *appetitus elicitus* of will. Desire fundamentally is of thing for thing; the beginning and the end, Alpha and Omega, lies behind and beyond the formal distinction of *auctor naturæ* and *auctor gratiæ* introduced by the theologians.

Soto agrees in effect with Cajetan in abolishing the problem. However it can be fairly argued that St Thomas himself meant more than their interpre-tations allow. Hence most commentators follow the line proposed by Ferrari-ensis (1474–1528), developed by Bañez (1528–1604) and John of St Thomas (1589–1644), broadened by the Salmanticenses (1631–63), and defended in our days by A. Gardeil (1859–1931).[9] What St Thomas had in mind, they say, is a desire of the will, that is an *appetitus elicitus* for a good somehow perceived, but one which is impotent of itself, *inefficax*, in this sense, that it presupposes no active natural power proportionate to the object, but only a *potentia obedientialis* to the action on it of a supernatural cause, and is furthermore a conditional desire, one that can be frustrated when a condition is not given, namely God's free act of will, which alone makes its achieve-ment possible. Its object is wholly supernatural, but the desire is natural on the part of the subject, for it rises from our knowledge of created things; is free, for it can be withheld or committed otherwise than to the thought of seeing God; and is an authentic expression of a mind and will open to the whole of reality without reserve. That this interpretation amounts to a com-plete solution would be too much to claim. It has been criticized for treating the desire as conditional, for God's promises are not in doubt to a Christian believer. Then again, it seems to prove the desire by the possibility, not, as St Thomas does, the possibility, or better the non-impossibility, by the desire. Perhaps it is the best we can do for an answer that goes no further than the terms of the question. Or perhaps the matter is better left with Cajetan or Soto.

---

[9] *La structure de l'âme et l'expérience mystique.* I, pp. 271–307. Paris, 1927.

GLOSSARY

accident, accidens: 1. A predicable accident, in logic a predicate that is attributed to a subject in fact but not by necessity, that is *per accidens* or incidentally; the two happen to be connected. 2. A predicamental accident, a real category of being, but not a thing, for it exists in another as in a subject, and this is the thing or substance. Often translated in this volume as a modification or quality or property of a thing.

act, action, activity: are used in this treatise ordinarily without discriminating between action, *actio,* as initiating change and producing an effect, and activity, *operatio,* an active quality immanent in its subject, e.g. knowing and loving.

appetite, appetitus, orexis: an inclination or bent to a good, used 1. of any potentiality with respect to its actuality; 2. of any being to its fulfilment though not mediated by knowledge (natural appetite); 3. of conscious desire of emotional appetite: 4. of rational appetite or will.

category, prædicamentum: a heading from Aristotle's division of reality into substance and nine sorts of concomitants, of which quantity, quality, and relation are the most important. These are the ten predicaments or categories of being.

cause, causa: a positive principle on which a reality depends for its existence. Material cause, that out of which it is composed and in which it exists; formal cause, that which shapes it as a kind of thing it is. Both these causes lie within the thing, which also depends on what is not itself. Final cause, why it is; efficient cause, makes it to exist. The exemplar cause is the idea of it in the mind of the maker.

end, finis, telos: the first of the causes, the why something is, and in this treatise the objective purpose of human activity. It is an end because the mind conceives it as good. The essential note is that it is wanted for itself, an integral note that for its sake other things are wanted too. The choosing of these should be guided by right reason, *recta ratio, orthos logos.* An end is a cause as an intentional object, not as a terminal result or finish.

Goods are traditionally divided into real values in themselves, *bona honesta,* which as such are enjoyable, *bona delectabilia,* and the means that serve to secure them, *bona utilia.* Since there are real goods other than the *Summum Bonum,* who is their final, efficient, and exemplar cause, there are real ends other than the ultimate end: hence the distinction, capital in St Thomas's thought, between the ultimate end and non-ultimate ends.

Other distinctions that occur are: 1. the end as intended, *in ordine intentionis,* and as executed, *in ordine executionis.* The first starts the process of acting for an end, and is a concept and desire of mind and will; the second is achieved when the process is translated into effective action and finishes by attaining and enjoying its object. 2. The objective end, *finis objectivus*, sometimes called the *finis qui*, which is the thing itself which is desired, andt he subjective end, *finis subjectivus, finis formalis*, called the *finis quo*, the activity of possessing it. 3. The end as abstract, sometimes called the *finis cujus gratia*, the reason why it is desired, and as concrete, *finis cui*, the person for whom it is desired. 4. The intrinsic purpose of a deed considered in its kind, *finis operis*, e.g. for murder the direct taking of an innocent human life, and an extrinsic purpose or personal motive attached to the doing, e.g. murder out of mercy.

Other terms as well are found in some authors. Thus they speak of a *finis remotus* in contrast with a *finis proximus*. But while 'proximate' will do in English, and St Thomas uses it to designate the immediate object or *finis operis* of a moral act, there is about 'remote' a suggestion of distance which makes it inapplicable to divine causality, for God, though ultimate, is not remote. Some also call the 'proximate' the 'intrinsic', and the 'remote' the 'extrinsic', but this can be the source of confusion between internal and external finality.

Internal finality is the bearing of an action from within itself towards its proper goal; external finality its bearing within a scheme or pattern composed of many agents. Why mosquitoes? Or more precisely, Why do mosquitoes bite? The answer in terms of internal finality is not difficult, if not comfortable for us. External finality, however, raises the difficulty of seeing a plan in the world, certainly one designed for our benefit. The difficulty may not be insoluble, but it can face the argument for the existence of God from design, though not that from teleology. cf 1a. 2, 3. Vol. 2, Appendix 10.

execution: in this treatise the giving effect to the intention of a human act. It starts from the effective command of the mind, *imperium*, the application of the will to the matter in hand, *usus activus*, the performance by the appropriate powers, *usus passivus*, and ends with some satisfaction, *quies*.

form, forma: 1. the shaping principle within an object, the substantial form of a thing, the accidental form of a thing's modification. 2. The idea or meaning of an object, intelligible form, or its sense-image, sensible form.

formal-material: a not uncommon analogy from Aristotelean hylemorphism to apply to twin principles in a topic, one shaping, determining, specific, the other receptive, indeterminate, generic.

freedom is attributed to non-necessitated activity. Improperly to any unforced activity, but this, if conscious, is better called voluntary. The term is properly attributed to activity which is not necessitated by its object, but where, as we say, a person makes up his own mind. It is helpful to distinguish different stages: the liberty 1. to act or not to act; 2. to act for this or for that; 3. when the alternatives are all good; 4. when they are right or wrong. Stage 1 constitutes freedom. Stage 4 is incidental.

freewill: the Latin term is *liberum arbitrium*, free decision, which better indicates its nature as the joint conclusion of mind and will adapting themselves to a non-compelling environment.

imagination, phantasia: the internal sense which composes an image, *phantasmum,* from the objects of the other senses, which can be charged with intelligence and so become a concept. Sometimes used by synechdoche for all sensation.

intellectus agens, nous poiētikos: usually translated 'active intellect', but 'factive' would be nearer the mark. Both have disadvantages, and the term is probably best left in Latin. The human mind's active power of heightening the images we receive from our environment so that they may be understood as meanings.

intellectus possibilis: the human mind as able to become its objects by understanding them. The term is often paired with *intellectus agens.* The transation 'passive intellect' is to be avoided.

intention: from *tendere,* to stretch forth, the relationship of mind and will opening out to the objective things that are known and loved; thus a concept is said to be an intention, so also a desire. The term is also more narrowly applied to the will's wishing, *intentio inefficax, velleitas,* and willing, *intentio efficax, volitio,* of an end, in contrast to its choosing, *electio* the means to it: in this sense it is particularly considered by moral theologians. cf 1a2æ, 1, 7 note f.

intentional: the term is wider and stronger in scholastic than in current usage, and refers to the truth-content and goodness content in acts of mind and will, not to their standing among the natural categories. Thus the knower becomes the known *in esse intentionali,* though his knowing is but a quality of himself *in esse naturali.* The early stages of a human act, before it is carried into practical effect, the 'order of execution', are said to be in the 'order of intention'.

means to an end, media ad finem: as such are pure utilities, holding no worth or pleasure in themselves. As soon as our actions are admirable to others or are to our own enjoyment we may be sure that they are no longer engaged with pure means, although they may be performed for the sake of a higher purpose. Thus the works of moral virtue, or a pleasant gossip with a friend. St Thomas often calls these non-ultimate or, if you like, intermediate ends, *ea quæ sunt ad finem,* things which are for an end, which may be translated as 'subordinate objects', but rarely as 'means'.

nature, natura: 1. a typological concept, a thing's species; 2. a dynamic concept, the source of its motion from within. Hence 'natural' may refer to an activity in accordance with a thing's constituent elements, in which case the love of God from grace is supernatural, not natural. Or it may refer to spontaneous and congenial activity, not forced, artificial, or against the grain, but voluntary, in which case the love of God from grace is natural.

obediential potentiality: see *potentia.*

objective: used of an object which confronts and engages a subject, and especially in the activities of cognition and appetition. The object is real when the subject is real. 'Object' is a key-word in the present treatise, especially for the theme that a finite or creaturely subject may have an infinite or uncreated object.

objectual: a seventeenth-century term, the equivalent of the Scholastic *objectivalis*, used by Cajetan and others to refer to a subject-object, not an effect-efficient cause relationship, proper to cognition and appetition. Also called intentional.

physical: in scholastic terminology is not necessarily restricted to the objects of the physical sciences or to phenomena of the material world, but is applied to what is of the *phusis* or nature of a thing. Thus God is said to act on us by 'physical premotion'. Efficient causality is sometimes described as physical causality, and contrasted with final or moral causality. The term, however, usually means belonging to material nature, except, sometimes, when it is being contrasted with intentional and moral.

pleasure, delectatio: the final phase of an activity which has attained its end. Joy, *gaudium*, and *fruitio*, are usually applied to the finer pleasures, *voluptas* to sensuous pleasure. All are presumed to be innocent until in some contexts they are found guilty.

potentia: has both an active and a passive sense, the power to do and the power to become; usually potential being is signified by contrast with actual being, and renders the Aristotelean *dunamis* and *entelecheia*. Where change is involved two principles are present, first, the principle of change in another as another, or the thing which sets in motion, second the principle of change from another as another, or the thing which is set in motion. The first is called *potentia activa*, active power, and sometimes in our translation, potency; the second is called *potentia passiva*, passive power or potentiality. Both principles can be present in the same substance, as when a man sets himself to endure the dentist's drill. In the *actio-passio* exchange between different things the potentiality is said to be natural when both the coming to be, *generatio*, and the passing away, *corruptio*, refer to forms on the same level of nature, thus wood can become ashes. But the form resulting may be of a higher level than the original, as when wood becomes a carved figure. Such potentiality is called obediential, but in theological usage the term is not applied to the capacity to receive artificial forms or even to be enhanced by participation in a higher order of created being, but is reserved for the capacity of rational beings to be acted on by God in such a way that they are drawn into communion with him by grace.

ratio: 1. the power of intelligence; 2. of reasoning; 3. the meaning, *logos*, of an object under consideration, sometimes translated 'quality' or 'character'.

subjective: is used of a subject, and does not carry the sense of being unreal. Thus subjective happiness refers to the active condition of the subject holding and enjoying his highest good, or objective happiness.

subsistent: that which is self-grounded, exists in itself, not in another.

substance, substantia: a being, *ens*, not an 'of a being', *entis*. It is not in another as in a subject. Contrast with 'accident'. The use of 'substance' for *ousia* or 'nature' occurs only once in this volume.

universal, universale: applicable to many. 1. And therefore can be treated as a diffused concept, as when we apply 'animal' to gnats, pythons, trout, magpies, elephants, and men; then it is so spread out as to be rather thin, and to relate only to part of the object in question. It is a matter of predication, and is called the *universale in prædicando.* 2. It is a richer concept when it refers to the single and simple principle of what is distributed and mixed among many, thus the universal good comprehends and causes all sharing in good, down to every snatch or shadow. This is a matter of causality or 'participation', and is called the *universale in causando.* In the first sense we speak of goodness in general, in the second of the subsisting good.

utility, bonum utile: an object chosen merely for the sake of something else, not of itself; a pure means to an end. It has no grounds of attraction within itself, in fact it may be disagreeable, as in St Thomas's stock example of unpleasant medicine.

will, voluntas: 1. the power or faculty of loving good presented by the mind; 2. the activity of that power; 3. and especially of intending the good as an end, by contrast with choosing an object for an end.

Index

(Numbers refer to pages. Italics to notes and appendices)

INDEX

useful *3, 23, 145, 149, 160*
usus *16, 17, 28, 97, 157*

utilia *3, 23*
utilitarianism *147*

V

Valentia, G. de *69*
Vasquez, G. *69*
Vatican Council I *129*
via negationis et eminentiæ 85
vicissitudes 129
virtual intention 25
virtue, moral & happiness 99

not end 37, 51, 53
vision 91, 93, 97
  beatific *5*, 83, 85, 87, *98*, 99, 127,
    131, *152*
voluntarism 151
voluntary act *5*, 21
voluptuousness 47, 49

W

Wallace, W. A. *113*
Walsh, P. G. *37*
wealth 31, 33, 35
whole & part 57, 101, 105
  well-being *35, 43*
will *5*, 9, 55, 69, 71
  as free 7, 143
  as necessary 129, 143
  moral goodness & happiness 97, 99
  through mind 7, 9, 21, 99, 125, 141

willing, not itself an end 7
wisdom
  intellectual virtue of 77
  practical 79
Wisdom, Book of 17, 49, 113, 129,
  160
wonder 85
world, this 123, 125
worth 3, 150
  and delight 93

VOLUMES

General Editor: THOMAS GILBY, O.P.

PRIMA PARS

PRIMA SECUNDÆ

SECUNDA SECUNDÆ